Present Tense

PRESENT TENSE

Rock & Roll and Culture

Edited by Anthony DeCurtis

Duke University Press

Durham and London 1992

Printed in the United States of America
on acid-free paper
The text of this book was originally published without
index or the present preface as volume 90,
number 4 of the *South Atlantic Quarterly.*

"The Eighties," by Anthony DeCurtis, originally
appeared as "The 80's" in *Rolling Stone* #591. By
Straight Arrow Publishers, Inc. © 1990. All Rights
Reserved. Reprinted by Permission.

"A Corpse in Your Mouth: Adventures of a Metaphor,
or, Modern Cannibalism," by Greil Marcus, is an
excerpt from his book *Dead Elvis: A Chronicle of a
Cultural Obsession,* © 1991 Greil Marcus. It is reprinted
here by permission of the author.

"Signposts on the Road to Nowhere: Laurie Anderson's
Crisis of Meaning," by Mark Dery, © 1989 by Mark
Dery, is reprinted here by permission of the author.
Portions of the interview originally appeared in a
November 1989 cover story published in *Keyboard*
magazine. By Mark Dery, © 1989 Miller Freeman
Publications, Inc. Reprinted by permission of *Keyboard*
magazine.

Library of Congress Cataloging-in-Publication Data
appear on the last printed page of this book.

This is for you, Frank.

Contents

Preface

In 1990 a younger colleague asked me what I perceived to be the biggest changes that had taken place in American culture since I was in college. I entered college in 1969—need more be said? Still, I'd long since gotten over any Sixties nostalgia I may ever have felt, and, fifteen years younger than me, he'd grown up heir to the full range of sophisticated critiques of Sixties-style leftism that had gained currency over the past two decades—the absence of any meaningful class analysis by the New Left easily being the most obvious and important.

After agreeing on the most pervasive change that had taken place—that what was considered the political right in the late Sixties and early Seventies had become the center—we began to talk about the Sixties as a kind of symbolic era, less important for the successes or mistakes of the movements of the time than for the belief instilled in many young people that all social structures were malleable and could be transformed for the better. How many people, young or old, believe anything like that now? To what degree should they believe it, and was it true even then?

Because both my colleague and I spend a good deal of our time writing and thinking about popular music, the talk then turned to how the meaning of rock & roll has shifted. It was hard to convey to someone who had grown up in the late Seventies and Eighties how much rock & roll mattered in the period between, say, 1964 and 1972. Every album by Bob Dylan, the Beatles, and the Rolling Stones during that time seemed infused with messages about how to live. Most of those records—with some notable exceptions—hold up quite well to this day, but they have taken on the sanctioned power of classics. From its earliest days, rock & roll has never been about sanctioned power. In the wake of the money culture that took shape in the Eighties, would it ever be possible for rock & roll to assume again a progressive role in American culture? By the time of our conversation, many observers had even begun to wonder if rock was dead. Is it?

In a partial attempt to address those questions—and to answer my friend's original question—I accepted Frank Lentricchia's invitation to edit a special issue of the *South Atlantic Quarterly* on rock & roll. That issue, which came out in the fall of 1991 and which was titled "Rock & Roll and Culture," eventually became this book. The ironies, of course, were ruthlessly apparent from the start—and still are. After all, what could be more an expression of sanctioned power than an editor at an enormously successful mass circulation consumer magazine editing a book on a titillating subject and having it published by a prestigious scholarly press?

But sanctioned power is power nonetheless and, like the subject it covers, rock criticism has often found ways to subvert the status quo, to avoid conforming to standards of acceptance that would dull its edge. Like much academic writing these days, rock criticism has routinely assumed that art is created in a social context; that hard distinctions between elite and popular art are ill-advised; that art created by minorities and working-class people is worthy of serious discussion; that writing criticism is itself a form of "creative writing"; and that critical writing can be a means of exploring broader questions about life in the culture at large. In fact, if the quality and variety of responses it generates is one important indicator of the ongoing vitality of an art form, rock & roll is very much alive.

In that regard, demonstrating the extraordinary range and quality of writing about rock & roll is one of the most significant purposes of this volume. As someone who enjoys doing both types of work, I have been saddened by the degree to which academic and journalistic writing have been forced apart since the late Seventies. That, it seems to me, was another subtle, but no less pernicious, effect of the money culture. If campuses were at the very heart of what was happening in America in the Sixties and early Seventies, that certainly was not the case during the Reagan years, when Wall Street was the center of the action. Pushed to the margins by the go-go economy of the Eighties, academics struck back by retreating into a cult of the obscure—and thereby accelerated their movement out of the mainstream. For their part, journalists allowed their writing to become increasingly ephemeral, a gloss on the glossy surface of the decade, just another twitch of the pulsating celebrity fanfest that popular culture became.

I was determined to try to bridge that gap, if only by getting a group of academics and independent critics to mingle together between the covers of the same book. I wanted the book to be a combination of a smart scholarly enterprise and a special issue of *Rolling Stone*, a resource from which both specialists and intelligent general readers could draw sustenance. Consequently, *Present Tense: Rock & Roll and Culture* is the furthest thing possible from a manifesto, at least as far as I'm concerned: there's too much in it with which I disagree! I was more concerned with suggesting potential directions for thinking about popular music than enforcing any particular one.

I was also determined to achieve a mix of theoretical, speculative, technical, and practical approaches to rock & roll. This extended to including a work of fiction—rock & roll as a purely imaginative experience. Additionally, a number of the contributors to *Present Tense* are active musicians, as well as being writers. This linking of ideas to action appealed to me—the ideas gain force through some semblance of realization in the world, the actions gain substance from being the subject of serious thought. Some of the pieces that follow are historical; some are experiential; some are wildly abstract—all are valid.

This desire on my part to create a kind of intellectual utopia with a rock & roll soundtrack is challenged, of course, by the fact that many of the approaches taken in this book fully contradict each other.

That's part of the tension the title is meant to suggest. Beyond that, at this point in its development, rock & roll stands in a tense relationship with its own mythology, its own musicological history, and with the broader culture in which music plays a part. It is both fully woven into the fabric of the American corporate structure and endlessly the subject of efforts to censor its rebellious, anarchic impulses. It is safe as milk and a clear and present danger.

It is unlikely that anyone could come up with a definition of rock & roll that every contributor to *Present Tense* would endorse. That such a basic question, the very nature of our subject, is still up for grabs is part of what makes this music—and writing about it—exciting. Doing it first, defining it later is a true rock & roll gesture. Believing that the more deeds and the more definitions the better is another. Keep on rocking, make more meanings: *Present Tense* is dedicated to both those propositions.

Anthony DeCurtis
New York City

Present Tense

Anthony DeCurtis

The Eighties

In November of 1980, Ronald Reagan was elected to his first term as president of the United States. A little more than a month later, on 8 December, John Lennon was shot to death outside his apartment building in New York City. Each of those events had its own all-too-real causes and consequences. But each has also come to bear the weight of symbol; each is a lens through which the mood and the manners of the 1980s, the cultural climate of the decade that followed, may be read.

Some say the 1960s died at Altamont; others say the 1960s died at Kent State. But whatever vestige of 1960s-style visionary thinking and progressive politics managed to survive the 1970s—when, after all, the Watergate revelations and Nixon's resignation at least partly vindicated 1960s radicalism and inspired a brief resurgence of idealism among the young—who can deny that the election of Ronald Reagan proved to be the fatal blow to the 1960s dream? Even the liberal values of the Great Society, which were little more than an extension of the civilizing efforts of FDR's New Deal, were anathema to Reagan—let alone the wild utopian urges that were meant to transport us to the Gates of Eden, or the road of counter-culture excess that would lead us to the Palace of Wisdom.

The generous collective impulses of the 1960s may ultimately have yielded to the Me Decade hedonism of the 1970s. But who knew that the next stop would be the pinched privatism, the smug selfishness, the glib pragmatism, the grim status consciousness, the greed masking as taste, the brutal superficiality of the 1980s? Who knew that the hung over sybarites of the Me Decade would transform, as if in the course of a nationwide Night of the Living Dead, into the desperately sober workaholics of the Gimme Decade?

Could there possibly have been a place for the likes of John Lennon in such a world? The point is not that Lennon was a saint, too good to live among the gleefully solvent sinners of the 1980s. It's just that he was too ungovernable, too unlikely to play by the rules, too interested in the margins to succumb to the savage mainstreaming of the last decade. The willful experimentalism, loopy romanticism, and smiling politics that Lennon represented—this was a man, you will recall, who believed that bed-ins and planting acorns could bring about world peace—are not virtues that would have carried much weight in an era during which greed was the ultimate good.

The characteristics that define the personality of Lennon's assassin, Mark David Chapman—an obsession with Lennon's media image to the point of obliterating the reality of Lennon the person, a worship of Lennon's power and celebrity so intense that it shaded into violence and hatred, a need to destroy the ideal he could not himself attain—are far more central to an understanding of the past decade.

Like the killings at Kent State, Lennon's death struck at the very souls of a generation and made idealism seem senseless, even dangerous. The vacuum left in those dead souls was filled in the 1970s with a craving for pleasure that could be kindled in a moment and extinguished just as quickly, pleasure not as a means of self-discovery—not even to be enjoyed for its own delicious sake—but as a distraction from numbness, a way to feel something, however briefly. Money and possessions—things that could be counted, measured, and used and that, for those reasons, provided the illusion of certainty—filled the vacuum in the 1980s. That so many of the people who wept and lit candles to mourn John Lennon's death eventually fell into step with the unforgiving individualism of the Age of Reagan is only one of the innumerable contradictions of the decade.

Musically, the 1980s got off to an unsteady start indeed. The punk explosion of the late 1970s had succeeded in stalling the alienating superstar juggernaut that had defined the earlier years of that decade, but punk itself became too self-infatuated and failed to gain much of a popular audience. Progressive artists like Talking Heads and Elvis Costello found a niche, but many of their contemporaries had either burned out or simply fallen by the wayside. In the early years of the decade, the economy was poor, video games—a technological harbinger of the very real war games to come—had seized the imagination of the young, and record sales were down significantly. It hardly seemed as if music mattered at all.

Then an event occurred that would energize the music scene once again and set in motion all the forces that would go on to shape the popular culture of the 1980s. On 16 May 1983, before a viewership of nearly fifty million people, Michael Jackson performed his Number 1 single "Billie Jean" on *Motown 25: Yesterday, Today, and Forever*, the television special that commemorated the twenty-fifth anniversary of Motown Records. After that, for better or worse, nothing was the same.

To that point, Michael Jackson's *Thriller*, which had been released on 1 December 1982 and had hit Number 1 during Christmas week, seemed as if it were going to be a successful record in the manner of *Off the Wall*, Jackson's fine previous solo album, which was released in 1979 and had sold more than six million copies. But Jackson's electrifying performance of "Billie Jean" sent fans streaming into record stores, where they often purchased another album or two before leaving, giving the music business a much-needed economic shot in the arm. *Thriller* would go on to sell some forty million copies worldwide, making it the best-selling album in history, but its significance is far greater than even this astonishing number would indicate.

It must be remembered that Jackson's appearance on the Motown special was not exclusively, or even primarily, a musical performance. Jackson lip-synced to a recorded track—the better to execute his breathtaking dance steps, including the mind-boggling Moonwalk— and there were no musicians onstage even to create the illusion that a band was playing. For imagery, atmosphere, costuming, and choreography, Jackson drew on the video he had made for "Billie Jean"— a prescient strategy that would go on to become conventional wisdom for artists like Madonna, Paula Abdul, Jackson's sister Janet, and a host of other acts in the coming years. In a decade in which visuals meant as much as music, and live performance aspired to mimicking the static perfection of videos, Jackson's rendering of "Billie Jean" on *Motown 25* was a watershed.

Just about a month or two before *Motown 25* aired, MTV had broken its de facto boycott of videos by black performers and begun showing Jackson's "Billie Jean" and "Beat It" clips. In the "Beat It" video, Jackson's audacious fusion of heavy metal—Eddie Van Halen played guitar on the track—and black street-gang imagery proved forward-looking, and Jackson and MTV proved to be a peerless match.

Founded in 1981, MTV had been flexing its muscles for a couple of years, finding a primarily youthful audience for a seemingly endless series of visually striking British bands of questionable talent like Duran Duran, Thompson Twins, and Men Without Hats and, to far more desirable effect, shaking up radio's monopoly on hit making. Still, MTV's standing was sufficiently precarious at the time that, rumor had it, CBS Records pressured the network into showing Jackson's videos by threatening to pull the clips of all its other acts. By the end of the decade, MTV's preeminence was so thoroughly established that such a threat would have been tantamount to filing for bankruptcy.

Quite apart from its considerable musical merits, *Thriller* defined both a strategy and a standard for success in the 1980s. The Beatles, Bob Dylan, and the Rolling Stones had liberated recording artists from the tyranny of the hit single in the 1960s and had established the album as a means of making an artistic statement. That tyranny returned in spades in the 1980s. Artistic statements or not, albums were seen as little more than collections of singles in the wake of *Thriller*'s seven Top 10 hits—and this was as true of *Born in the U.S.A.* and *The Joshua Tree* as of *Like a Virgin*, as true of *Purple Rain* as of *Forever Your Girl*. You might be a brilliant songwriter and a stunning musician, but after *Thriller*'s ground-breaking videos and the apotheosis of MTV, you'd better be something of an actor, too—or at least a pretty face.

And about those sales figures: a gold record—earned by sales of more than five hundred thousand records—might have impressed people in the 1960s and 1970s, but those days are long gone. After *Thriller*, platinum sales—earned by selling a million or more copies— were a prerequisite for stardom. Except for rare prestige acts—performers whose recognized status as important artists made them valuable to record companies despite their relatively low sales—the notion that you could have a productive career selling a few hundred thousand albums with each release was dead.

To a greater degree than ever before, marketing—the creation and selling of an image—became an essential component of an artist's success. Videos, video compilations, long-form videos, corporate sponsorships, product endorsements, T-shirts, book deals, interviews, television appearances, movie tie-ins, songs for soundtracks—all that began to envelop what was once considered a rebel's world, the world you chose because you had no other choice or you hated the idea of working for the man, because you wanted independence and freedom and nothing less, because you wanted that greatest of all possible goods, that most sublime of all possible states: to be a rock & roll star. Being a rock & roll star became a job, and true to the 1980s ethic, you'd better be willing to put in the hours and produce—to smile and make nice with the powers that be—or you might as well go back to the bars.

≡≡≡

By the mid-1980s, rock & roll was well on its way to becoming terminally safe. Joining a rock band had become a career move like any other, about as rebellious as taking a business degree and, if you got lucky, more lucrative. Your accountant was likely to be as hip as your lead singer. And far from resisting the marketing demands made of them, artists seemed to be tripping over themselves in their eagerness to sell out, to lease their songs to sell products, to put their dreams in the service of commerce.

Then, just as it seemed that rock & roll was incapable of offending anyone, Tipper Gore discovered the line about masturbation in "Darling Nikki," on Prince's *Purple Rain* album, and founded the Parents' Music Resource Center (PMRC). The drive to place warning stickers on albums was underway. Due to the influential standing of Gore, who is married to Albert Gore, Jr., the Democratic senator from Tennessee, and her colleague Susan Baker, wife of Secretary of State James A. Baker III, Senate hearings were held in which members of Congress pondered the meaning of rock lyrics. Rock & roll was the first target in the war on the arts that would soon escalate.

Eventually—and predictably—the controversy over lyric content and the effects of popular music on young people centered on the two musical forms that, despite their massive sales, still retained something of an outsider's edge: rap and heavy metal. Given how polarized our society became during the Reagan years, it is impossible not to see elements of racial and class prejudice in that development. While both genres have very much entered the mainstream, the core audience for rap is still black and the core audience for metal still consists largely of working-class whites. These constituencies are typically not given much credit for being able to tell the difference between the dramatic situation in a song and the realities of their own lives.

For that matter, the performers who speak to those constituencies are not thought capable of that distinction, either. If Eric Clapton— who is white and, better yet, English—covers a Bob Marley song and sings about shooting the sheriff, it's understood that he's an "artist" and doesn't really mean it. He can enjoy a Top 10 hit unhindered by questions about his motives or the effect on his listeners of the song he is singing. If the members of N.W.A, who are black, rap about a violent confrontation with the police, as they did on their blistering 1988 album *Straight Outta Compton*, they are presumed to be too primitive to understand the distinction between words and actions, between life and art. Their reward is organized boycotts and FBI harassment. In the case of 2 Live Crew, the reward is arrest and potential imprisonment. In many ways, the response that those groups have ignited— along with the legal difficulties endured by Ozzy Osbourne and Judas Priest in cases involving the effects of their songs on listeners—lends validation to the provocative content of much rap and heavy metal. The closest parallel to this persecution is the Nixon administration's effort to deport John Lennon in the 1970s because of his activism and the political content of his music.

But if rock & roll succumbed to the ethos of greed that charac-terized the Gimme Decade, and if it is still struggling to find the conviction to battle the incursions of bluenoses, it also helped restore a semblance of social consciousness to a period that, for the most part, borrowed its attitudes toward the less fortunate from Ronald Reagan and Margaret Thatcher. It took Bob Geldof, the charmingly brash leader of a failing Irish rock band, for example, to focus the attention of the entire world on the famine in Africa with Band Aid and Live Aid.

In response to a statement Bob Dylan made from the stage during his performance at the Live Aid concert in Philadelphia, John Mellen-camp, Willie Nelson, and Neil Young organized a series of concerts to assist the struggling farmers in America's heartland. U2 headlined a series of shows in 1986 that helped bring a little-known London-based human rights organization called Amnesty International to the fore-front of political awareness in the United States. Bruce Springsteen, Sting, Peter Gabriel, and Tracy Chapman carried Amnesty's banner around the world—often to countries with frightening human rights records—two years later.

Those high-profile actions were not universally celebrated, how-ever. They occasionally drew criticism—some of it justified or at least understandable. The big show could be seen as a kind of quick fix, and the quick fix, preferably as executed by internationally known celebrities, was a very 1980s phenomenon—as was the sense of bore-dom and even resentment that just as quickly set in when the quick fix inevitably failed to work.

Consequently, it was important that mammoth gestures on the order of Live Aid and the Amnesty tours were backed up by hun-dreds of artists like Jackson Browne, KRS-One, Living Colour, R.E.M., Simple Minds, and 10,000 Maniacs. These performers consistently played benefits and supported causes in quotidian ways that demon-strated that problems do not disappear because a bevy of superstars fill a stadium and move their fans to dial an 800 number.

If rockers looked beyond the borders of their cities and countries and addressed the larger issues in the world around them, they also looked beyond their aesthetic borders for inspiration in their music. Talking Heads, led to African rhythms by their producer Brian Eno, stunned the music world in 1980 with the release of *Remain in Light*, an album whose relentless drive and thematic reach set the stage for similar experiments by other artists. Peter Gabriel's solo records and performing bands through the 1980s borrowed a host of sounds from musicians around the world. Gabriel returned the favor in 1989 by establishing his Realworld label, distributed by Virgin Records, to bring the sounds of what had become known as "world music" to the West.

Certainly the most commercially successful—and controversial—cross-cultural fusion was Paul Simon's *Graceland*. Released in 1986 in a charged political atmosphere, the album drew critical raves but also incited a firestorm of protest because Simon had visited South Africa to record the album, violating the cultural boycott declared by the United Nations and the African National Congress, the organization leading the struggle against apartheid. The debate that ensued was bitter and prolonged. The musical merits of the album often seemed beside the point as the discussion centered on the proper role of artists in the political battles of their time. Undoubtedly the experience was unpleasant for everyone involved, but it provided further evidence of popular music's vitality and its ability to comment on and even enter the essential struggles of the age.

In addition to his political activism in support of Amnesty International and efforts to help preserve the rain forests, Sting broadened his musical palette in the 1980s, leaving behind the Police to work with jazz musicians like saxophonist Branford Marsalis and pianist Kenny Kirkland on two ground-breaking solo albums: *The Dream of the Blue Turtles* and . . . *Nothing Like the Sun*. Onstage, Sting's bands played like *bands*—a virtual miracle in a decade in which improvisation, not to say playing instruments at all, was held to an absolute minimum so as to make sure musicians did not fall out of time with prerecorded accompaniment or computerized lighting cues.

Bruce Springsteen, U2, and R.E.M. also played an essential role in preserving the human element in rock & roll at a time when technology threatened to overwhelm flesh and blood. Springsteen ran the gamut from the stark, acoustic balladry of *Nebraska* to the booming rock & roll of his massively popular breakthrough album, *Born in the U.S.A.*, all the while keeping the lives of his characters in rich focus with all the skill of a masterful short-story writer. U2 came roaring out of Dublin in 1980 with a message of hope, faith, and passion that eventually reached an audience of millions with *The Joshua Tree* in 1987. The anemic British synth-pop that U2 blew off the international stage early in the decade with fervent albums like *Boy* and *War* is now, for the most part, a dim memory.

Just as U2 put Dublin on the pop-music map, R.E.M. emerged from Athens, Georgia, in 1981 with the independently released single "Radio Free Europe"/"Sitting Still" and gradually built an audience through relentless touring and an inspiring refusal to compromise with the more absurd edicts of the music industry. To this day, R.E.M. stands as a model of how a young band can remain true to its own idiosyncratic vision and still reach large numbers of listeners.

By the end of the 1980s, rap—which got its start in the mid-1970s in the South Bronx and took the country by storm in 1986 when Run-D.M.C. (with the help of Aerosmith on the smash single "Walk This Way") and the Beastie Boys each racked up multi-platinum albums—was bearing much of the brunt of criticism for how soulless music had become. Indeed, rap's reliance on prerecorded rhythm tracks and sounds borrowed—some would say stolen—through sampling continues to make the genre all too vulnerable to such charges.

But at a time when most pop songs featured lyrics that were hardly worth any attention at all, rap placed words and the human voice at the very center of its sound. All talk about the irresistibility of hip-hop beats aside for the moment, what could possibly be more human than the insistent, demanding voices that came blasting out of tracks like Grandmaster Flash and the Furious Five's "The Message," Run-D.M.C.'s "King of Rock," or Public Enemy's "Bring the Noise"? Among its many other contributions to music in the 1980s, rap gave the big lie to the view—so common among rockers and some tediously hip rock critics—that lyrics don't matter.

A black rocker in the tradition of Jimi Hendrix, Prince was perhaps the artist who moved most gracefully amid even the most dangerous currents of the 1980s. Before it became fashionable—or even fashionably controversial—Prince shattered sexual stereotypes in 1980 with *Dirty Mind*, a bold rock-funk fusion that boasted songs about incest, oral sex, and troilism, and a cover that featured Prince himself in black bikini underpants, all without seeming the slightest bit sensational. The urgent staccato riff that drove that album's title track—the essence of Minneapolis funk—would prove to be one of the most influential sounds of the decade. His work was a major target of the censorship brigade, but Prince never condescended to enter the fray, even mustering, presumably on the basis of his spiritual beliefs, some sympathy for his tormentors.

Prince also managed the visual demands of the decade with flair, offering up both a terrific feature film, *Purple Rain*, and a string of exciting videos. Shifting styles in ways that only rarely seemed contrived, he set certain trends, trailed after others, followed daring statements with vapid ones and, at a time when many artists were all too willing to pander, did pretty much whatever the fuck he pleased. It was heartening.

═════

The 1980s more or less ended in January of 1989 when Ronald Reagan left office. The vicious presidential campaign of 1988—in which the Republican party gleefully played on white racial fears, wrapped its candidate, the insipid George Bush, in the flag and used McCarthyite rhetoric to make even the most centrist views seem seditiously un-American—now seems like the last dying gasps of cynical 1980s values.

So far the 1990s seem as if they will be characterized by an eager sense of penitence driven by a secret fear that it really may be too late to turn things around. Suddenly, after a ten-year rape of the earth, everyone is an environmentalist, but reports on such issues as global warming, ozone depletion, waste disposal, and the pollution of oceans and rivers are increasingly dispiriting. Suddenly, after eight years of simply outrageous tax breaks for the well-to-do, everyone wants the economy to be brought under control, but the size of the deficit and the cost of the savings-and-loan bailout grow ever higher and seem to defy comprehension, let alone remedy. Just when we were happily celebrating the death of communism, capitalism teeters precariously on the verge of recession or worse.

Everyone has grown more compassionate—kinder, gentler—but the staggering desperation and crushing numbers of the homeless and needy to whom the largess of the Reagan administration somehow never trickled down seem completely overwhelming. Once the hostages came home from Iran, it seemed convenient to forget about the Middle East—and American dependence on foreign oil. Now the Middle East is back on the front burner, and burning hot. The long-term implications of the war with Iraq are frightening to consider.

As often happens, the uncertainty of the future has sent people scurrying to the past for reassurance. This tendency achieved a certain crazed extreme in 1989, a year that spent most of its time trying its damnedest to be 1969—or at least an airbrushed version of 1969, blurring all the wrenching complexities of that year.

Twenty years after Altamont, the Rolling Stones filled stadiums around the country and were the most popular show on the road. Nearly twenty years after the breakup of the Beatles, Paul McCartney dusted off a healthy bunch of Beatles songs and launched a highly successful American tour. Twenty years after they sang about how you "got to revolution," the members of Jefferson Airplane reunited for a series of shows so impossibly lame that it seemed like a Las Vegas lounge act's rendition of the greatest hits of the Summer of Love. And, of course, the twentieth anniversary of Woodstock inspired endless commentaries about the days of peace, love, and granola in the mud.

Looking to the past, though, does not need to be an act of escapism or nostalgia, particularly in a country that is so extremely in need of a meaningful sense of history. An appreciation of the 1960s would be better served by allowing that decade's lessons to be enacted, not simply packaged and sold back to us as a sitcom. Those lessons are simple and important: the belief that we are not simply individuals but part of a larger culture that requires our most earnest efforts and ideas; the conviction that the worlds within and outside ourselves are subject to transformation, that our actions can shape the future, that what we choose to do matters deeply; the insistence that America has a place for our best selves, and to the degree that it doesn't, it must be changed; the notion that music can help formulate a vision toward which we can aspire.

And if we must look back to Woodstock, remember that Jimi Hendrix, the black man who closed the show that last morning, once wondered what would happen if six turned out to be nine. What if.

Robert Palmer

The Church of the Sonic Guitar

Accept that music is not sealed to passion, nor to
piety, nor to feelings; accept that it can blossom
in spaces so wide that your image cannot project
itself within them, that it must make you melt
within its unique light!
—Louis Dandrel

Current cosmology (the study of the universe as
an ordered whole) considers that there was an
original moment of creation. I propose to call that
moment the "Big Ring" since the old term is modeled on the noisy violence of our own culture. At
the time of the "Big Ring," unknown forces brought
the universe into being. The sounding itself, the
ringing of that first note *is* the creation, which ever
since has been expanding, dividing, and echoing.
It is reverberating even now.
—David Hykes

I had a hot blues out, man. I'd be driving my
truck . . . and pretty soon I'd hear it [my first electric blues hit] walking along the street, I'd hear
it *driving* along the street. . . . I would be driving home from playing, two or three o'clock in the
morning, and I had a convertible, with the top
back 'cause it was warm. I could hear people all
upstairs playing that record. It would be *rolling* up

there, man. I heard it all over. One time I heard
it coming from way upstairs somewhere, and it
scared me. I thought I had died.
—Muddy Waters

Guitar Slim . . . was gettin' a fuzz tone distortion
way before anyone else. You didn't hear it again
until people like Jimi Hendrix came along. Believe
it or not, Slim never used an amplifier. He always
used a P.A. set, never an amplifier. He was an
overtone fanatic, and he had these tiny iron cone
speakers and the sound would run through them
speakers and I guess any vibration would create
that sound, because Slim always played at peak
volume. . . . If Slim was playing, you could hear
him a mile away.
—Guitarist Earl King

'Scuse me while I kiss the sky.
—Jimi Hendrix

The electric guitar was the last crucial ingredient to find its proper
niche in the fundament of rock-&-roll-as-we-know-it. Since the 1960s,
rock & roll fanatics have been, ipso facto, guitar fanatics. Whether
their ideal of rock & roll heaven was Eric Clapton's blues feel, melodic
invention, and tonal purity; or Jimi Hendrix's vocalizing of the instrument's expressive capabilities in the course of turning its sound
into an elemental force; or the pure-toned, long-lined elegance, lyri-
cism, and coherent thematic development of Duane Allman's mara-
thon improvisations; or the gritty crunch and bite of Keith Richards's
power chording, 1960s rockers have invariably been worshippers in
the church of the sonic guitar.

Post-1960s rock has only solidified the electric guitar's position as
rock's sonic and iconographic summum bonum. Its identity as a religious emblem has become ever-more pronounced. It is impossible
to hear the from-the-gut riff-thrash of Metallica, Slayer, or Megadeth without visualizing the symbol of the inverted cross and the
hand sign of the double horns (representing pre-Christian nature
worship and the horns of Pan, rather than the devilry of fundamentalist Christian propaganda). In what might be termed the punk art

wing of modern rock, the sonorous resonating properties of feedback-sustained guitar textures have assumed an explicitly spiritual association through their development by bands and performers such as Lou Reed and the Velvet Underground, Tom Verlaine and Television, and more recently Sonic Youth. To attend a show by one of these groups is to immerse oneself in a clanging, droning sensurround of guitar harmonics, to enter a precisely demarcated, ritually invoked sonic space. This is the movable church of the sonic guitar, a vast, high-vaulted cathedral vibrating with the patterns and proportions of sound-made-solid. Perhaps the most appropriate analogue for this invisible but highly audible sacred architecture is the Gothic cathedral, designed according to traditions of mystical mathematics, such as the proportion of the golden mean. And they were designed to resonate music, specifically the chanting of monks. One finds the same sonic concerns in the sacred architecture of Islam: the courtyard of one medieval mosque was designed to resonate any sound made within it seven times, in overlapping waves of slap-back echo. And of course there are the legendary acoustical properties of Eastern structures such as the Taj Mahal. Impressively thorough sonic explorations of some of these architectural wonders have been made by composer David Hykes and the Harmonic Choir, whose album *Hearing Solar Winds* was recorded inside the twelfth-century Abbey of Thoronet in Provence, and by Paul Horn's solo flute recording *Inside*, made on the sly (without official permission) inside the Taj Mahal. Listening to these recordings at high volume must be something like experiencing Hykes's "Big Ring" from inside the sound box of a truly humongous electric guitar.

This is a far from idle comparison. The *acoustic* guitar's flexibility in terms of tuning made it the ideal instrumental vehicle for the non-tempered, microtonal melodic language of the blues, in which key intervals such as the third, fifth, and seventh are not *flatted*, as a black key flats the tone of the adjacent white key on a piano, but *flattened*, with the degree of the flattening bearing a direct relationship to the level of emotional intensity. As among the Akan of Ghana and other tribal groups speaking pitch-tone languages, falling pitch corresponds to intensifying emotion. The *electric* guitar can merely make the instrument's single note lines a little louder, so that the musician can solo like a saxophonist or brass player. But once a certain volume threshold has been passed, the electric guitar becomes another instrument entirely. Its tuning flexibility can now be used to set up sympathetic resonances between the strings so that techniques such as open tunings and bar chords set the entire instrument humming sonorously, sustained by amplification until it becomes a representation in sound of the wonder of Creation itself—the "Big Ring."

A piano, whose strings are tuned to the fractional, rationized intervals of so-called "equal temperament" (the tuning standard for most post-Bach classical music), cannot achieve this effect without being radically retuned, as modern composer La Monte Young (a founding father of the rock tradition initiated by the Velvet Underground) has done in his epic composition "The Well-Tuned Piano." But an electric guitar, properly tuned to resonate with everything from the hall's acoustics to the underlying 60-cycle hum of the city's electrical grid, is forming its massive sound textures from harmonic relationships that *already* exist in nature; compare this to the arbitrary "equal temperament" system which causes decidedly unharmonious harmonic interference patterns and dissonances when certain tones are allowed to ring together. In electric music—rock & roll—one of the first proofs of this theory was the engineering experiments conducted at Chess Records in the late 1940s and early 1950s. A tile bathroom adjacent to the studio was chosen as a resonating chamber for guitar amplifiers, resulting in sounds on early records by Muddy Waters and other artists that can still raise the hairs on the back of your neck. A piano in equal temperament, placed in the same bathroom, produced nothing but a tonal muddle, so the studio john was reserved for the amps of guitarists and, occasionally, harmonica players.

T-Bone Walker, the bluesman who popularized the electric guitar in his work fronting the Les Hite big band and on his signature tune "Stormy Monday," had recorded in Dallas in 1929 as Oak Cliff T-Bone. His move into amplification in the mid-1930s seems to have hardly affected the style heard on the 1929 disc, at least at first. His picking on his early and mid-1940s sides for the Black and White label was clean, with a terse, dry tone, and minimal vibrato and sustain. Of the other guitarists who first plugged in during the years 1935–37, Eddie Durham, who tripled as arranger, trombonist, and guitarist with Count Basie, contributed some bluesy solos to 1930s sides by Basie small groups featuring Lester Young. But again, though these solos could have been conceived on an acoustic guitar, they simply wouldn't have been audible in a band context without an amp.

The most experimental of the early electric guitarists, as far as we can judge from the recorded evidence, was Bob Dunn, who built a pickup and patched together an amp for his lap-steel guitar while working with one of the jazziest and most musicianly of the Southwest's white western-swing bands, Milton Brown and his Musical Brownies. Dunn's solos on Brown's mid-1930s discs are so startlingly futuristic that this listener feels he has been thrust abruptly into a different century. Using his slide bar to sculpt and color horn-like melodic phrases, with apparent influences from the French gypsy jazz guitarist Django Reinhardt and the leading black jazz hornmen of the day, Dunn created a revolutionary electric guitar sound that was so utterly idiosyncratic he seems to have inspired few if any imitators. The work of Bob Wills's steel guitar man, Leon McAuliffe, was much more conservative and stolidly country-swing-rooted, though McAuliffe was responsible for one electric guitar showpiece that became popular with black and white orchestras near the end of the big band era, "Steel Guitar Rag."

In *San Antonio Rose*, his exhaustive study of the life and music of western-swing kingpin Bob Wills and his Texas Playboys, Charles Townshend offers fragmentary but suggestive evidence that T-Bone Walker and Charlie Christian, the front-runners in the first generation of black electric guitarists, were inspired, at least in part, by the early amplified playing of white musicians such as Dunn and McAuliffe. Walker, who was born in 1910, and Christian, six years his junior, were friends and musical partners during the early 1930s, playing together on Texas street corners for tips, and trading licks and chord voicings. Walker's heritage was that of a classic Texas bluesman; as a child, he guided Blind Lemon Jefferson around Dallas from street corner to tavern, picking up on Jefferson's discursive, horn-like single string playing at the same time. Christian, who like Walker was from Dallas, also spent several years working out of Oklahoma City with popular territory bands like Alphonso Trent's.

Though Walker has found his niche in history as the father of electric blues guitar and Christian is revered as the first great electric guitarist in jazz, their backgrounds and teenage friendship would have outweighed any considerations of genre in their own minds; for a time they even studied with the same teacher, the otherwise obscure Chuck Richardson. In the southwest territory, blues and jazz had been intimately related from the beginning. Country bluesmen recorded with jazz band backing and learned chord voicings from more harmonically advanced jazzmen. Jazz bands regularly featured shouting blues singers like Joe Turner, and, after the mid-1930s, blues-singing guitarists such as T-Bone Walker. Western-swing and jazz present a similar continuum on the white side of the tracks, with men like McAuliffe representing a jazzy but heavily country-inflected style, while mavericks like Dunn played a kind of pure, futuristic jazz all their own. And every one of these players, black and white, was solidly grounded in the blues. Indeed, there is plenty of evidence of black and white players freely trading ideas and techniques, including the skills of fashioning some of the earliest homemade amplifiers and pickups. But the differences in race were keenly felt; white musicians usually got the better-paying jobs, and social custom prevented race-mixing on public bandstands. During the 1930s heyday of the swing bands, black territory outfits like Count Basie's early Kansas City combo made radio broadcasts, but white musicians got the lion's share of radio exposure.

It seems likely that Walker and Christian would have heard electric lap-steel players like McAuliffe and Dunn on local radio shows. Whether this listening had any effect on their playing, aside from opening their ears to some of the possibilities of amplification, is debatable. Of all the early black electric guitarists, Basie's man Eddie Durham sounds like the most likely candidate for western-swing influences on his 1938 Commodore recordings with Basie small bands. Walker's earliest electric recordings are squarely in an updated Blind Lemon Jefferson Texas blues tradition, colored with a scattering of jazzy chord voicing he most likely picked up in Christian's company. As for Christian, he took to the amplified guitar like a duck to water, rapidly developing a fleet, horn-like style that sounds a great deal closer to the work of Basie tenorman Lester Young than it does to Bob Dunn. Christian's rhythmic flexibility and harmonic savvy made him one of the most popular participants in the celebrated Harlem jam sessions at Minton's that midwifed the birth of bebop. He was easily a match for Thelonious Monk, Dizzy Gillespie, Charlie Parker, and the other early bop firebrands. Unfortunately, most of the recordings he made before his death from tuberculosis at the age of twenty-five were as a sideman with Benny Goodman, who gave his remarkable guitarist ample solo space but was prevented by his own hostility to bebop from hiring a rhythm section that could have effectively seconded Christian's flights of improvisational genius.

How loudly did these early electric guitarists play? Here, alas, the recorded evidence is practically useless. Certainly by the late 1940s, guitar bluesmen in the South and Southwest were blasting away. Sam Phillips's early 1950s recording policy at Sun, which involved capturing bluesmen playing on the equipment and at the volume they were accustomed to, leaves little doubt that in boisterous southern juke joints, amp settings were frequently turned up to 10, an impression further strengthened by some of Elmore James's early 1950s Flair and Meteor sides, recorded in Mississippi clubs and home studios with Ike Turner at the controls. Houston guitarist Goree Carter was playing jacked-up, hell-for-leather jump figures, associated later with Chuck Berry but actually derived by Berry from earlier T-Bone Walker, on his rampaging 1949 single "Rock Awhile." If one is inclined to search out "the first rock & roll record"—a dubious pursuit at best, since it all depends on how you define rock & roll—Carter's "Rock Awhile" seems a reasonable choice. The clarion guitar intro differs hardly at all from some of the intros Chuck Berry would unleash on his own records after 1955; the guitar solo work crackles through an overdriven amplifier, and the boogie-based rhythm charges right along. The subject matter, too, is appropriate—the record announces that it's time to "rock awhile" and proceeds to illustrate how it's done. To my way of thinking, Carter's "Rock Awhile" is a much more appropriate candidate for "first rock & roll record" than the more frequently cited "Rocket 88," recorded for Sam Phillips almost two years later by Ike Turner's Kings of Rhythm, hiding behind the pseudonym of Jackie Brenston (the lead vocalist) and his Delta Cats. (The respective dates as given in discographies are "circa April, 1949" for "Rock Awhile" and 5 March 1951 for "Rocket 88," but the issue is of more interest to record collectors than to anyone else—one might as well call the first rock & roll record Trixie Smith's "My Man Rocks Me [With One Steady Roll]" from 1922, citing its unmistakable lyric intent, and be done with the whole thing.)

But we were talking about electric guitars, *loud* electric guitars, and when they first appeared on record. If recording had simply documented the music of the juke joints and taverns, we would have examples of jacked-up guitar sizzle and the edgy hum of over-driven amps from the 1940s—the noisier the gig, the louder an electric bluesman like Muddy Waters would play, just to cut through the din. The problem was studio recording technology. Imagine a hyperamplified electric guitar blazing away in the tiny J&M studio where Fats Domino and Little Richard recorded their hits. The precise instrumental balance and exact microphone placement engineer Cosimo Matassa and the musicians had worked long and hard to perfect would have been blown away by a single guitar chord, the VU meter on the studio's primitive tape recorder would have red-lined, and a welter of distortion—not controlled distortion but noisy, cacophonous, runaway distortion—would have been the recorded result. There are, in fact, guitar solos on late 1940s and early 1950s discs cut at J&M, but the guitarists, team players to a man, simply edged up their volume controls a bit, according to a prearranged plan, and fitted their solos neatly into the ensemble textures the way horn soloists like Lee Allen did. Occasionally there is a notable exception to prevailing trends: Billy Tate's "You Told Me," recorded at J&M in 1955 with Fats Domino on piano, builds up to a gloriously dirty, snarling guitar solo.

There were other, more deliberate exceptions, and here Chess in Chicago and Sun in Memphis led the way. Muddy Waters's early recording career at Chess is one of the earliest examples of a producer, engineer, and musician working together to create an electric guitar sound suitable to the recording medium—a sound that consciously creates the illusion of a cranked-up-to-10 juke joint guitar sound but is in fact an illusion, the guitar sound being modified not only by the amplifier but by the judicious application of both room acoustics and recording technology. When Waters came to Chess in 1947, he ini-

tially recorded backed by piano and bass, giving his records a sound
not dissimilar to the pre–World War II records of Chicago bluesmen
such as Tampa Red. But Leonard Chess was an experimenter. And
besides, he was a businessman—those early records didn't sell. So in
April 1948 he recorded Muddy playing electric guitar with only Big
Crawford's bass to back it up. The resulting record, "I Can't Be Sat-
isfied" / "I Feel Like Going Home," was the most traditional record
Waters made since arriving in Chicago as far as its basic musical materials were concerned—Delta blues the way Son House or Robert
Johnson might have played it. Yet this record was something entirely
new. The reactions of the record-buying public told Chess that much.
The initial pressing was sold out in a matter of hours, and enterprising
porters riding the Illinois Central down South from Chicago did brisk
business carrying copies of the record and selling them in southern
cities and towns at vastly inflated prices. The difference, of course,
was amplification: not just amplification but an ingenious new way
of recording voice and electric guitar and bass, and blending them
together into a new sound so powerful, so vibrant with presence, it
was *scary*—scary enough for Waters himself, driving home alone after
work, to hear "people all upstairs playing that record. . . . One time
I heard it coming from way upstairs somewhere, and it scared me. I
thought I had died."

The Chess repertory of idiosyncratic recording techniques grew
to include using the studio's tile bathroom as a resonating chamber
for guitar amps, mixing directly miked amplifier and room ambience with artificial reverb, and recording both guitar and lead vocal
"hot"—so close to the upper end of the VU meter that the very loudest notes pushed the needle just a shade into the red. The records created in this way jumped out at you. They were scary enough as *songs*,
with their tales of hoodoo hexes and gypsy fortune-tellers. Everything about the production amplified and focused that scariness, the
archetypal blues scariness of standing at a pitch-black Delta crossroads in the middle of the night, waiting for the Devil—or Legba, the
Yoruba/hoodoo god of the crossroads, the opener of paths between
the worlds—and feeling your blood run cold with every whispered
susurration of the roadside weeds. Get a little too drunk, punch up
one of *those* records on the jukebox, and you've got The Fear.

Muddy Waters was already working in the Chicago taverns with a full electric band when he made those records, but Leonard Chess built up his studio sound instrument by instrument, adding Little Walter's harmonica in the summer of 1950, but not allowing him to bring his amplifier (which he'd been playing through since the 1940s) until July 1951; Jimmy Rogers's second electric guitar was added by the end of that year. By perfecting his single electric guitar sound first and then adding to the ensemble instrument by instrument, Leonard Chess showed that he was one of the first to understand the necessity of capturing the raw live sounds of electric bands on tape, and one of the most methodical as to how he went about it.

Down in Memphis, Sam Phillips's approach was also methodical, though in a different way. According to Phillips, his motivation for recording the black and hillbilly combos that came trouping into his studio as soon as he opened its doors in 1950 was "the freedom we tried to give the people, black and white, to express their very complex personalities. . . . I just hope I was part of giving the influence to the people to be free in their expression." This motivation, or method, had certain corollaries that were part of the actual recording process: "I didn't want to get these people in some stupid-assed studio and lead them astray from what they had been used to doing. To put it another way, I didn't try to take them uptown and dress them up. If they had broken-down equipment or their instruments were ragged, I didn't want them to feel ashamed. I wanted them to go ahead and play the way they were used to playing. Because the *expression* was the thing. I never listened to the sound of one instrument. I listened for the effect, the total effect."

An early instance of Phillips's philosophy in action was the recording of "Rocket 88" by Ike Turner and his Kings of Rhythm in March 1951. Turner and the band had driven up to Memphis from the Delta town of Clarksdale to audition, and on the way guitarist Willie Kizart's amplifier had fallen from the top of the car. When the band set up in the studio and Kizart plugged in, the amp began emitting fuzz and crackling with static. Phillips recalls that "when it fell, that burst the speaker cone. We had no way of getting it fixed. . . . It would probably have taken a couple of days, so we started playing around with the damn thing. I stuffed a little paper in there where the speaker cone was ruptured, and it sounded good. It sounded like a saxophone. And we decided to go ahead and record."

What Phillips fails to add is that this jury-rigged fuzztone guitar sounded good to *him*—an engineer at Savoy or Regal or King would probably have thrown the band out of the studio. Phillips enjoys giving an impression of himself as a more or less passive medium, ushering talented musicians in his door and giving them "the freedom . . . to express their very complex personalities." The role he played in the development of Elvis Presley shows him to have been a master psychologist as well, an impression further strengthened by his celebrated "Devil's music" argument with Jerry Lee Lewis during the recording of "Great Balls of Fire."

But there is more to it than this. Stan Kesler, a canny observer of Phillips's working methods, played pedal steel guitar on early Sun country recordings, switched to bass for rock & roll sessions, helped craft early songs for Presley to record, and became a seminal Memphis producer himself, including among his triumphs Sam the Sham and the Pharoahs' "Wooly Bully." I once asked Kesler to explain Phillips's success, and he said unhesitatingly that the "very *first* thing to remember about Sam is that he was one hell of an engineer." Certainly Phillips was competent enough to have engineered national network radio feeds for big bands broadcasting from the posh rooftop club at Memphis's Hotel Peabody before he opened his studio. Once he secured the studio location at 706 Union—a small storefront, bigger than Cosimo's J&M in New Orleans but not by much—he began by gutting the insides and rebuilding according to his acute ear for acoustics. The studio's ceiling had a peculiar slope to it; Phillips maximized its quality as a sound resonator by installing a ceiling of corrugated tiles that was an unending line of ridges and valleys. The shape of the ceiling and the setup of the studio were augmented by an ingenious and entirely original system of "slap-back" tape echo that involved feeding the original signal from one tape machine through a second machine with an infinitesimal delay. This artificial ambience, and Phillips's exceptional ear for balancing instruments and voices, enabled him to give his artists "the influence . . . to be free in their expression" while actually recording an illusory, idealized representation of their customary live sound.

Phillips hadn't started his own Sun label when he recorded "Rocket 88," which was booted along by Kizart's fuzztone guitar booming out a distorted but not overloaded boogie-bass figure. Little Richard thought enough of "Rocket 88" some five years later to appropriate its signature riff as a lead-in to "Good Golly Miss Molly." Of more immediate interest to Phillips was the original record's commercial performance. He leased it to Chess, and it became one of the biggest r&b hits of the year, reaching Number 1 on the r&b charts and remaining on the charts for seventeen weeks. It was a catchy, rocking tune, but that fuzzed-out guitar doubling the boogie-bass line was clearly one of its chief selling points, the single ingredient that differed significantly from the other rocking automobile blues that were becoming popular around the same time.

From then on, when Phillips was recording a blues combo, he let the guitarist wail. B. B. King's earliest recordings for Phillips have an exciting, dirty guitar tone that was smoothed out of his later records. Howling Wolf and his West Memphis-based combo, whom Sam caught one night broadcasting live on West Memphis radio station KWEM and sought out, recorded a series of blues classics at Sun. On every one of them, guitarist Willie Johnson's slashing rhythm licks and jazzy fill-in runs cut through the band sound like a hot knife through butter. When Johnson really let loose—turning up his amp until it crackled, slamming out dense and distorted power chords—he kicked the band into savage overdrive. With Wolf moaning, growling, and howling his traditional Delta lyrics and punctuating the rough combo sound with harmonica wails, they sounded like a blues band from Hell. Their first single, "Moaning at Midnight" / "How Many More Years," has all the eerie hoodoo of Muddy Waters's early discs and then some. On "How Many More Years," Johnson's slamming power chords crashed like thunder. On a slightly later Sun studio side, "House Rockers," Wolf kicked Johnson into his guitar solo by hollering, "Play that guitar, Willie Johnson, 'till it smoke . . . blow your top, blow your top, blow your TOP!"

Still without a label of his own, Phillips leased these first Wolf recordings to Chess, who recognized a winner when they heard one, drove South, and spirited Wolf away to Chicago and an exclusive Chess contract. For Phillips, losing Jackie Brenston and Wolf to Chess and B. B. King to Modern/R.P.M. (whose local talent scout, Ike Turner, seemed to dog Phillips's footsteps) was devastating. Short on funds, still depending on location recordings of weddings and funerals and the sort of souvenirs Elvis recorded for his mother's birthday when he first walked into Phillips's studio, Sam nevertheless started a label of his own. His first venture, the Phillips label, issued only one known release, and it was one of the loudest, most overdriven, and distorted guitar stomps ever recorded, "Boogie in the Park" by Memphis one-man-band Joe Hill Louis, who cranked his guitar while sitting and banging at a rudimentary drum kit. Finally, in 1953, Phillips launched Sun.

Among the talents attracted by Sun were two harmonica-playing singers from the West Memphis area, James Cotton and Junior Parker. Both recorded with Auburn (Pat) Hare, an Arkansas-born guitarist Phillips had been using on various recording sessions since a June 1952 date with blues singer Walter Bradford's combo. Hare was a Memphis-area guitarist cut from the same bolt of cloth as Willie Johnson. Both men were blues players to the core but had obtained some familiarity with jazzy chord voicings. Both played single-note lines in fills and solos, a staple among electric guitarists since the mid-1940s' success of T-Bone Walker ushered in the era of electric blues guitar. But they were also slicing, savage rhythm players. Other guitarists in other towns may have developed similar ideas at the same time or even earlier, but on the basis of recorded evidence (which is just about all we have to go on), Johnson and Hare were the originators of one of the most basic gambits in the rock & roll guitarist's arsenal, the power chord.

A chord—several notes harmonized and played together—can be inserted at any appropriate place in a performance. A *power* chord is fundamentally rhythmic rather than harmonic in purpose and character. Usually, a power chord is accented for maximum impact. As it has become a more and more venerable device in the rock & roll guitar lexicon, its uses have become more various. Figures are built around power chords, which follow one another in quick succession in an incisive, cutting riff or phrase but are rarely allowed to lose their identity as individual accents, however cleverly or densely they are strung together. If you're still not entirely sure what I'm talking about, go listen to Keith Richards's guitar figures on "Jumpin'

Jack Flash." Richards once told me he got ideas for several of the power chord figures on Rolling Stones records from the acoustic guitar power chords that propel 1950s Everly Brothers singles like "Wake Up, Little Suzie." Robbie Robertson of The Band says he picked up the practice from hearing Willie Johnson's work on the early Howling Wolf discs being broadcast over Nashville's WLAC. Although the Wolf discs from Memphis had been recorded in the early 1950s, Chess had stockpiled a number of them and released them in the late 1950s or early 1960s on the enormously influential Wolf "rocking chair" album (titled *Howling Wolf* but remembered more often for the rocking chair on the cover).

But back in the Sun studios, in the years 1952–54, Pat Hare was the power chord king. One of the most gripping examples of his style was "Cotton Crop Blues," released in 1954 under vocalist James Cotton's name. Whatever equipment Hare was playing through, there must have been more wrong with it than a burst speaker cone. Rarely has a grittier, nastier, more ferocious electric guitar sound been captured on record, before or since, and Hare's repeated use of a rapid series of two downward-modulating power chords, the second of which is allowed to hang menacingly in the air, is a kind of hook or structural glue. This figure turns what could have been a merely good blues record about the indignities of a life spent picking cotton—an explanation (as if one were really needed) for the then-ongoing mass exodus of black southerners north to Chicago—into something extraordinary and unforgettable. The first heavy metal record? I'd say yes, with tongue only slightly in cheek.

At the same session, or the day after (the dates are 13 and/or 14 May 1954), Hare cut a single of his own, and all the pent-up violence and emotional intensity that had been evident in his playing from the beginning came pouring out. I'm speaking of scary records: Hare's "I'm Gonna Murder My Baby" is *The Texas Chainsaw Massacre* on a three-minute vinyl disc. Again, Hare used hard-slammed power chords to structure the half-spoken, half-sung, entirely threatening performance. His spoken asides are along the lines of "I'm gonna kill 'er tomorrow." Some years later, after playing on Junior Parker's Sun and Duke sides and then moving to Chicago, Hare joined the Muddy Waters band and was reunited with his longtime partner James Cot-

ton. Hare played on one spectacular Waters record after another between 1957 and 1960, from "She's 19 Years Old" and "Walking through
the Park" (the latter has a classic Hare solo) to the *Muddy Waters
at Newport* album of 1960, which introduced a new generation of
young white rockers to electric blues and was especially influential
in England among groups such as the Rolling Stones and the Yard-
birds. And then life caught up with art: Hare was arrested, tried,
and sent to prison for allegedly murdering his girlfriend. Although
he was occasionally let out to play a local gig, he never finished his
sentence; he died behind bars. This circumstance makes "I'm Gonna
Murder My Baby" even scarier to listen to than it must have been at
the time. No wonder the power chord has been most fundamental in
modern rock as the basic structure for riff-building in heavy metal
bands. "I'm Gonna Murder My Baby" is as heavy metal as it gets.

Meanwhile, electric blues-based guitarists were barnstorming
across the South, sometimes meeting in large big-city clubs for
"battles of the blues" that inspired them to pull out all the stops.
Of the Texas guitarists most directly influenced by T-Bone Walker,
Clarence "Gatemouth" Brown was either the flashiest and most resourceful user of the electric guitar's sonic resources, or he had a particularly sympathetic recording situation at Duke/Peacock records.
His early and mid-1950s singles abound in volume and sustain effects,
deliberate amplifier overloading, wildly stuttering scrambles up the
neck, screaming high-note sustain, and other rock & roll devices.
"Dirty Work at the Crossroads" is probably the most inclusive single
representation of these effects. In concert, everyone from T-Bone and
Gatemouth to less renowned but no less gonzo Texans such as Goree
Carter and Bobby "Blue" Bland's ace axman Wayne Bennett sometimes gave these stars a run for their money.

But in the annals of early and mid-1950s electric guitar lore, Guitar
Slim's legend looms large indeed. Earl King related a typical story to
interviewer Jeff Hannusch:

> Gatemouth Brown, T-Bone Walker, Lowell Fulson and Guitar
> Slim were all performing one night at the White Eagle in Opelou-
> sas, Louisiana. Slim was headlining because "The Things I Used
> To Do" [his 1954 r&b smash with piano and arrangement by Ray

Charles] was a scorcher. They were all sitting in the dressing room and Guitar Slim walked up to 'em and said, "Gentlemen, we got the greatest guitar players in the country assembled right here. But when I leave here tonight, ain't nobody gonna realize you even been here." Well, they all laughed but that's exactly what happened. Slim come out with his hair dyed blue, blue suit, blue pair of shoes. He had 350 feet of mike wire connected to his guitar, and a valet carrying him on his shoulders all through the crowd and out into the parking lot. Man, he was stopping cars driving down the highway. No one could outperform Slim.

Eyewitnesses also agree that nobody could out*blast* Slim when it came to volume. Earl King's story about Slim disdaining amplifiers and playing directly through a P.A., whose iron cone speakers would further enrich the sonic overtones of his ringing guitar strings, means in effect that he had a setup offering him virtually unlimited feedback and sustain, all of which he could rigorously control with the volume and tonal settings on the guitar itself once the P.A. was properly adjusted. "He had a lot of melodic overtones in his solos," King confirms. "Slim tuned standard, but he used that capo to get the effect of open strings. . . . I've seen Slim play many a time without it. He just used it for effect." And what an effect it must have been. Early and mid-1950s r&b audiences were still accustomed to bands that featured honking saxophones as their primary solo voice, fronted by blues singers who kept their guitar work subordinate to the impact of the vocals. Slim reversed the priorities. He was a bluesman by birthright; born Eddie Jones in the Mississippi Delta town of Greenwood (or possibly Hollandale), he combined early training in gospel singing with a beginning guitar style that led early commentators to dismiss him as an imitator of T-Bone Walker and, especially, the flashier Gatemouth Brown. The blue suits, shoes, and hair, the 350-foot guitar cords, and the Jimi Hendrix-like sonic effects soon made it clear that he was an original. In retrospect, he was every inch a rock & roller.

Accounts of some of Slim's exploits are almost uncannily reminiscent of the Stones's Keith Richards. In the mid-1970s, when I was covering part of a Stones tour for *Rolling Stone*, the band arrived by private jet in the early hours of the morning and checked into a Hilton

Inn. It was one of those mammoth inside-out structures. The interior of the building was entirely hollow, and the door to each room on each of the hotel's many levels opened directly onto a balcony that ran all the way around the inside of the hotel, with parallel balconies above and below it. In other words, you could stand in the door of any room and see the door of every other room in the place. Soon, a sound began blaring out of a room across the void from mine, around fifteen stories up. It was a Fender amp and it was unmistakably Keith Richards. Before long, he emerged from his room, guitar in hand, and perched precariously on the balcony, where he kept threatening to plunge to his death but somehow never did, and he kept jamming all the while, the sound pouring out the open door of his room.

Compare that to the following Earl King story from Hannusch's invaluable *I Hear You Knockin': The Sound of New Orleans Rhythm and Blues*: "You knew Slim was back in town [New Orleans] 'cause early in the morning, around seven-eight o'clock, if he was tanked up, you'd hear them amps and P.A. going off. People'd be calling the police, 'cause you could hear Slim three blocks away! And here's Slim up in his room with his shorts on, goin' through his stage routine. . . . If you went up there, there'd always be about seven or eight different women up there. He'd have his songs written with eyebrow pencil on pieces of paper tacked to the wall."

When solid-body Les Pauls appeared on the market, Slim immediately realized that with a solid body guitar he could more easily control the feedback and sustain than with the electric hollow-body he had been using. According to his bandleader, Lloyd Lambert, he would also turn the bass controls on his guitar and P.A. as low as they would go and crank the treble up to 10. Lambert realized that standing in the middle of this sonic firestorm every night wasn't helping his hearing, but he couldn't tell Slim anything, either about the volume he played at or the pace at which he lived his life. By 1958, his drinking had reached a debilitating stage that made it more and more difficult for him to travel. "I wouldn't say he was a pretty good drinker," Lambert told Hannusch. "He was the best! Slim just wouldn't take care of himself. He lived fast, different women every night. I'd try and tell him to eat good and get his rest, but he'd say, 'Lloyd, I live three days to y'all's one. The world don't owe me a thing when I'm gone.'" He died in New York in February 1959 at the age of 32, from bronchial pneumonia complicated by alcoholism.

If Slim was one of rock & roll's original Kings of Excess, and the first saint in the Church of the Sonic Guitar, he was also, during his lifetime, a nightmare to record. One of the most hauntingly beautiful of his sides, the 1952 "Feeling Sad," has no guitar on it at all, but the purity and passion of its down-home gospel vocal, the plaint of a soldier in Korea that "I was sending you my money baby, and all the time you was doin' me wrong," make listening to it an experience not likely to be forgotten. Slim began recording for Specialty in 1953, scoring almost immediately with the biggest hit of his career and one of the top r&b records of 1954, "The Things I Used to Do." But Specialty's Art Rupe and his man in New Orleans, Johnny Vincent, later the colorful proprietor of his own Ace label, had little patience for a guitarist who would wait patiently while studio balances were carefully adjusted, wait for the count-off, and then jack his amplifier right on up to 10. If Spinal Tap had already invented the Number 11 amp setting, there is little doubt that Slim would have used it, anywhere, anytime.

The Guitar Slim album issued by Specialty in the United States some years ago is a major disappointment. Not only was Slim's guitar deliberately buried in some of the original mixes, but some selections had questionable additions, such as organ and vocal chorus overdubs after Slim's death. Finally, in 1984, England's Ace label leased the original tapes from Specialty and turned them over to the superb remastering engineer Bob Jones. Jones was able to strip away the later additions, bring up the guitar, give its sound more presence and bite, and generally restore the performances to at least some semblance of the artist's original intent. For listeners interested in the roots of rock guitar, the British Ace label's *Guitar Slim: The Things I Used to Do*, is required listening. Among its highlights, "The Story of My Life" has a thrilling guitar solo that rings out proudly, with Jones's remastering bringing out every nuance of phrasing and tonal subtlety. One album isn't much, but it's an album I, for one, wouldn't be without.

Earl King was not simply Slim's traveling companion and posthumous keeper of the flame. He was and is a formidably talented singer, songwriter, and guitarist in his own right; his New Orleans-made singles of the late 1950s and early 1960s are themselves solid links in the rock-into-soul chain. And like many talented performers of the time, King paid his dues by sometimes being called in at the last minute to impersonate an indisposed star at an already booked engagement. In this case, the star was Guitar Slim, and King reportedly was every bit as convincing as James Brown or Otis Redding impersonating Little Richard. But King also left us a recording legacy that helps put Slim's true contribution to the music in perspective. His 1960–62 sessions for the Imperial label, which include some of his most accomplished and enduring compositions in "Trick Bag" and "Mama and Papa," also include a modern reinterpretation of Slim's "The Things I Used to Do." More important, these sessions yielded a classic two-part single that is, in effect, the missing link between Slim and modern rock guitar, "Come On," an irresistibly funky dance tune highlighted by a riveting, extended guitar solo. King begins playing bluesy, more like the Slim we know from records, but he soon begins to stretch up to screaming, liquid high-note phrases that are uncannily reminiscent of Hendrix's recordings made more than five years later. There can be little doubt that Hendrix, a veteran of the r&b circuit with stints backing Little Richard and the Isley Brothers to his credit, heard "Come On" and took its lessons to heart. Not only did he build a certain aspect of his style from King's revolutionary, screaming high-note melismata, he also recorded his own versions of Guitar Slim's "The Things I Used to Do" and Earl King's "Come On," thus forging another link in the chain, and explicitly laying bare the roots of his art as they extend back through King to Guitar Slim to the likes of Gatemouth Brown to the father of electric blues guitar, T-Bone Walker. Working the other way from the watershed of Hendrix's brief but brilliant career, we can follow this influence into the work of every accomplished rock guitarist playing today. This is what we mean when we call rock & roll a *living* tradition.

If Guitar Slim is the patron saint of our Church of the Sonic Guitar, Ike Turner can only be its fallen angel, the Dark Prince. Most of the publicity he has received in recent years has had to do with cocaine, alleged gangsterism, and his supposed physical and mental cruelties to Tina Turner; emerging as the long-suffering Angel of her New Morning, Tina has painted Ike as her Lucifer, in the original sense of the light-bringer. Light, in the form of musical tutelage and inspiration, he certainly gave, but like all who mess with the Lucifer of legend, Tina paid a heavy price. Whether the story is as cut-and-dried and morally unambiguous as Tina's confessional bio and celebrity interviews have made it appear need not concern us here. Ike's character certainly has a bearing on his importance as an originator of sonic-stun flash-blues guitar. His personal life is his own business.

Indisputably, Turner was a young man of more than average intelligence, resourcefulness, musical acumen, and business savvy. Born in Clarksdale, Mississippi (the Delta town that gave us John Lee Hooker, Sam Cooke, and from its immediate outskirts the likes of Muddy Waters) on 5 November 1932, Ike could easily have grown up a conventional bluesman, learning from his elders and forging his own style from traditional elements in the time-honored tradition. He did seek out his elders, taking early piano lessons from musicians such as King Biscuit Time ivory-tickler Pinetop Perkins, and gleaning lessons and advice from the formidable Sonny Boy Williamson II. But when he was in high school, the fast-talking, smooth-dressing Turner landed a regular disc jockey slot on Clarksdale radio station WROX. On his show he played the latest jumping r&b discs from Los Angeles and New York, as well as from Chicago and closer to home, listening carefully and developing a musical orientation more influenced by the energy and ferment of the late 1940s national r&b scene than by Delta doings. While in high school, he also joined the Tophatters, a student big band drawn together by their love of modern jazz. As so many black performers had discovered so many times, there was little money to be made playing modern jazz—especially in Clarksdale, Mississippi. So Ike and a few of his closest musical cohorts from the Tophatters broke off and formed the Kings of Rhythm. All of them were capable interpreters of deep Delta blues, but being younger and having been at work assiduously expanding their musical horizons and slicking up their image, they preferred playing jumping band blues with a rocking boogie beat and a section of riffing, big-toned saxophones. Ike himself played piano; the guitarist, Willie Kizart, was the son of a well-known Delta blues pianist, Lee Kizart, and the guitar pupil of one of the area's earliest musical modernists, Earl Hooker.

With this band, Turner recorded a number of sides for Sam Phillips, including the 1951 Number 1 r&b hit "Rocket 88" that Little Richard was to find so inspiring five years later. But to this band of bright young upstarts local opportunities for regular work and growth seemed as limited as Sun Records's erratic distribution. After spending the early years of the 1950s doubling as a musician and record company talent scout (he recorded B. B. King, Junior Parker, Bobby "Blue" Bland, Howling Wolf, and others at the beginning of their careers, often at his Clarksdale radio station gig or in a studio he'd rigged up in his own house in Clarksdale), Turner reformed the temporarily dormant Kings of Rhythm and moved the entire group to St. Louis in mid-1954.

Like Memphis, St. Louis was a mecca for black southerners who'd hoed one too many rows of cotton and had boasted a vital and diverse black music scene since the 1920s. By 1955 two St. Louis bands were running neck and neck as local favorites—the Kings of Rhythm and Chuck Berry's trio. Possibly their closest competition was another transplanted Mississippian who was to become one of the most durable and influential blues guitarists of the 1960s, Albert King. But King, whose fluid phrases moved like oil oozing over stone and cut with a deceptively relaxed-sounding viciousness, appealed mostly to a somewhat older blues crowd. Turner and Berry were competing for the patronage of all-nighters in St. Louis, and the wide-open East St. Louis, Illinois, just across the river, where the clubs opened when the Missouri clubs shut down and kept rocking into the morning hours. Turner and Berry were also in competition for the growing white audience then beginning to embrace rocking black r&b, and were great favorites with the white teen crowd at spots like George Edrick's Club Imperial.

Bill Stevens, then a white teenager planning to go into his father Fred's paint business, remembered his St. Louis club-hopping days recently for British interviewer Bill Greensmith, the most thorough historian of the St. Louis scene:

"There were about three of us who bummed together when we were kids," he said. "And we couldn't get served in the white tavern but we could get served in the black tavern—we were underage. So these fellows were all playing at your local clubs on the east side, Ike included. They would come over and play at the Imperial or the [other] clubs in St. Louis until 1 o'clock in the morning, then they would go over to the east side and start playing at 1:30 and play to daylight. And this is where we all ended up. Kingsbury's is actually where Ike got his start—Kingsbury's Lounge. Very nice couple—older. Miss Kingsbury was a friend of my mother's maid and that being the case I could get away with being in there and sit there all night, drink and listen to the music, get involved with it. I enjoyed the music, enjoyed the partyin'. To me it was good times."

Stevens and his father became so enthusiastic about the local music scene, and the lack of local recording activity, that they started Stevens Records in the late 1950s, recording some wild and crazy instrumental and vocal burners by Ike Turner and other St. Louis luminaries. Because Turner was still under contract to Sun as a recording artist, his agreement having a few more months to run, he appeared on Stevens as Icky Renrut.

At first, Turner and the band lived in a big house, where all-night partying never seemed to keep him from waking everyone up in the morning and organizing a highly efficient rehearsal with a single-minded authority and military approach to organization that probably makes James Brown his only real rival in the field of band-leader martinets. But everyone agreed that the rehearsals were worth it—the band was *tight*, as can be heard on a series of recordings made between 1955 and 1959. By this time, with the help of lessons from Willie Kizart and, undoubtedly, a great deal of practice, Turner had transformed himself from a pianist into a gonzo guitarist. Sam Phillips's memories of his early 1950s Sun sessions, not surprisingly, reveal that already "Ike had the best-prepared band that ever came in and asked me to work with them. And," he added, "Ike! What a piano player he was! People don't know that Ike Turner was the first stand-up piano player. Man, he could tear a piano apart and put it back together again on the same song." But this was nothing compared to the over-the-top ravings Turner unleashed on electric guitar when the Kings of Rhythm traveled to Cincinnati to record for Federal in August and September of 1956.

Turner projected a flashy, bad-ass persona. Guitarist Bobby King, who was playing around St. Louis in 1957, recalls that

> Ike was never performing, he always had the band performing— he would always be back in the crap game shooting dice with a whole lot of money—$1500—$1600. I'd never seen that much money in my life! He was always the sharp guy and . . . he kept his band clean and sharp, beautiful suits and attire, they were always together. Ike always had a good band and a variety of vocalists, he had a hell of a reed section, they were some of the leading sax players in the city.

There was also his carefully cultivated sharpie/hustler image, his evil look (practiced, perhaps, in front of a mirror?), and his reputation for getting the most out of his musicians by any means necessary: one of his singers from the St. Louis days, Bobby Foster, remembers that Turner "told me he was gonna stick the guitar up my ass if I didn't do it right. And he was serious." Turner and the Kings of Rhythm already had a fearsome reputation around St. Louis when they took off for Cincinnati to record for Federal, the biggest label they'd yet worked for.

After absorbing the basics of blues guitar technique from Willie Kizart, Turner became fascinated by the tremolo or "whammy bar" that was a new technological innovation on certain solid-body electric guitars. The player struck a note or chord with his right hand, then quickly reached down and gave the curved metal bar sticking out of the sound box near the bridge a nice energetic shake that shivered the note or chord with a vibrato-like quaver, the degree of vibrato and distortion depending on how violently the guitarist manhandled both the bar and his strings. Turner manhandled with a crazed abandon that belies his cooler-than-cool image, and that must have been something to see in the studio.

On Federal sides like "I'm Tore Up," featuring vocalist Billy Gayles, and the steamroller rockers "Sad as a Man Can Be" and "Gonna Wait for My Chance," with singing by Jackie Brenston of "Rocket 88" fame, Turner unleashed his full power, wresting twisted, tortured, bent, and shattered blues notes and chords out of his guitar not just for emphasis but in practically every bar of every solo. This was a wildness that simply hadn't been heard before, one well ahead of its time— the whammy bar's heyday in the late 1950s and early 1960s never produced music approaching such savage urgency. Overtones rang out bell-like, only to be shattered by violent manipulations of the whammy bar, giving way to lines of screaming high notes that began sounding bluesy and then began bending and distorting themselves until the guitar sounded, for a moment, like a primitive synthesizer.

Several additional examples of Turner's playing from this period are, if anything, even more gonzo. Tommy Louis's furiously rocking "Wail Baby Wail," a shouter in the Little Richard mode, sets up a guitar solo that seamlessly blends the then-popular Chuck Berry intro-and-break style with all the furious string-bending and whammy-barring of which Turner was capable, suggesting at least some stylistic connection between the two doyens of mid-1950s St. Louis guitar, Berry and Turner. In 1958, Turner and at least some members of his band were in Chicago doing session work as well as their own records for the somewhat shady Cobra/Artistic operation, whose owner reportedly lost the company in a poker game. In any event, Turner showed up playing one of two electric lead guitars on "Double Trouble," the first recorded masterpiece by one of the greatest of all modern blues guitarists, Otis Rush. Rush's eerie moan about hard times and hoodoo paranoia is punctuated by his own crying, fluid phrases, and periodically the mood escalates from dread to pure terror as Turner inserts a quivering shard of a glassy blues chord. "Double Trouble" is the single most striking performance in a series of Otis Rush Cobra sides that later played a key role in inspiring the British blues revival. A comparison of Rush's original "All Your Love" with the John Mayall/ Eric Clapton version reveals the latter as a nearly literal homage, and Led Zeppelin was only marginally more creative in their remake of "I Can't Quit You Baby."

By 1958, Ike Turner had discovered Annie May Bullock, a.k.a. Tina Turner, and from that time on he became the Svengali behind her, directing the band with his usual iron-fisted methods and parading Tina in her skimpy costumes like a pimp displaying the merchandise. His guitar playing receded into the background, although there is one fascinating album of guitar instrumentals by Turner on the Crown label, and he plays a mean blues solo on a live Ike and Tina performance in Africa captured in the film *Soul to Soul*. Since then, there's been a well-publicized split, accusations, arrests. It's too bad, because Ike Turner deserves a prominent place in rock & roll history, and not just as a guitarist whose wildman strategies were rarely heard again until the advent of the Velvet Underground and later punk groups like Richard Hell and the Voidoids, with equally gonzo, equally resourceful guitarist Robert Quine. Turner's remarkable accomplishments as a talent scout, the classic blues records he produced in the early 1950s for the Modern label, his bands, Ike and Tina albums, spin-off projects—all add up to a rich and varied career. Suspected criminal or even psychopathic tendencies should have nothing to do with it—what about Pat Hare's chillingly fulfilled prophecy of "I'm Gonna Murder My Baby," something Ike Turner has never been accused of doing, though he may have tried? Forget it. Art is art, and great rock & roll is great rock & roll no matter what kind of maniac is playing it.

What matters, in this necessarily brief and fragmented account of the rise of sonic guitar, is that virtually every innovation associated with rock guitar playing in the 1960s can be traced back to black musicians of the middle and late 1950s—from the "heavy" sound and power chording of men like Willie Johnson and Pat Hare to proto-funk rhythms, from the "black rockabilly" and rhythm guitar styles derived from gospel-trained players to the sainted founder of our Church of the Sonic Guitar.

Trent Hill

The Enemy Within:
Censorship in Rock Music in the 1950s

The traditional approach to censoring the objectionable in the realm of "high" culture tends to pit the heroic censor and the forces of the Good against the transgressing and villainous autonomous producer/author. The very structure of the opposition suggests its weakness; it is all too easy to reverse the valences of the opposition, so that the producer becomes a heroic soul attempting to stand up to the censor, who has all the machinery of state repression on his side. The writer working in solitude is a sympathetic figure; his book may represent the work of years, presenting itself as a compelling vision that must be respected, even if it cannot be accepted, by its audience. Moreover, prosecuting literary obscenity cases in trial is something of a nightmare; in order to win such cases, the prosecution has to establish that the work in question is both obscene and utterly lacking in any redeeming social value. And as has been shown repeatedly since the 1930s, the brute fact that obscenity trials gather into a courtroom a group of educated, authoritative voices who have definite arguments about the worth of a work tends to establish the worth of a work, and therefore its right to be disseminated. So literary obscenity prosecutions generally undermine the very social and legal consensuses upon which they are supposedly based, and ironically establish the validity of and interest in the very works they are meant to proscribe.

On the other hand, there are many reasons why, for shrewd censors in the 1950s, pop cultural productions seemed such an appealing aesthetic, ideological, and political target. It is harder to argue that rock & roll records are the productions of a heroic creator; they cannot support the myth of either the autonomous author or the autonomous *auteur*. The material conditions of pop culture production are more readily apparent; even the most naive fan knows that pop culture creators are deeply dependent on the material support of complicated corporate networks for their success, and that they are indeed the products of these same networks. Senators at the 1960 "payola" hearings would find that the pop star Fabian served as a double indictment of the recording industry: he was notorious for lacking anything resembling raw musical talent, but was attractive, charismatic, and marketable. Fabian's recording company therefore took great pains to use every means available to mask the many flaws in his voice, proving to the assembled senators both that he was simply a creation of the recording industry and that the record companies were force-feeding the American public inferior music.

Another advantage in pop culture productions, from the point of view of censorious power, is that in general they do not take long to produce, and their techniques of production are closely aligned with the technologies of mass production. Relative to "objectionable" literature, the character of pop culture productions as a commodity is easier to establish, and it is therefore easier to tar them with the brush of Mammon. Indeed, the accusation "they're only in it for the money" forms a litany intoned by censors from Senator Kefauver in 1954 up to Paula Hawkins's contemptuous dismissal of Frank Zappa at the Parents' Music Resource Committee hearings in 1985:

SENATOR HAWKINS: So you do make a profit from the sales of rock
                   records?
MR. ZAPPA: Yes.

SENATOR HAWKINS: Thank you. I think that statement tells the story to the committee. Thank you.[1]

But this aesthetic/ideological problem presents censors with a substantive practical problem as well: it is not so easy to censor these cheap gauds, since they multiply so easily and rapidly. The task of censoring them demands a radically different strategy from that of censoring "high" cultural productions, and therefore they have typically been the subject of a different kind of censorship than have novels and movies.

It is relatively easy to stop the dissemination of a novel or a movie by direct means, by intercepting and proscribing it in a series of judicial and police actions, because their mode of production is intensely organized and hierarchical; the censor has available to him efficient points of intervention by which to stop the publication and dissemination of the outlaw text. Rock & roll records are products of a much less highly organized system of production. A single individual could perform a variety of functions in different places in an amorphous, loosely defined productive network. Dick Clark, for instance, was at the same time disc jockey, label owner, TV star, songwriter, publisher, and part-owner of a record-pressing plant. And, arguably, 1950s rock & roll relied much less on publicity and much more on presentation. You did not hear the new single advertised on the radio, but heard the song itself. A would-be censor could not easily point to any place in the network at which the entire flow of texts or records could be stopped. Confronted with the bewildering concatenation of individuals and businesses with different stakes and functions in the record industry, the congressional investigators looking into the intricacies of payola in early 1960 could only imagine that the whole thing ran by a mixture of luck, fraud, and conspiracy. Indeed, one way to read the payola hearings is as an attempt—an attempt that was ultimately successful—to force a greater degree of organization and hierarchical responsibility onto the record industry so that the flow of music/product could be more easily regulated.

The censorship of pop culture—or at least those efforts at censoring it that have proven successful—has relied largely on the methods and strategies that we have come to associate with McCarthyism: the direct confrontation between the censor and the accused in a court

of law, or before a duly empowered commission, not in order to legitimate the political repression of isolated individuals, but to mandate
the social and economic repression of an entire system of material
and cultural production.[2] Which is to say, to draw on a contemporary
example, that it was inevitable that Luther Campbell, the voice of
2 Live Crew, would be found innocent in court; it is not inevitable,
however, that his distributors will be found innocent; and it is even
less inevitable that retailers will choose to continue to carry such a
controversial product.[3] Censors since the 1950s have consistently relied less on the legal supports for censorship and political repression
that exist within the body of American common law (and these supports, even if they are contested, are still quite substantial), than on
the ability of censors to draw on the resources for repression that
exist in the American discursive body politic and to identify successfully those critical economic nexuses, where pop culture's mode of
production "comes together," so that they may be severed and so that
the noise, be it audio or visual, may be silenced.

In many ways, the censor cannot be contented by establishing this
peaceful community. Censorship battles have the effect of exposing,
not just the enemy within, but a whole set of cultural power relations
and antagonisms. Censorship is always, in the end, an elite response
to a politically threatening situation, a profound if not always articulate mode of cultural criticism. It is the least democratic kind of
criticism, one that few of us can indulge in. It is the response of a person or a group who has access to money and power and the splendid
variety of "bully pulpits" that money and power can buy; it is the response of the responsible, of those who can make decisions as to what
can and will be disseminated, who can defend these decisions if they
are contested, and who can enforce these decisions (or see to it that
they are enforced) once they have been made. Censors almost never
claim to enjoy what they feel compelled to do; their task is always an
unpleasant one, always one that they would rather not have to perform. They would much prefer it if people were reasonable enough
and responsible enough to practice self-censorship. No, these messy
spectacles of court trials, congressional oversight hearings, trustees'
board meetings, and the like are things that the censors, those most
sensitive antennae of the Good and the Proper, would rather avoid

having to put themselves and us through. Perhaps this delicacy shows consideration for the feelings of the silenced, and a desire to avoid the public exposure that these proceedings inevitably bring. Perhaps, on the other hand, it has more to do with a desire to avoid exposure of the antagonisms that give rise to the insecurities, along with the ambiguity of outcome once the spectacle of antagonism is made public. If it is made public. No, it is better if these things are decided in the privacy of the corporate office or, even better, in the silent star-chamber of the human heart. That way, there can be an end to all the uncertainty, a "resolution" of all these conflicts, before they even arise.

≡≡≡

What we should notice first about early rock & roll music is that it was less a breakthrough at the level of musical form or language than a series of transformations in the way in which popular music was produced and disseminated. Some of these transformations are chiefly technological and economic in nature; the demise of radio as a medium for the presention of dramatic and theatrical material after the advent of TV created a space that could be filled by music. Likewise, the development of the vinyl record, which could be produced more cheaply than the older shellac discs, enabled small record companies to spring up with greater ease and made it easier to release a variety of records.

Yet these changes in the technical and economic infrastructure of the music business are not so important for the development of both rock & roll and the reaction to it as are changes in the class-specific character of music dissemination. Rock & roll is a hybrid of early 1950s blues, r&b (the sophisticated, dance-oriented rhythm & blues that was popular among urban blacks), and country music (then known as "folk" or "hillbilly" music: it, too, was essentially a dance music). These Ur-musics were well established among groups that did not bear the full burden of the campaigns of repression: poor and working-class blacks and whites.[4] They were both the chief producers and the chief consumers of these musics, which were profitable genres that represented economically important submarkets and socially important subcultures. Before World War II, the primary markets for these musics, and therefore the only places where they could readily be heard, were the South and select urban areas where blacks had migrated in search of better economic opportunities. During the war, however, these opportunities spread and diversified geographically, luring southerners of both races up to the cities of the industrialized North and West. As a result, these culturally homesick internal immigrants set up a demand for the music that they knew, and worked unselfconsciously to disseminate it and generalize the demand for it.

But even though both country and blues musics were growing in popularity, they were still considered to be class- and race-specific. This specificity was not merely a specificity of marketing categories, but of cultural sanction and meaning as well; it would not be considered wholly proper for a "cultured," urban, middle-class white teenager to listen to (or, heaven forbid, dance to) Hank Williams or Muddy Waters, no more so than it would have been for him or her to hang out on the street corner, fornicate, shoot pool, or read *Tales from the Crypt*. In spite of the cultural interdictions placed upon them—or perhaps because of these interdictions—the musics powerfully appealed to the thoroughly silenced majorities of young people in the 1950s: they defined spaces in which teenagers could exercise the body and, to a limited extent, indulge its sexuality.

In short, you could dance to them. They had a powerful, pulsing beat, unlike most mainstream white popular music of the early 1950s. Their problem was that if you liked them, you could hear them only with difficulty, only if you were either lucky enough to live within range of any of the small radio stations that served the market for "race" music, or if you were willing to go to record stores in those parts of town where the primary market for these musics lived, the home of those cultural Others of the McCarthy era.

There was, in the 1950s, both a cultural and economic space waiting to be filled, a kind of sociopolitical poem waiting to be written, driven on one side by the possibility of a market for a new, strange (or estranged) commodity, and on the other side by an imperative that developed in response to the stifling range of controls placed on American society by the political projects of McCarthyism and the campaign to eradicate juvenile delinquency. And it is striking how achieving this poem required no new theory or ideology of language—musical, modernist, or other—to transform utterly the cultural landscape of 1950s America. What it did require was that people in positions of institutional, cultural, and economic power serve as vectors for this new virus: that they disseminate the music, establish networks for its distribution, and argue for its legitimacy.

A rich variety of people was willing to step into this role in the mid-1950s. There were disc jockeys, such as Alan Freed, a man who was even better equipped for his chosen role as cultural and ideo-logical nightmare for the scared American middle class than was William Gaines, Jr.;[5] there were record-label owners, such as the Chess brothers at Chess Records, and Sam Phillips at Sun Records, who were sensitive to the opportunities for disseminating a music that seemed bound to a specific market into other sectors of the culture and the economy; and, finally, there were the musicians, who at times seemed less like messengers of a deliberately bold new musical message than accidents of a fate they did not control. And it is rather fitting that they were "accidents"; they were manipulators of musical codes that predated them temporally and transcended them culturally. If any of these agents of social and musical catalysis were "original," it was in their ability to reorganize existing material and discursive networks into new configurations, thereby demonstrating that there were some limited spaces of freedom available to Americans living in that most proper decade. The early career of Elvis Presley is the perfect example of these new, culturally subversive affiliations. The son of hardscrabble working-class parents, steeped in a musical background of blues, country, and gospel musics, Elvis became an example of (and an example for) crypto-delinquents, who would ultimately seem to include just about everybody: "Those who dress sharply, 'hip,' and 'jazzy,' and affect 'off-beat' haircuts." He was positioned to do so in part by virtue of his background and his abilities, but perhaps even in larger part because Sam Phillips, who seems in retrospect perhaps the closest thing America has had to a prophet in the twentieth century, saw that the children of Tail Gunner Joe and Dr. Wertham were ready to hear a white man sing "with the Negro sound and the Negro feel."[6]

Rock & roll music established social contexts in which subterranean social forces could assert themselves, find an outlet for expression, and resolve their various antagonisms (or, perhaps, reinforce these antagonisms). Just as all of these forces were not "progressive," neither were all of these resolutions. But that is not what is at issue in the movements to contain rock & roll; the issue is that these various contending tendencies were given a voice, that they came into the open, established connections, and found reinforcement for their sense and practice of applied (if unreflective) antinomianism: rock & roll seemed to call for a realignment of energies at both the psychic and social levels. While that may have been fine for the kids, for their parents and the other authorities rock & roll was a threatening reminder of the existence of others and otherness that set a dangerous precedent that had to be examined, understood, criticized, and controlled. Gertrude Samuels, writing for the *New York Times Magazine*, stated what was the critical question that parents, congressmen, preachers, and other wielders of power and authority deliberated, at times obsessively, throughout the mid-to-late 1950s: "What is it that makes teen-agers . . . throw off their inhibitions as though at a revivalist meeting?"[7] The answer to this question—and the implications drawn from it—took many forms:

(1) *The Beat*. Both its admirers and detractors agreed that one characteristic defined rock & roll as a musical genre (even if they disagreed as to whether or not it was truly music): its beat. It was the beat—repetitive, powerful, and pulsating—that both energized the kids and enraged the censorial Mammadaddy. Alan Freed's understanding of the beat was relatively historical and complex: "It began on the levees and plantations, took in folk songs, and features blues and rhythm. It's the rhythm that gets the kids. They are starved for music they can dance to after all those years of crooners."[8] The music was always described in terms of its beat; the only question was whether this beat bore with it a positive or negative ideological valence. Not all the authorities shared Freed's optimism. According to one "expert," the dancing inspired by rock & roll was "primitive," of a sort that "demonstrated the violent mayhem long repressed everywhere on earth"; in conclusion, he warned that if "we cannot stem the tide with its waves of rhythmic narcosis and of future waves of vicarious craze, we are preparing our own downfall in the midst of

pandemic funeral dances."[9] If this piece of Cold War era "expertise" strikes us as a finely wrought bit of hysteria, we should note that this hysteria in the face of the beat, along with the confused network of middle-class anxieties that made it seem like a sensible reaction, was quite widespread among critics of rock & roll, and indeed has continued as a theme in criticism right up to the present day. According to Allan Bloom, rock & roll is indeed no more and no less than the savage and primitive rhythm of darkest Africa; furthermore, "[y]oung people know that rock has the beat of sexual intercourse."[10]

Much of the fear associated with rock & roll did in fact derive from its mimetic affinities to sex, and the associated fears that it (and the culture that surrounded it) encouraged and legitimated sex outside of marriage. Yet there were other anxieties that attended to the beat. It worked to consolidate large, amorphous gatherings of youth (as well as the even larger, amorphous culture of youth), providing 1950s teenagers with a cultural focus that encompassed wide areas of appearance, attitude, and behavior. Some observers thought that this power of the music proved that it was a new form of mind control with dangerous affinities to fascism. Herbert von Karajan, the conductor of the Berlin Philharmonic, was precisely vague when he summarized all of these anxieties in his attempt at "explaining" rock & roll: "Strange things happen in the blood stream when a musical resonance coincides with the beat of the human pulse."[11]

Even within the music business, there was much anxiety about the new music (which was really not so new after all). In an influential unsigned article in its 23 February 1955 issue, the editors of *Variety* magazine issued "A Warning to the Music Business." The occasion for this warning was the sudden popularity of r&b songs, such as "Sixty-Minute Man" and "Work with Me, Annie," whose rhythms underscored the scantily clad sexual message of the lyrics—or, as the editors described them, "leer-ics":

> What are we talking about? We're talking about "rock & roll," about "hug," and "squeeze," and kindred euphemisms which are attempting a total breakdown of all reticence about sex.[12]

The record labels most widely associated with the dissemination of all these "blue notes" were the smaller labels, such as King and Imperial, that were "heedless" of responsibility, as might have been expected, since they did not operate within the social and ideological boundaries of respectability as defined by the legitimate major labels. But major labels were guilty of the same sins as the independent operators, and were, due to the greater degree of trust and responsibility invested in them as known quantities, even "guiltier" in a large social sense.

The effect of the *Variety* editorial (and a similar one that ran in *Billboard* magazine) was immediate and striking, at least at the level of the grand sociopolitical gesture. Some newspapers reprinted parts of it and added their voices to the call for cleanliness on the nation's airwaves. Record labels disavowed that they ever intentionally released discs that contained double entendres, and fell all over themselves endorsing *Variety*'s position. The Boston Catholic Youth Organization began to police record hops (which were suspected of providing fronts for illicit sexual behavior) and monitor radio stations more closely. And, while Boston has traditionally been the site of the most extreme episodes of censorship (going back to the banning of John Cleland's *Memoirs*), stations all across the country announced that they would no longer program "off-color" records.[13]

(2) *Jungle Strains.* These records were "off-color" in both the moral and the racial sense; while sexually frank lyrics had long been accepted in r&b songs, it was only when these records became objects of consumption for white kids that anybody (least of all *Variety* magazine) had any kind of problem with them. According to the February 1955 piece in *Variety*, music of the past contained the same kinds of coded reference to matters sexual; the "only difference is that this sort of lyric then was off in a corner by itself. It was the music underworld—not the mainstream." Its success, that is, established its guilt, identified it as a threat, and demonstrated the necessity of controlling it. This new outbreak of cultural miscegenation could only spell trouble for white America, which lived in a guilty fear of African-Americans and their culture. Guilty, because of the growing consensus that racism and segregation were evils that had to be remedied; fear, because this culture of poverty was ambiguously coded as a source of both liberation and delinquency. It (and its musical expressions) stood for what was, in McCarthyite America, coded as

"primitive." Beyond the reach of modern society, deemed too unimportant to warrant direct surveillance by those in positions of power and responsibility, African-American culture seemed to be a repository where sexuality, supposedly untouched by social convention and bourgeois ethics that allowed it to function only within marriage and property relations, flourished unfettered. White intellectuals found this repository irresistible. According to Norman Mailer,

> . . . the Negro had stayed alive and begun to grow by following the need of his body where he could. . . . [T]he Negro . . . could rarely afford the sophisticated inhibitions of civilization, and so he kept for his survival the art of the primitive, he lived in the enormous present, he subsisted for his Saturday night kicks, relinquishing the pleasures of the mind for the more obligatory pleasures of the body, and in his music he gave voice to the character and quality of his existence.[14]

And of course this valorization of the Negro as culturally independent comes through to some degree in Alan Freed's defense of rock & roll. The music that "began on the levees and plantations" was to be the means by which teenagers could be restored to their bodies in the vehicle of the dance.

Not everybody in white, middle-class America—the ruling class that supplied society with its ruling ideas—took very kindly to this democratic and market-driven Negrification of its youth. One of its responses was only somewhat more subtle than it was doomed: record companies, concerned with the economic and ideological viability of marketing yowling black folk to white kids, originally sought to allay their fears and the fears of parents by having "safe" white songsters produce dessicated cover versions of the real Negro thing. But these ersatz productions were not successful for long: Pat Boone was not Little Richard, and despite all apparent similarities, the song they sang was not the same, even if the title of both of their records was "Tutti Frutti," their chord progressions the same, and their lyrics identical. In addition, overt racism was at least occasionally an important component in white American power's reaction. Some whites felt that the goal of the Negro was to overrun the white race by a long campaign of miscegenation. According to Edwin White, a member of the Mississippi House, "the normal and inevitable result through the years will be intermarriage and a mix-breed population."[15]

Some white southerners felt that rock & roll music was a part of this campaign, and traced the music's popularity to part of a fiendish plot by the NAACP to "infiltrate" southern white teenagers. In Birmingham, Alabama, the local White Citizen's Council petitioned juke box owners to remove the "immoral" records, which were "the basic, heavy-beat music of Negroes [that] appeals to the base in man, brings out animalism and vulgarity." The author of that description, Asa Carter, was an authority on the music based on his having "swung a few niggers [him]self." As might have been expected from such an organization, the White Citizen's Council immediately put their theory into practice; the day after this proclamation, a few of its members rushed the stage at a whites-only Nat King Cole concert, assaulting the singer and injuring him slightly before they were dragged off the stage.[16]

This episode suggests something that is, so far as I know, unique to rock & roll among forms of pop culture: it has throughout its career been identified with social movements and tendencies that represent the boundaries of the permissibly progressive (which is what the civil rights movement was in the 1950s). It is perhaps this political affiliation that the music has maintained up until the present, and what has spared it from the severe and overt repression that some other pop culture forms (such as movies and comic books) have faced during the same time period. Indeed, all of the rock and rock-related records that have been brought to trial for or accused of obscenity in the 1980s—from the Dead Kennedys' *In God We Trust, Inc.*, to N.W.A's *AmeriKKKa's Most Wanted*, to 2 Live Crew's *As Nasty as They Wanna Be*—have been defended and acquitted on grounds that they are political discourses and are protected as such under current law.

If rock & roll was identified with the expansion of rights for African-Americans during the 1950s, we must not overlook the fact that this identification was not unambiguously positive, even in the more liberal sectors of the society. The history of exclusion that Mailer draws on is one rich in consequences: if the Negro is a repository of drives excised from white America by means of the methodical application of paranoia, the Negro has been freed from this fate by an economic and social exclusion that has made him a victim of poverty and a candidate for delinquency. Most of the positive, liberating character-istics that Mailer uses to define his white/black hipster are, after all, characteristics that would mark a white teenager as a delinquent. And African-Americans were always regarded in the 1950s as a group "at risk" for delinquency; it was their schools that had the most prob-lems with student discipline, their neighborhoods that had the most problems with gangs, their insertion into former white enclaves that gave rise to social unrest. Just as their culture was a resource for lib-eration, their very existence was a catalyst for social upheavals and racial tensions.

(3) *Rock & Riot.* If the release of the presocial (or at least pre-McCarthy), primitive, and negroid id was an indirect affinity that rock & roll had with juvenile delinquency, white America worried even more about what seemed to be direct and blatant connections between rock & roll and teenage savagery. According to Frank Sinatra,

> Rock 'n' roll smells phony and false. It is sung, played, and writ-ten for the most part by cretinous goons[,] and by means of its almost imbecilic reiteration, and sly, lewd, in plain fact, dirty lyrics . . . it manages to be the martial music of every sideburned delinquent on the face of the earth.[17]

While Sinatra's pronouncement here may strike us, as does so much other "respectable" opinion of the time, as the sign of an ideologically overdetermined frenzy much more dangerous than the phenomenon that inspired it could actually be, his opinion is quite unexception-able viewed in the light of the 1950s press. According to that press, rock & roll was a fad like most other fads except more dangerous, steeped as it was in the violent energies of the Negro, the poor white, the delinquent, and the hoodlum, all of whom found, in the spaces defined by the music, room for the free play of desires and drives that were antagonistic to those of civilized society, and that could spill over to affect (or afflict) otherwise "good" teenagers, if it were allowed to develop unchecked.

For starters, the culture of rock & roll consisted of a rich iconography of delinquency. The styles we associate with it—leather jackets, blue jeans, the "ducktail" haircut, the preference for the motorcycle —were all associated in the consciousness of the 1950s with rebellious, discontented, working-class teenagers who were always "at risk" for delinquency. In the words of some in attendance at the National Association of Secondary School Principals: "You can't put a kid into a monkey suit like one of these blue jeans outfits and expect him to make any kind of good record for himself."[18] These associations were solidified by such movies as *The Wild One* and *Rebel without a Cause*, which suggested to parents and other emissaries of power that this manifestation of working-class youth culture denied the validity of those long-term life projects—the "American Dream"—that so many of the other battles of the period tried to affirm. Rock & roll culture was a culture of the immediate, of physical pleasures affirmed as ends-in-themselves, all of which evoked a dangerous denial of interest in long-term consequences and responsibilities, and a death of ambition that could only be an ominous sign in a scruffy prole teenager. And it was even more worrisome that rock & roll offered a system of objects and roles that were both attractive and accessible to middle-class youth.

The nascence of rock & roll indeed appeared to offer not only a theory and iconography of delinquency and teenage rebellion, but its practice and fruition as well. The early accounts of the new music in newspapers and journals are all descriptions of a struggle, if not a riot. According to the *New York Times* account of one Freed show in New York, thousands upon thousands of teenagers lined up on Washington's Birthday (a school holiday) for hours to see the show, in the process smashing windows, crashing barricades, and destroying the ticket seller's box at the theater where the show was held. All of this was the doing, according to the headline, of the "blue-jean and leather-jacket set," a headline that supplied for the parents the sartorial codes that defined the meaning of the music. (In case the connection wasn't obvious enough, the story ran on a page alongside stories of slain young robbers, exhortations to establish dress codes, and a host of denunciations of the music.) [19]

Indeed, in the mainstream press of the day, all signs indicated that rock & roll and violence were directly and irredeemably linked. One rock & roll riot at Fort Bragg was cut short with tear gas; in Cambridge, a rock & roll fundraising event at MIT turned into a fracas after it became evident that there would be no dancing allowed. The culprits were "these kids . . . that you knew weren't from any college."[20] Riots in Asbury Park, San Jose, Dallas, and Boston destroyed property and sent some people to the hospital; and after the riot in Boston (which, as Martin and Segrave argue, was as likely a police riot as anything else), Alan Freed was indicted for "inciting the unlawful destruction of property."[21] Apparently, after a night of exceptionally tight crowd control by the police, the teenage audience at Freed's show in Boston got out of their seats and rushed into the aisles to dance, at which point the head of security ordered the lights turned on. Freed allegedly told the audience: "I guess the police here in Boston don't want you kids to have a good time," which set off a riot. Worse, people were mugged, robbed, and stabbed outside the arena (which was in a high-crime area) before, during, and after the show, which for many confirmed the connection between crime, violence, and rock & roll.

But the problems with violence at rock & roll shows were not so much attributable to the music as to the fact that these shows were large gatherings at which a whole host of class conflicts played themselves out. Early rock & roll shows were interracial affairs; African-Americans made up between one- and two-thirds of the audience, which also contained white working-class kids who found the more "hillbilly" aspect of the music appealing. This was a highly volatile concatenation of class and race antagonisms that neither the music nor the police could easily contain, and the sexually charged atmosphere of these shows and record hops provided the spark that could set off conflagrations at almost any time. We could argue that, just as these shows provided arenas in which repressed hostilities could return to the psychosocial surface, the incidence of these explosions provided rare occasions in which hostilities could be discussed, albeit in a highly mediated fashion. Moreover, it should not surprise us that the music was held accountable for these explosions of hostility.

They were symptoms of a disease that was too shameful, too fraught with consequences, to be discussed in the light of day, and as a result the only therapy allowed was to make the symptoms disappear.

These attempts to come to grips with the nature and menace of rock & roll are all from the perspective of power, from the point of view, that is, of people and groups who saw the new music as a threat to the hierarchies and hegemonies that ensured their continued social domination. We can see this as the ideological flip side of rock & roll's liberating potential. The rise of rock & roll and the other youth-oriented forms of popular culture was, in the broadest sense, a critique and renunciation of what Herbert Marcuse called affirmative culture. It restored culture to the realm of use-value, tied it back in to a complex of other activities (dancing foremost among them), removed culture from its traditional function as an affirmation of the life of the exalted spirit over and against the life of the body that has been defined and constricted by the imperatives of capitalist production. That is what it might have seemed to the mobs of bopping kids. But to their parents—especially if these parents were scared, conservative, cautious middle-class parents—the music was a threat.

During the early development of rock & roll, nobody seemed to crystallize this new threat, this new avatar of the enemy within, better than Elvis Presley did. The career of Elvis in the 1950s turns out to be exemplary not only for the sort of social forces that he inspired and signified, but also as a catalyst and focus for the wrath of power in the face of the noise. While Elvis would define the parameters of style and desire for teenagers by the end of the 1950s, at the time of his first recordings (1953–54), he attired himself in the sartorial code of the delinquent or the "cat," as stylish, tough young men called themselves in Memphis. From the beginning, Elvis occupied a space of class and race anxiety that would define his image and his music; the son of poor white trash, he carried himself, on Sam Phillips's account, with a degree and kind of uncertainty associated with Memphis blacks: ". . . [H]e felt so inferior. He reminded me of a black man in that way. His insecurity was so markedly like that of a black person." His first record bore the trace of this same ambivalence: the a-side was a cover of "That's All Right," a song by the blues singer Arthur Crudup, while the b-side was a cover of Bill Monroe's "Blue Moon of Kentucky." [22]

All of Presley's recordings with Sun Records did quite well, even though they were on an independent label and therefore did not have either the distribution or the ideological clout of a major-label endorsement behind them. In spite of this success, newspapers and magazines did not see fit to speak of Presley or the menace he represented until he did receive this clout, in December of 1955, from RCA Records, which was so desperate to get into the rock & roll market and get Presley's services that they bought out his contract for the staggering sum of $45,000. It was at that point that the threat of Elvis, as the poor white messenger of poor black sexuality, became a material force, a kind of virus that had to be reckoned with by any means necessary. At first, he seemed to be merely the grotesque punchline to a cultural joke that people were taking too seriously. The 30 April 1956 issue of *Life* called him "A Howling Hillbilly Success" and suggested that his music was a travesty of the traditional male role; his music had "a sob around every note." But as his popularity increased and his appearances multiplied, the opposition stiffened. *Life* claimed in an issue later that year that Presley was "A Different Kind of Idol," one who set potentially dangerous precedents, who legitimated both the personal style and sexual expressiveness of delinquents (or of blacks), whose career was pushing the boundaries of American acceptability perhaps farther than it should be allowed to go. [23]

Elvis was culturally and politically dangerous not only because of his particular reconsolidation of the codes of class and race, but of gender as well. Perhaps the most common complaint in the demonography of Elvis is that he was a marginally literate pedagogue whose chief lesson was sexual confusion. The writer for *Life* and Jack Gould of the *New York Times* both agreed that Elvis's signature stage mannerism—his wild, grinding, abandoned hip movements—were not so much suggestive of a new masculine sexuality as they were reminders of the old spectacular presentations of female sex: the burlesque, the bump-and-grind, the hoochy-koochy. And, Gould implied, that was the only reason (or excuse) for his fame. [24] Gould's assessment seemed to be borne out by the famous broadcast of Elvis's first appearance on the *Ed Sullivan Show*. The network censors would allow only the upper part of his body to be broadcast, although the studio audience could see him as a gyrating totality. This carefully censored broadcast of Elvis is perhaps the best figure for the attitude of power toward the rock & roll of the 1950s. Elvis there became a bivalent text, exoteric and esoteric at the same time: while the surface Elvis, his "front," if you will, was not terribly frightening or exceptional, this front was supported by a "secret" Elvis, darkly sexual, capable of generating an outbreak of mass hysteria that all could see at home, leaving its cause to the imagination. But even this bit of social prophylaxis was too suggestive. The networks were roundly condemned later for "exploiting" teenagers: "On the Sullivan program he injected movements of the tongue and indulged in wordless singing that were singularly distasteful." [25]

The fault here did not lie with Presley, who was presumed to be too stupid to chart the course of his fate (he was, after all, just doing what came naturally), nor with the teenagers, who were simply poor dupes, but with the sober, responsible men of the ruling class who were in a position to decide what would and would not be represented in the legitimate and legitimating cultural markets of the day. Elvis was a "blue note" that did not belong in respectable music or in respectable society, a dissonance that was too appealing and suggestive of a new form of musical and social equilibrium radically at odds with the prevailing one of the day. The reaction to Elvis was severe, at all levels of society: police departments sent out vice squads to his concerts; religious organizations held prayer rallies to counterpose his pernicious influence; *America* (the magazine) warned America (the nation) to "Beware Elvis Presley," calling on TV stations and talent agencies to cease "handling such nauseating stuff." [26]

There seemed to be no way for the culture to contain or control the menace that was Elvis; he was, in the words of a writer at *Newsweek*, an "inextinguishable" flame that threatened to set American society burning, despite the best intentions and efforts of critics. When things seemed darkest, however, the army came to the rescue: Elvis was drafted. The political implication of his induction is still widely discussed. The draft board in Memphis seemed quite delighted at the prospect of causing this white-trash boy a little trouble; Dave Marsh has argued that this was a deliberate move on the part of the government to teach Elvis a lesson: "The government's intention in drafting Elvis was to rob him of everything—not just fame but also his wealth and whatever new dignity he had acquired." [27] I am in no position to evaluate Marsh's argument, although it seems to me that it smacks too much of a conspiracy theory of power that sees its action and its agency being transacted at all times behind closed doors, with its members (the people with the ability to make decisions that shape and transform other people's lives) operating in perfect consensus, in perfect secrecy, and with perfect efficacy.

Whatever the merits of that theory, in this particular case it overlooks the fact that the actual effect of Elvis's tenure in the army was not to silence him, but to reclaim him for the benefit of a constellation of political and economic forces to which he at first seemed iconographically antipathetic. Before, he represented all that was threatening in American youth culture; he scrambled the codes of sexuality, class, and race in a manner that suggested dangerous new linkages and reconciliations among them. His stint in the army enabled him to "clean up his act"; it was the perfect way to make him safe for democracy. His manager, Col. Tom Parker, insisted that he take no special privileges, and that no concessions be made for him; he entered as a normal soldier, as a "grunt," and when he emerged, he had been purified of his socio-semiological sins. As though to demonstrate that newfound purity, his first performance—televised, of course—after his (honorable) discharge was with Frank Sinatra. Elvis was a sideburned delinquent no more.

During the 1950s, it was quite rare for censors to attack specific individuals, except insofar as they were readily available, culturally strategic targets; perhaps the only other incidents of the full weight of power brought down on an individual rock & roller were Chuck Berry's conviction on a Mann Act charge of transporting a minor across state lines for the purpose of committing an impropriety, and the arrest of Alan Freed and some others on charges of commercial bribery following the payola hearings. Such confrontations always gave the target of censorship access to too many means of institutionalized resistance. In general, the censors did not fare so well when they relied on direct confrontation with the enemy within. Several cities and communities across the country tried to ban rock & roll shows: Jersey City, Asbury Park, Boston, Cambridge, Los Angeles, San Jose, Newport. Yet the futility (and in some cases the illegality) of this project must have been apparent. At best, proscribing public concerts could only affirm the sense many young people had that rock & roll was their music, that there was indeed something special about it, and that the authorities were merely acting out of terror and a rage to order out of proportion to the chaos that was threatened. Even if shows were banned, this would at any rate interdict only one leg of what was rock & roll's nuclear triad of delivery systems. Rock & roll concerts were spectacles at which the tensions that comprised social life in the American 1950s were displayed and resolved, true, but they were not nearly as omnipresent nor as insidious as the music's other two delivery systems: records and radio. Due to the "bad taste" of the American public, as well as the irresponsibility of those in positions of power in the music industry, containing rock & roll at that level would require a much more concerted effort that would specify it as a disease, isolate and expose its causes (or its agents), and destroy its capacity to replicate and transmit itself both economically and culturally.

The form that therapy took was two series of hearings held in the late 1950s. The first, in 1958, was held in the name of investigating a possible conflict of interest in the radio industry. There were two large, competing organizations that managed the lucrative publishing rights to recorded music: the American Society of Composers, Authors, and Publishers (ASCAP), and Broadcast Music, Inc. (BMI). ASCAP had held a virtual monopoly until the 1940s in the field of music licensing, which was the mechanism by which publishers collected royalties on songs they owned. Like any good monopoly, they used their position to maximize their profits, setting royalty fees at figures that seemed exorbitant to broadcasters and other firms that used licensed music. These broadcasters and record companies therefore formed BMI in the 1940s in an effort to break ASCAP's monopoly.

ASCAP was not only a music licensing company, however, but also a critical gatekeeper in the music business, one that carefully selected which publishers they would represent and that paid royalties based on the depth of a songwriter's catalog and seniority within the company. Neither of these practices worked to the benefit of "race," "hill-billy," or (later) rock & roll songwriters, whose publishers were routinely denied access to ASCAP's near-essential services. Naturally, then, these publishers and songwriters flocked to BMI. When these previously marginal musics assumed places of economic and cultural centrality in the 1950s, BMI profited enormously. The problem with this success was that BMI was a nonprofit organization owned by several of the major players in the broadcast industry: many large radio stations and record companies were BMI affiliates. The stage was set, then, for the hearings, which were at one level an inquiry into possible conflicts of interest on the part of businesses (such as radio stations) that held public licenses; on another level, they were an inquisition into the guilt or innocence of rock & roll.

But perhaps I should not say "levels" here, which implies that the two projects are in some way separate. In the hearings they were both aspects of a seamless totality in which the survival of the music was expressly at stake. The popularity of rock & roll was held to be a direct function of merchandising; according to such an unbiased expert as Oscar Hammerstein, rock & roll songs "die as soon as the plug stops."[28] Ephemeral and culturally degraded, rock & roll's dissemination was wrecking America's capacity to appreciate good music, which was defined not just as music in the high European art tradition, but also as the "ageless treasures" of the American popular song (which ASCAP licensed, for a fee): the compositions of Cole Porter, Jerome Kern, Irving Berlin, and, yes, Oscar Hammerstein. The reason this worthy music did not even have the chance to fall on deaf ears was that disc jockeys, with only avarice in their hearts, weren't giving it a chance to be heard and appreciated.

Vance Packard suggested to the committee that it was the disc jockeys, those master manipulators, the hidden persuaders, who were corrupting America's children by operating as advance men for broadcasters, who held a multifaceted interest in rock & roll. They owned the licensing agency that paid out royalties for the music. Moreover, rock & roll was "cheap." Not just cheap in the cultural sense; that much was obvious. But it was economically cheap as well. Mr. Packard pointed out that recording rock & roll did not require the use of expensive, union-scale studio musicians or orchestras, did not require the services of expensive, legitimate songwriters, and did not demand the use of trained singers with expensive fees. Not only were those things not necessary, they were positively useless in that musical context. The outcome of this new musical economy of scale?

> Our airways have been flooded in recent years with whining guitarists, musical riots put to a switchblade beat, obscene lyrics about hugging, squeezing, and rocking all night long. This is the diet served up daily to young Americans whose tastes are still forming.[29]

In these hearings, or at least in the testimony of the witnesses who favored legislation, "BMI" became a complicated signifier for not just rock & roll but the entire apparatus by means of which it is produced and disseminated. For it is by means of that total apparatus that American minds were being rotted out by the menacing noise of rock, race, and hillbilly music, all of which were considered similarly cheap and worthless. Indeed, the senators at that hearing repeatedly stated that they were not really interested in what was the nominal subject of the hearing, the squabble between those two economic giants, ASCAP and BMI. The senators wanted to argue about that great aesthetic question that had such dire political consequences: what to do with rock & roll. In the words of Senator John Pastore from Rhode Island: "What difference does it make who is doing the poisoning? Does it not become the responsibility of the Congress to remove the cause and the source?"[30]

"The cause and the source" was BMI, the poison was rock & roll and its related musics, and the witnesses were quite concerned to point out that these conspirators were not only culturally inferior and economically suspect, but were, quite frankly, un-American:

> In short, a shrewd newcomer to this country came to BMI and pointed out a neglected lode of cheaply mined music. BMI set him up in the business of exploiting this long-scorned vein, and almost overnight the sound of the "heartbeat of America" came wailing and stomping over the airways, from thousands of radio stations.[31]

This particular definition of "un-American" is quite expansionistic, well able to encompass all sorts of difference from the norm established by and in reference to white middle-class professionals such as Mr. Packard himself. The music was deeply suspect because it came from people who had no warrant or right to promote their culture as being the spontaneous song of the American Adam: Negroes, Latin Americans, "a milk-truck driver, a pair of teenage schoolgirls, a publicity man," not to mention Elvis Presley, who was a critical agent in the "heavy infiltra[tion]" of the popular song charts by music that had the bad taste to be popular.

Mr. Packard's testimony was extreme, a brittle ideological crystallization of an attitude shared by most of the witnesses at the hearing who were critical of rock & roll. The music was always cheap, always the product of inferior songwriters, and its popularity (which was held to be the exclusive work of a broadcasting industry that was utterly effective at forcing its wishes on the American public) was won at the direct cost to the work of the "trained, willing, able, and accomplished" who, by virtue of their membership in ASCAP, were demonstrably of cultural value.

If Packard and his colleagues focused the issue of the hearing, they also polarized it in such a way that there was nothing the committee could have done about stopping the menace. The position, as stated, was too easy to object to for all the best reasons. Senator Albert Gore, Sr., of Tennessee came by after Packard's testimony to denounce his "gratuitous insult to thousands of our fellow Tennesseans, both in and out of the field of country music."[32] More important, if in the testimony of the critics "BMI" became a coded expression for the cultural depravity that rock & roll represented, "ASCAP" became, all too easily and all too legitimately, a coded expression for cultural elitism. Numerous witnesses from all walks of life gave testimony before the committee of their personal experiences of exclusion from ASCAP: songwriters, publishers, milkmen, hillbillies, and the veteran schoolteacher from Jacksonville, Florida, who happened to be the composer of "Heartbreak Hotel." All of these people told similar stories: while, technically, membership in ASCAP was open to all, in practice the applications of those who did not fit into the company profile were never answered, their requests for information never recognized, and their songs never published, or if they were, the royalty structure favored songwriters who were old and established over all others. The disc jockeys laughed off the conspiracy model that the ASCAP witnesses relied on to explain the predominance of rock & roll on the radio. In the end, ASCAP's arguments were refuted and their image as cultural guarantors was rendered ambivalent: guarantors, yes, but of a remote, elite, exclusive culture, as concerned with keeping the helots out as with keeping the treasures in. Which were, after all, two aspects of the same project.

Looking at that round of hearings, we could say, following Jacques Attali, that one of the threatening qualities of rock & roll was that it represented a revolution in the mode of production of "popular" music. It threatened an entire system of rigid hierarchies that dominated and defined all phases of musical production: the abyss between performer and audience, songwriter and performer, disc jockey and record publisher, as well as the hierarchies that existed within each of those fields, such as that between "independent" record labels and "major" labels. Along with opening up the production of music to would-be musicians, rock & roll opened up the production and distribution of records to would-be entrepreneurs. Anybody with some capital (not a lot, necessarily—*some* would do quite well) could put out a record, and small record labels could successfully compete with big labels.[33] But this democratization of production had a profoundly ambiguous political meaning. As democratization—as a demonstration of the possibilities of socioeconomic fluidity and mobility in America—it was something to be valued and praised, which is exactly what happened during the 1958 BMI-ASCAP hearings. But as a vector of cultural, libidinal, and political chaos and rebellion, as an agent for the confusion of the values, mores, and assumptions of power that guaranteed the "American way of life" as it stood in the late 1950s, it was a force to be reckoned with in the only way that power in the 1950s could reckon with any kind of dissent: by stifling it.

The method of stifling it was not the old way, the way of Anthony Comstock and his Society for the Suppression of Vice, which would have required that some spokesman for good American taste drag each of the offending records—all thousand or so of them a year, recorded and distributed by a whole host of geographically diffuse labels—into a court of law, and establish the guilt of each individual record. That was not the way that power in 1950s America worked, or needed to work. What was needed was the production of the spectacle of consensus, some compelling proof that the whole business of rock & roll was corrupt and in need of surveillance, containment, and strict regulation.

This was precisely the function of the second round of hearings aimed at establishing the guilt of rock & roll as a totality: the payola hearings of 1960. The hearings were held concurrently with a series of hearings aimed at uncovering corruption in TV game shows, and were aimed at similar breaches of ideological faith: whereas the TV hearings investigated charges that game shows were rigged, the payola hearings sought to establish that radio programming was "on the fix." The investigators (which included the FCC, the FTC, and a House subcommittee) were on rather more substantial legal ground than the ASCAP/BMI committee had been; while payola was not a federal crime at the time that the hearings began, it was a crime in several states, and the consensus in the news organs (as well as on the floor of the committee room) was that the representatives were investigating a system of criminal conspiracy rather than holding an inquiry into aesthetics. But these two apparently unrelated projects wove in and out of the hearings as their necessary and sufficient motifs. The targets of the hearings were not songwriters, but rather the men (and they were mostly men) who were responsible for record production, marketing, and dissemination. These were the people who were ultimately to blame for the music's existence and reproduction in a commodity economy, and who were therefore a much more efficient target for regulatory zeal. They included many of the "big fish" of the industry: presidents of major distribution companies, record company CEOs, and some of the most important disc jockeys in the country, including Alan Freed and Dick Clark.

Held ostensibly to investigate whether or not rock & roll disc jockeys had accepted money in exchange for playing records on their radio shows, the hearings were a grand social theater of the confessional, a spectacular confirmation of the presence of the enemy within and a means by which this enemy could be anatomized and purged. Disc jockeys were called before the assembled representatives and asked to confess their sins, which began with playing rock & roll in the first place, and only ended with the taking of money. One of the first witnesses to testify, DJ Norm Prescott from Boston, was formerly known best for having held a write-in contest for a lock of Elvis's hair at his radio station, a promotion that earned him a place in *Life* magazine. In front of the committee, however, he expressed regret for having played the music; he had done so, he said, chiefly from economic necessity. According to him, payola was rampant in the business, and was "the backbone of the radio station."[34] Prescott (and many of the penitent disc jockeys who followed him) confirmed the suspicions many responsible Americans had about rock & roll: that the claims that it was genuinely popular were a sham, that the ratings for popular records were based on whim and nonsense (or payola), and, in general, that the music, which was by and large brazen, ludicrous, and rather degraded, would not have a ghost of a chance unless it was sustained by a conspiracy of bribery and fraud:

MR. BENNETT: Well, do you think without payola that a lot of this so-called junk music, rock 'n' roll stuff, which appeals to the teenagers would not be played, or do you think that kind of thing would be played anyway regardless of the payola?

MR. PRESCOTT: Never get on the air.

MR. BENNETT: Do you think payola is responsible for it?

MR. PRESCOTT: Yes; it keeps it on the air, because it fills pockets.[35]

Witness after witness testified that rock & roll was the sound of payola. In the words of Alan Dary, another Boston-area disc jockey: "I do my level best to play the type of music that an adult audience would enjoy. Consequently, I do not get into the raucous kind of sound that I had always associated payola with."[36]

The collusion between the disc jockeys and the promotion men was nothing less than a ruthlessly effective "thought control operation," according to the committee. Record producers and distributors would cut deals and make payoffs to disc jockeys (to give special consideration to a label's records) and to record stores (to report high sales of a company's records to trade journals and sales-tracking agencies); this would lead, by the iron logic of mass brainwashing, to teenagers buying the records in question, which would in theory lead to more payola, more sales, and more money for all concerned. Except, of course, for the poor duped public, which was doubly deprived: of its money, which was bad, but also of its right to hear good music, adult music, on the radio, which was worse.

The unspoken conviction throughout these hearings is that the success of rock & roll represented a local abdication of market forces in favor of a pure conspiracy. The committee was convinced that it was only through payola that a music so self-evidently inferior could become so popular, and their interpretation developed the force of truth as the hearings progressed: rock & roll was at once a cause and a symptom of a cultural scandal; it was the function of an insidious conspiracy aimed at those too intellectually and morally weak to avoid its clutches, a conspiracy that worked without opposition at the level of either the individual conscience or social responsibility. And the work of the committee was therefore twofold: to establish the moral guilt of both the industry and the music. Indeed, it is hard to read the massive transcript of the payola hearings without being reminded time and again of the spectacle of confession that McCarthy and his acolytes had made a part of the political and cultural landscape of the 1950s. The committee sought to rid society of a dangerous menace that lurked within its legitimate channels: the morally corrupt disc jockey who was responsible for ruining American teenagers; the record company that released the raucous stuff in the first place, and then bribed the disc jockeys to play it; and the distribution companies that functioned as the nervous system by which the entire productive network communicated with itself and with the outside world.

The point was, ultimately, this enemy's exposure. Since payola was legal, nothing could be done directly against the disc jockeys who had accepted it, nor against the record labels and distributors who had offered it in the first place. But, as was so often the case, the direct punishment of the "guilty" by the full mechanism of the law was not necessary. In the committee's mind, the subterranean practice of payola was linked with all of the multiform evils of rock & roll music, its popularity and its proliferation. And the committee was convinced that the exposure of this corruption, and the ensuing national consensus on its threat, would work to purge the country of its cultural menace.

As it turned out, the project succeeded in its aims. Many of the disc jockeys who appeared before the committee lost their jobs, and others throughout the country had to forfeit their positions in order to satisfy the consensus of power that, finally, something had to be done, and could be done. Alan Freed, "the Pied Piper of rock & roll," was unrepentant before the committee, and was arrested along with several others and charged with violating New York's commercial bribery laws. Defending himself against these charges broke him both financially and physically, and he was never again to play a majcı role in the development of the music he had in many ways pioneered. Indeed, such was the power of the hearings as a theater of guilt that they succeeded in their cultural goal—the general containment of rock & roll—even when they failed to expose the culpability of a particular witness. This is perhaps clearest in the case of Dick Clark, who was one of the main targets of the investigation. Clark's national TV show *American Bandstand* was a powerful force for the transmission of both the sound and the culture of rock & roll. Every day after school, American teenagers could see people just like them trying out the latest dances to the newest songs, and Clark was their interpreter. In addition, he had extensive financial investments in the business: in a variety of publishing houses, independent record labels, distributors, and a record-pressing plant. Therefore, not only was Clark a most important vector by which the music was transmitted, he was also emblematic of the nefarious connection between money interests and rock & roll that supposedly enabled the music to get off the ground in the first place and establish its hegemony. It stood to reason that he would be the most guilty of payola.

A great deal was at stake in his testimony, and both he and the committee prepared extensively for his appearance. Clark retained the services of Computech, a statistical-analysis service, to demonstrate that he did, indeed, play records according to their popularity, and not according to the degree of his financial stake in them; the committee employed the services of government statisticians to criticize the methodology used by Computech and to refute its analysis. Both the committee and Clark prepared a descriptive catalog of his investments. There is a critically fascinating difference between his affidavit (which did not appear in the hearings transcript) and the presentation of the committee (which did). Clark's affidavit is a narrative of the history of his involvement in these companies; the committee chose to present the information in the form of several large charts which show the music industry as a large, synchronic web at the center of which was Dick Clark.

Clark's defense, which succeeded in saving his career, would hold substantial consequences for the future development of the music. He argued for a narrow definition of payola that demonstrated to the satisfaction of the committee-as-court-of-law (if not to the satisfaction of the committee-as-confessor) that while he regarded the work of the committee as helpful to the industry, he did not think that he had taken part in any practices he regarded as immoral or illegal. And this argument was mutually supportive of his representation of himself as a middle-class Everyman who just happened to get involved with rock & roll because he liked teenagers and thought the music was a solid business opportunity. He claimed that he had invested so broadly in the business as a means of providing for himself and his family in the event his TV and radio career came to an end. He worried about his reputation. He was, in short, capable of defending himself and the music as a legitimate, sober, American business enterprise that would be quite willing to work within the constraints set for it by the legal and aesthetic guardians of American culture.

And Clark was not alone. Networks and radio stations established conflict-of-interest policies that would protect them from suspicion, although it limited the degree to which people could involve themselves in the music and its production. (Clark, for instance, would have to sell practically all of his holdings at a substantial loss.) As if it were necessary after the hearings, practically all major record companies signed consent decrees to stop offering any financial consideration for the playing of its records. The investigation even touched the investigators themselves; when it became public knowledge that FCC Chairman John Doerfer had accepted a plane and yacht trip from a broadcasting company official (with whom he happened to be friends), he had to resign his position.

The effects of the payola hearings on rock & roll would be many and manifold. Economically, the hearings worked to force a consolidation of power and hierarchy in the music business; conflicts of interest that had resulted from the limited number of qualified people performing a variety of institutional and economic functions disappeared by force. The hearings worked, as it were, to bring the music industry from the age of liberal/competitive capitalism into the age of monopoly capitalism. As a result, it became harder and harder for small labels to compete for talent; indeed, by the mid-1960s, they would no longer be factors in the marketplace. Payola had been a force that increased competition in the record business; without payola the small record labels lost the means by which they could compensate for the major labels' promotional weight. Not coincidentally, the small labels were responsible for much of the music in the first place.

The hearings also affected the direction of rock & roll as a "pure" cultural form (if we can allow ourselves, for a moment, to imagine what such a thing might be). They sent a powerful message to the keepers of the cultural gates—the presidents, A&R men (talent scouts), and managers of record labels and distribution firms—that it was no longer safe or really even acceptable to squander these valuable material resources on the manufacture and dissemination of such cheap and "raucous" music. At least they sent a word to the wise, to the men and women who had survived the scandal with their positions intact; after all, the hearings drove many of the most knowledgeable and committed people out of the profession. They would be replaced by more sedate and cautious people who would use their power responsibly; while Chuck Berry, Negro and cradle robber, was in prison, America could have good, talented singers such as Pat Boone, who used to drive his Corvette to Columbia (where he studied "Art for Art's sake" while looking dreamily into the future), and who wrote inspirational books for confused adolescents in between interpreting and selling songs written by Negroes and white trash.[37] The result of the hearings, then, was a containment of the menace far more effective than the mere silencing of it could ever have been. Rock & roll was a powerful, contrary voice in 1950s American cultural discourse, a voice that bore with it disquieting news not only of the existence of others, but of the possibility of Otherness, of a different configuration of both personal and social energies. The achievement of the hearings was to recuperate and co-opt that voice to make it not only safe for the tender ears of the children of power but an effective soundtrack for its collective reveries of stability.

Notes

1   *Hearings before the Committee on Commerce, Science, and Transportation, United States Senate, Ninety-Ninth Congress, First Session, on Contents of Music and the Lyrics of Records* (Washington, 1985), 61.
2   In a sense, I am recasting Michel Foucault's argument against adopting the repressive hypothesis at the level of repressive state apparatuses: even at that level, the tendency of those in power is to avoid direct and spectacular confrontation and antagonisms in favor of using more diffuse methods for controlling discourse and practice.
3   Of course, it is possible to use both strategies to devastating effect. Retailers are much more susceptible to legal pressure than are record labels, who can better afford the legal defenses necessary to prosecute and win a censorship case. The flip side of this is that if a producer—be it a record label or a book publisher—is willing and able to fund defenses for accused retailers, the case against these retailers will fall as the case against the artifact falls. But if the censor's legal strategy fails, the political and economic effect of these cases all too often works in his favor: by drawing attention to the retailer's dubious wares, the censor manages to subject him or her to the community's wrath.
4   I do not mean to say here that these groups *escaped* repression; after all, it was their unions that were observed and infiltrated, their organizations that were suspected of harboring closet Reds and functioning as their fronts. Moreover, it was their children who were the iconic embodiments of the perils of delinquency. But within the elite cultural milieus that decided who and what would be censored, that examined the culture of the proles and found it perilously inadequate to the task of raising children who could "fit," it was commonly assumed that these proles were incapable of real agency; they were not masters of their destiny, but raw material to be mastered either by forces of American capitalism or The Enemy. Many of the episodes of censorship in the 1950s would be carried out in the name of their protection; others, in the name of their containment; but none in the name of their suppression. The targets of these episodes were always members of the same cultural and political elites to which the censors belonged themselves. So long as the prole remained at his level—so long as he did not seek any position of power or responsibility from which he could challenge the order of things—he was considered beyond suspicion. Or, perhaps I should say, *beneath* suspicion.
5   Freed was a college-educated classical music disc jockey at a radio station in Cleveland who was tipped off, by a friend in the know, that white kids were venturing into black neighborhoods in droves to buy records cut by black r&b artists. He began playing these records on his late-night radio show, which rapidly became

the most popular one in Cleveland. Freed invested a great deal of showmanship in broadcasting the music; while a record was playing on the air, he would pound on a telephone book that he kept by the mike, sing, moan, and howl along with the music.

William (Bill) Gaines, Jr., won fame and notoriety during the early 1950s as the publisher of EC Comics, a line noted for its crime, horror, and science-fiction titles, *Tales from the Crypt* among them. These books were condemned by a variety of "experts," critics, and social commentators (chief among them Dr. Fredric Wertham, author of *Seduction of the Innocent*) as being responsible for the enormous rise in juvenile delinquency during the period. These comics (and Gaines) were the subject of several days' worth of Senate hearings in 1954 whose result was the passage of the Comics Code of 1954.

6   Ed Ward, "The Fifties and Before," in Ed Ward, Geoffrey Stokes, and Ken Tucker, *Rock of Ages: The Rolling Stone History of Rock & Roll* (New York, 1986), 77. I do not want to lay out the early history of rock & roll in extensive detail here, if only because there are so many excellent works that do the job better than I could ever hope to. Besides *Rock of Ages*, Charlie Gillette's *The Sound of the City* is perhaps the classic text. For a brief, concise, and specific introduction, see *American Popular Music: Readings from the Popular Press, Volume II: The Age of Rock*, ed. Timothy E. Scheurer (Bowling Green, 1989). Greil Marcus's "Presliad" (in *Mystery Train: Images of America in Rock 'n' Roll Music* [New York, 1975]) is the seminal article in the field of Presley studies.

7   Gertrude Samuels, "Why They Rock 'n' Roll—And Should They?" *New York Times Magazine*, 12 January 1958, 16.

8   Edith Evans Asbury, "Rock 'n' Roll Teen-Agers Tie Up the Times Square Area," *New York Times*, 23 February 1956.

9   Milton Bracker, "Experts Propose Study of 'Craze,'" *New York Times*, 23 February 1956.

10   Allan Bloom, *The Closing of the American Mind: How Higher Education Has Failed Democracy and Impoverished the Souls of Today's Students* (New York, 1987), 73.

11   *New York Times*, 26 October 1956.

12   *Variety*, 23 February 1955, 2.

13   I am indebted here, as in many other places in this article, to the work of Linda Martin and Kerry Segrave, whose *Anti-Rock: The Opposition to Rock 'n' Roll* (Hamden, Conn., 1988) is an impressively researched, comprehensive chronicle of both criticisms of rock & roll and efforts at censoring it. It is an excellent introduction to the problem of censorship in the music, as well as a good factual account of the general history of the music, which has since the 1960s tended to define itself in opposition to the efforts made to control and contain it.

14   Norman Mailer, *The White Negro* (San Francisco, 1957), 4. While Mailer is here directly discussing jazz music, this music was itself losing its appeal among African-Americans, who were turning more and more to r&b and other dance musics to gratify the "obligatory pleasures of the body."

15   *New York Times*, 1 December 1955.

16 "Segregationist Wants Ban on 'Rock 'n' Roll,'" *New York Times*, 30 May 1956; and "Who the Hoodlums Are," *Newsweek*, 23 April 1956.

17 Samuels, "Why They Rock 'n' Roll," 19.

18 "Principals Toss a Rock at Presley-Mimic Role," *New York Times*, 25 February 1957.

19 Asbury, "Rock 'n' Roll Teen-agers."

20 Laura Haddock, "Cambridge Acts after Teen Riot," *Christian Science Monitor*, 12 March 1956.

21 Martin and Segrave, *Anti-Rock*, 36.

22 Ward, Stokes, and Tucker, *Rock of Ages*, 79–80.

23 "Elvis—a Different Kind of Idol," *Life*, 27 August 1956.

24 Jack Gould, "TV: New Phenomenon," *New York Times*, 6 June 1956.

25 Jack Gould, "Elvis Presley: Lack of Responsibility Is Shown by TV in Exploiting Teen-Agers," *New York Times*, 16 September 1956.

26 "Beware Elvis Presley," *America*, 23 June 1956, 294–95.

27 Cited in Ward, Stokes, and Tucker, *Rock of Ages*, 162–63.

28 *Hearings before the Subcommittee on Communications of the Committee on Interstate and Foreign Commerce, United States Senate, Eighty-Fifth Congress, Second Session, on S. 2834* (Washington, 1958), 6.

29 Ibid., 109.

30 Ibid., 115.

31 Ibid., 135.

32 Ibid., 141.

33 In fact, during the early days of rock & roll, major labels were extremely reluctant to invest anything in something that was so obviously a "fad," so small labels did quite nicely, and indeed dominated the singles charts up until the middle 1960s.

34 *Hearings before a Subcommittee of the Committee on Interstate and Foreign Commerce, House of Representatives, Eighty-Sixth Congress, Second Session, on Payola and Other Deceptive Practices in the Broadcasting Field* (Washington, 1960).

35 Ibid., 39.

36 Ibid., 92.

37 Pat Boone's fullest statement as a social philosopher and counselor of youth can be found in his work, *'Twixt Twelve and Twenty* (Englewood Cliffs, N.J., 1958), which is a rather skillful translation of the Protestant work ethic into a series of analyses and prescriptions applicable to the American teenager in the late 1950s. It is full of helpful hints on "how to find your personal gold mine, how to work it, and what to do after it starts to pay," whether that mine be sexual or economic in nature.

Greil Marcus

A Corpse in Your Mouth: Adventures of a Metaphor, or Modern Cannibalism

> *People who talk about revolution and class struggle without referring explicitly to every-day life, without understanding what is sub-versive about love and positive in the refusal of constraint, have corpses in their mouths.*
> —Raoul Vaneigem, Paris, 1967

> The slaughter increases, and [people] cling to the prestige of European glory. . . . [T]hey cannot persuade us to enjoy this rotting pile of human flesh they present to us.
> —Hugo Ball, Zurich, 1916

"HURRAY, THE BUTTER IS GONE! Goering in his Hamburg address: 'Brass has always made an empire strong; butter and lard have at best made a people fat.' "
—John Heartfield, Prague, 1935

The only objective way of diagnosing the sickness of the healthy is by the incongruity between their rational existence and the possible course their lives might be given by reason. All the same, the traces of illness give them away: their skin seems covered by a rash printed in regular patterns, like a camouflage of the inorganic. The very people who burst with proofs of exuberant vitality could easily be taken for

prepared corpses, from whom the news of their not-quite-successful decease has been withheld for reasons of population policy.
—Theodor Adorno, Los Angeles, 1944

In an era when art is dead [the student] remains the most loyal patron of the theatres and film clubs and the most avid consumer of its preserved corpse.
—Association Fédérative Générale des Etudiants de Strasbourg/Internationale Situationniste, *De la misère en milieu étudiant (On the Poverty of Student Life)*, Strasbourg, France, Fall 1966, as translated by the Situationist International in *Ten Days That Shook the University: The Situationists at Strasbourg*, London, early 1967

People who talk about revolution and class struggle without referring explicitly to everyday life, without understanding what is subversive about love and positive in the refusal of constraint, have corpses in their mouths.
—Raoul Vaneigem, *Traité de savoir-vivre à l'usage des jeunes générations (Treatise on Living for the Young Generations)*, Paris, Fall 1967

People who talk about revolution and class struggle without. . . .
—Wall poster, Comité Enragés-Internationale Situationniste, Paris, May 1968

PEOPLE WHO TALK ABOUT REVOLUTION AND CLASS STRUGGLE WITHOUT. . . .
—Anonymous graffiti, Paris, May 1968

ART IS DEAD—DON'T CONSUME ITS CORPSE
—Anonymous graffiti, Paris, May 1968

People who talk about revolution and class struggle without. . . .
—Various unauthorized translations of Vaneigem's *Treatise*, published in pirate editions as *The Revolution of Everyday Life*, U.S.A. and U.K., late 1960s–early 1970s

People who talk about revolution and class struggle without. . . .
—Translation of Comité Enragés-Internationale Situationniste wall poster in *Leaving the 20th Century: The Incomplete Work of the Situationist International*, edited by Christopher Gray, designed by Jamie Reid, U.K., 1974

—Collage by Jamie Reid from *Leaving the 20th Century*

It's like someone just told me there aren't going to be any more cheeseburgers in the world.

—Felton Jarvis, record producer for Elvis Presley, on the occasion of Presley's death, U.S.A., August 1977

PRESLEYBURGER SHOCK

Shock. Horror. They are the only two words to describe the latest report from our Pick of the Poseurs correspondent in America. The recently described sensational attempt to steal Elvis' body was doomed to failure from the start, reason being a successful snatch has already been staged.

probe the sicker this bizarre situation has turned out to be. It seems even more rare and more sought after 'Dean burger specials', made from the remains of James Dean can be bought. Those who have tasted this speciality said they are rather tough but tasty. They are thought to be authentic however, as they still contain bits of the car wreckage.

'Disneyburgers' are quite a diff-

Shock. Horror. They are the only two words to describe the latest report from our Pick of the Poseurs correspondent in America. The recently described sensational attempt to steal Elvis' body was doomed to failure from the start, reason being a successful snatch has already been staged. What's happened to the body? It now appears certain that it was minced down and turned into the most bizarre cult food of all time. Certainly "Presleyburgers" have been selling to the New York and West Coast rock aristocracy at up to $1000 a throw. Unconfirmed reports suggest that a small consignment of frozen Presleyburgers have arrived in U.K. and that Cliff Richard ate one just before going on at his recent Dome gig.

P.O.T.P. reporters have questioned rock superstar Frankie Vaughn and though he declined to reply, his mouth was clearly seen to water. P.O.T.P. readers can draw their own conclusions.

The further we went with our probe the sicker this bizarre situation has turned out to be. It seems even more rare and more sought after 'Death Burger Specials,' made from the remains of James Dean can be bought. Those who have tasted this specialty said they are rather tough but tasty. They are thought to be authentic however, as they still contain bits of the car wreckage.

'Disneyburgers' are quite a different matter however, as they had the good sense to deep freeze him only twenty minutes after he had died. Walt Disney will have quite a surprise however when they wake him up in the year 2,000 AD and finds a couple of his arms and legs missing.

—Anonymous text (by Ray Holme and Joby Hooligan) in *Pic of the Poseurs—Magazine for Modern Youth*, London, 1977

—Back sleeve of Sex Pistols single "Satellite" (b–side of "Holidays in the Sun"), by Jamie Reid, London, Fall 1977

—Sleeve of Cortinas single "Defiant Pose," by TC + P/Hipgnosis, London, 1978

—Stickers enclosed with *A Factory Sample*, EP with recordings by Joy Division, the Durutti Column, John Dowie, and Cabaret Voltaire, Manchester, U.K., 1978

—Sleeve of "Mittageisen" ("Metal Postcard"), Siouxsie and the Banshees single ("pluck cogs from fob watches / for dinner on Friday"), London, 1979

—Sleeve of "C'mon Everybody," Sex Pistols single featuring the late Sid Vicious, by Jamie Reid, London, 1979

—Rough design by Jamie Reid for sleeve of "C'mon Everybody."

"The idea of the Vicious-Burger related back to the spoof we did as the Wicked Messengers. When Presley's body was lying in state at Graceland, there were loads of rumours about people trying to break in and steal it. We invented this little campaign—in a spoof fanzine called *Pick of the Poseurs*—saying that in fact his body had been stolen and had been turned into a commercial product—i.e., hamburgers. It also related to the old Situationist 'corpse' metaphor."
—Jamie Reid, in *Up They Rise—The Incomplete Works of Jamie Reid*

. . . the King's decaying body is exhumed and brought back for one last concert tour (unfortunately, it keeps falling off its stool and collapsing onstage in a heap). The corpse is trotted out for record-store autographing sessions. . . . Finally, slices of flesh are hacked off and sold in "Piece o' Presley" packages.
—*Rolling Stone*, on John Myhre's film *He May Be Dead, But He's Still Elvis*, U.S.A., 1979

OUR FOREIGN CORRESPONDENT WRITES:

Top show biz moguls and TV personalities were convicted last week of eating Viciousburgers at New York's prestigious Studio 54 Disco, after the latest of a series of Vice Squad raids on the "playground of the idle rich."

Virgin Record Company boss, Richard Branson, 37, TV personality Dick Clark, 55, David Frost, 42, and several journalists, including Michael Watts, 38, editor of a music paper, were seen consuming several burgers each in what has been described as an "orgy of vampirism." "It was horrific," said clubgoer Richard DeNunzio of Brooklyn, "They each had several corpses in their mouths." More showbiz and media names, including some well-known News Reporters, are expected to be convicted as the hearings continue.

The last few years have seen an increase in this bizarre cult of vampirism, of which the Viciousburger is only the latest example. Vampires are noteworthy for consuming star corpses in the form of burgers in the mistaken belief that some of the star's charisma will rub off on them; sadly, as you can see, these attempts are doomed to failure and these cultists deluded. The cult is said to have begun in the 50's with Deanburgers; these were very rare, and contained bits of Porsche wreckage and sunglasses—those cultists still alive who tasted them say "They were tough but tasty." Perhaps the worst outbreak of vampirism before the Viciousburger scandal was the Presleyburger scandal of 1977. The scandal was discovered when an attempt was made to steal Presley's body from the grave by occultists: the body was already stolen! It now appears that it was minced down and turned into the bizarre cult food, Presleyburgers. These are said to be very expensive ($1000 a throw) and high on fatty content, but it still didn't deter the thrill-seeking showbiz crowd: Mick Jagger was said to have eaten several before his recent Wembly concert. Heavy prison sentences imposed in Canada on Keith Richard, another vampire, stopped the spread of this disgusting cult, but with the present Viciousburger scandals it seems to be flourishing. And even now, there are unconfirmed reports of Curtisburgers, grisly burgers with hints of rope and marble. There is no truth, however, in the rumour

Hitlerburgers are freely available: they were only available post-war and reserved for VIP's.
—Anonymous text (by Jon Savage) found among the Jamie Reid Collection acquired by the Victoria and Albert Museum, London, 1979

. . . there was even talk of having Elvis's corpse dug up and the stomach analyzed for traces of drugs which led me to fantasize: Can you imagine anything more thrilling than getting to stick your hand and forearm through the hole in Elvis's rotted guts slopping whatever's left of 'em all over each other getting the intestinal tracts mixed up with the stomach lining mixed up with the kidneys as you forage fishing for incriminating pillchips sufficient to slap this poor sweating doctor 20,000 years in Sing Sing and add one more hot clip to Geraldo's brochure of heroically humanitarian deeds done entirely in the interests of bringing the public the TRUTH it has a constitutional right to know down to the last emetic detail which they in time get as you pull your arm out of dead Elvis's innards triumphantly clenching some crumbs off a few Percodans, Quaaludes, Desoxyns, etc. etc. etc. and then once off camera now here's where the real kick to end 'em all comes as you pop those little bits of crumbled pills in your own mouth and swallow 'em and get high on drugs that not only has Elvis Presley himself also gotten high on the exact same not brand but the pills themselves they've been laying up there inside him perhaps even aging like fine wine plus of course they're all slimy with little bits of the disintegrating insides of Elvis's pelvis

SO YOU'VE ACTUALLY GOTTEN TO *EAT* THE
KING OF ROCK 'N' ROLL!

which would be the living end in terms of souvenirs, fetishism, psychofandom, the collector's mentality, or even just hero-worship in general. Notice I am leaving out such pursuits as necrophilia and coprophagy—there are admittedly some rather delicate distinctions to be made here, some fine lines to be drawn, but to those so insensitive as not to perceive them I will simply say that calling this act something like "necrophilia" would be in poor taste and if there was one thing Elvis always stood for it was good taste and maintaining the highest standards that money could buy so fuck you, you're just jealous, go dig up Sid Vicious and eat him, but if you do please save some for me because I'd like if possible just a small say 3" × 3" hunk out of his flank because what I want to do is eat the flesh under the skin, then dry the epidermis itself which isn't all that tasty anyway and slip it in the sleeve of my copy of *Sid Sings* as a souvenir to show my grandchildren and perhaps take out and wrap around my dick every once in a while when I'm masturbating cause a little more friction always helps get the wank achieved and sometimes I have found that when I literally can't get it up to jerk off because I'm too alienated from everything including my own cock if I take a scrap of dried skin from a dead rockstar—trade you an Al Wilson in mint condition well as mint as dead can be anyway for a Jim Morrison I don't care how shot to shit—it really seems to do the trick.

But I digress. Jerking off with some of Sid's track-riddled forearm could not even be called child's play compared to the exquisite sensation of eating those pills and gore out of Elvis. I mean, I read Terry Southern's "The Blood of a Wig" too, but that was written before the age of the celebrity, as Marisa Berenson told *People* magazine when they put her on the cover: "My ambition is to become a saint." *My* ambition is to become a parasite on saints, which shouldn't be too difficult, I mean they're supposed to get holier through physical mortification and all that, right? Plus I know about how Idi Amin used to dine on the flesh and drink the blood of his onetime enemies while lecturing their severed heads in a line on the desk in his office concerning the improprieties they committed while alive so I don't need to go get *The Golden Bough* just to prove to everybody else what I already know because it's simple horse sense which is if I eat a little bit of Elvis (the host, as it were, or is that mixing mythologic metaphors?) then I take on certain qualities possessed by Elvis while he was alive and walking around or laying in bed with the covers over his head as the case may be, and when these pills make me high they'll put me on the Elvis trip to end 'em all as I'll be seeing what he saw and thinking what he thought perhaps up to the last final seconds before kicking the bucket and if all of this works well enough as it most certainly will I intend to be greedy when offered the chance of a lifetime and scoop out a whole giant rotten glob of his carcass that let's face it he's never gonna need again and I eat from deep in the heart of him as I fully intend to do, why, THEN I WILL BE ELVIS! I'll make several dozen unwatchable movies and that number plus a couple dozen more unlistenable albums! I'll know karate so I can kick out the eyeballs of my landlord next time he comes up here to complain I haven't paid the rent in three months! Like I'm sure he's gonna come complaining to Elvis about something as piddling as rent anyway! Ditto for Master Charge, Macy's, all these assholes hounding me for money I don't have and they don't need: I mean, seriously, can you imagine *Elvis* sitting down with his checkbook and a stack of unpaid bills, going through the whole dreary monthly routine, and then balancing his bank account? He'd just go out and buy a car for some colored cleaning lady he'd never met before instead! Then Master Charge would tear up the bill saying "Mr. Presley you are a real humanitarian and since we are too we want to say we feel honored to have you run up as high a tab as you want on us."

Lessee, now, what else can I do? Well, concerts. Kinda boring, tho, since all I've gotta do (all I'm ALLOWED to do if I'm gonna not insult Elvis's memory by breaking with tradition) is just stand there holding a microphone, singing current schmaltz with no emotion, and occasionally wiping the sweat off my brow with one of a series of hankies hidden away in the sleeve of my White Castle studded jacket and then toss the contaminated little rag to whichever female in the first few rows has walked more backs, blackened more eyes and broken more arms and legs in attempt to get up close to my godly presence. As my whole career has surely borne out, I believe with one hand on my mother's grave that aggressive persistence in the service of a noble cause should be rewarded. Still, all this, ah, don't *you* think it sounds kinda, well, *dull*? I mean, how many hankies can you throw out before you start to go catatonic? At least Sid Vicious got to walk onstage with "GIMME A FIX" written in blood on his chest and bash people in the first row over the head with his bass if he didn't approve of the brand of beercan they were throwing at him.

Sid got to have all the fun.

—Lester Bangs, "Notes for Review of Peter Guralnick's *Lost Highway*, 1980," published in Lester Bangs, *Psychotic Reactions and Carburetor Dung*, U.S.A., 1987

The words in this pamphlet are not set out in the order in which they appear on the record, instead I have laid them out in the 3 groups in which I conceived them.

    (1) 6 corpses in the mouths of the Bourgoisie

    (2) 4 songs

    (3) ALBION, AWAKE!

—Notes by Chris Cutler in booklet of lyrics enclosed with Art Bears LP *The World as It Is Today*, U.K., 1981

—Page on Lennonburger in "This Could Happen to *Your* City! The Northern California Underground Uprising of '82," included in the LP *Maximum Rock n Roll Presents Not So Quiet on the Western Front*, San Francisco, 1982

Well, that's my story—and I'm stickin to that. So let's have another drink and—let's talk about the blues.

Blues is about *dignity*. It's about self-respect, and no matter what they take away from you, that's yours for keeps. I remember how it was, how every medium, TV and papers and radio and all those people were saying, "You're on the scrapheap, you're *useless*," and I remember how easy it was to start believin that, and I remember how you'd hear people *take it for granted* that it was true, just because someone with ah, an *ounce* of power said so. That's a problem now: too many oddballs, *pocket-book* sociologists and would-be philosophers with an axe to grind—but there's a solution! It's not easy; it's a matter of comin to terms in your *heart* with the situation you're in, and not havin things *forced* upon you. There're plenty of forces against you, forcing you against your will and your ideals. You've got to hope for the best—and that's the best you can hope for. It's hope against hope. I remember something Sal Paradise said. He said, "The city intellectuals of the world are *divorced* from the folk bloody body of the land and are just rootless fools!" So listen—when the smile, the condescending pat on the back comes and says, "We're sorry, but you're nothing, you've got nothing for us and we've got nothing for you"—you say, *no*, and say it loud, NO! Remember: People who talk about revolution and class struggle without referrin *explicitly* to everyday life, without understanding what is *subversive* about love and positive in the refusal of constraints—such people have a *corpse* in their *mouth*.
—Pete Wylie/Wah!, "The Story of the Blues, Part One and Part Two," U.K., 1982

Dr. Allen Nadler reports that Chico has yet another claim to the title of culinary capital of the West: La Salle's, a great hangout, is now featuring the Belushi Burger—"Sloppy But Good."
—Herb Caen, *San Francisco Chronicle*, 1982

—Ray Lowry, *New Musical Express*, London, 1983

Pop is a frustration machine. And one of its most interesting mechanisms is the tension between the star's incitement of desire and passion (not to mention hysteria) and the bureaucratic and ideological apparatus erected to protect stars from the consequences of this incitement.

At one point we interview Adam Ant's manager, Don Murfet, an expert in personal security. . . . Don turned out to be a wise and benevolent man, as genuinely concerned for the well-being of fans as stars. One month after this interview, his protégé Adam Ant appears on the front cover of *Sounds*, glowering lustily at all and sundry with both hands tucked into gaping flies. What was a fan to think?

It is hardly surprising, when stars offer themselves so lavishly for *consumption*, that some fans will take the invitation literally.

Like Mark Chapman.

After all, the only plausible way to "consume" people is to annihilate them.

—Fred and Judy Vermorel, *Starlust: The Secret Fantasies of Fans*, London, 1985

Burger King can't be getting over on the food, it must be the artwork. Burger King does what the Comte de Lautréamont and his surrealist followers only dreamed about. It creates a decadence you can taste.

Burger King sells the whole world the same democratic hamburger and to each burger buyer they say, "Have it your way." . . . And the hamburger is the most symbolic of foods. It is round, like the body of Christ in the Mass, but it's also hot and juicy. Like Frankenstein, it is a body made of many bodies.
—Glenn O'Brien, *Artforum*, U.S.A., April 1986

Sable sauntered in to the Burger Lord. It was exactly like every other Burger Lord in America. McLordy the Clown danced in the Kiddie Korner. The serving staff had identical gleaming smiles that never reached their eyes. And behind the counter a chubby, middle-aged man in a Burger Lord uniform slapped burgers onto the griddle, whistling softly, happy in his work.

Sable went up to the counter.

"Hello-my-name-is-Marie," said the girl behind the counter. "How-can-I-help-you?"

"A double blaster thunder biggun, extra fries, hold the mustard," he said.

"Anything-to-drink?"

"A special thick whippy chocobanana shake."

She pressed the little pictogram squares on her till. (Literacy was no longer a requirement for employment in these restaurants. Smiling was.) Then she turned to the chubby man behind the counter.

"DBTB, EF, hold mustard," she said. "Choc-shake."

"Uhnnhuhn," crooned the cook. He sorted the food into little paper containers, pausing only to brush the graying cowlick from his eyes.

"Here y'are," he said.

She took them without looking at him, and he returned cheerfully to his griddle, singing quietly, "Loooove me tender, looooove me long, neeeever let me go. . . ."

The man's humming, Sable noted, clashed with the Burger Lord background music, a tinny tape loop of the Burger Lord commercial jingle, and he made a mental note to have him fired.
—Neil Gaiman and Terry Pratchett, *Good Omens: The Nice and Accurate Prophecies of Agnes Nutter, Witch*, U.S.A., 1990

———

A man dies and they want to serve him up for posterity. Serve him, so to speak, trussed up for our dear descendants at the table. So that they, napkin tucked under chin and armed with knife and fork, can dig in to the freshly deceased.

The deceased, as you know, have the inconvenient habit of cooling off too slowly, they're burning hot. So they are turned into aspics by pouring memories over them—the best form of gelatine.

And since deceased greats are also too large, they are cut down. The nose, they say, is served separately, or the tongue. You need less gelatine that way, too. And that's how you get yesterday's classic, a freshly cooked tongue-in-aspic. With a side dish of hoofs from the horse he used to ride.

—Blind fragment in untitled collage by Elvis Costello, 1989

Glenn Gass

Why Don't We Do It in the Classroom?

It could be a scene out of any college classroom at exam time: the nervous looks, head-pounding and frustrated I-knew-that-last-night expressions as the students grope to remember if Brian Jones was (a) the leader of the Beach Boys? (b) the Beatles's manager? (c) one of the original Rolling Stones? (d) none of the above?

Brian Jones?! The correct answer, by the way, is "c." The next question on more than a few minds might be, "Why is this being taught in a college class?" (a) because university standards have sunk to new lows? (b) because music departments need the money generated by large course enrollments? (c) because rock is a vital musical form and cultural force? (d) because Brian Jones was also a classical violinist of exceptional ability? Again the answer is "c," though opinions on that vary, to say the least (and "b" would, too often, be a correct response as well). In spite of the predictable complaints and resistances, classes on rock music, such as the series of rock history courses I teach at Indiana University, are being offered by a rapidly growing number of universities, re-flecting a general trend toward interdepartmental studies of popular culture that is only now reaching most music schools and conser-vatories. Roll over, Beethoven: thirty-seven years after Elvis's first recordings, rock has its own traditions and its own treasured "clas-sics."

Seeing Rock & Roll next to Symphonic Literature and Music Ap-preciation in course listings must seem like a nightmare come true for more traditionally minded faculty members whose view of culture involves a refined sensibility that must be learned and earned. Rock courses are still waging the same struggle for acceptance that jazz studies faced on their way to becoming standard offerings, and facing the same prejudices that view "popular" as synonymous with cheap, crude, and unrefined. I know I get my share of horrified looks when "Satisfaction" comes blasting out of my classroom. Composer Milton Babbitt once lamented that his students studied "serious" music all day, then went home and listened to "the same music the janitors liked."[1] As Allan Bloom put it, "[Rock music] ruins the imagination of young people and makes it very difficult for them to have a pas-sionate relationship to the art and thought that are the substance of liberal education. . . . [A]s long as they have the Walkman on, they cannot hear what the great tradition has to say."[2]

The Great Tradition is apparently in serious trouble, and rock music makes an easy target for those who need something to blame for the fact that classical music is losing the depressingly small audi-ence it had to begin with. On the other hand, the Great Tradition itself is an easy target in these politically correct times. Rock's as-sault on academia mirrors a heightened interest in world music and ethnomusicology and a general acknowledgment of the need to move beyond the near religious canonization of Western (white male) art music that has been the entire focus of musical higher education.[3] It seems, though, that the validity granted the popular musics of other cultures is only grudgingly granted that of our own, and that even when ours is approached, rock and pop still tend to be viewed merely as illegitimate offspring of "authentic" musics like the blues, country, and gospel. As a classical composer and rock fan who likes Milton Babbitt and Bruce Springsteen (and a lot of other things serious musicians and janitors listen to), I have a hard time understanding how anyone could argue with the simple assertion that the best of any type of music can reward repeated listening and, in a classroom, help to sharpen aural skills and musical awareness. Ideally, one could hope that studying one type of music will inspire students to explore another, that rock history will lead to jazz and classical appreciation courses. This happens occasionally and should surely be encouraged (this is often used as a rationale for nontraditional offerings). Most often, though, the students who enroll in rock courses would otherwise avoid music offerings and will probably not take another—all the more reason to reach them now, any way we can. Since they will listen to rock & roll in any case, why not help them to listen more creatively and with greater insight into the music's history, techniques, and cultural role?

Granted, it's still hard to compare "Tutti Frutti" with Beethoven's Ninth Symphony, but why compare them? Rock music—indeed, all music—must be approached and appreciated within the context of the era and aesthetic in which it was created, and at the same time made fresh and vital for today. The amateurish quality, in the best and worst senses, of most rock music does pose special problems in the classroom, but it also offers an opportunity to address and discuss the music on the type of straightforwardly emotional level too often neglected in traditional music courses. There are, of course, many musical elements to notice as well: songwriting and vocal styles, instrumental and production techniques, song forms, band arrangements, musical influences, lyrical references, and rhythmic patterns, to mention only a few. But rock & roll can be as dull and repetitious as some of my classical colleagues say if it is approached with the same methods and criteria one applies to a Mozart sonata—if Bob Dylan's voice is evaluated as if he were auditioning for the Met, or if the chord structure of "Louie Louie" and the melodic contours of "Mother Popcorn" are analyzed in terms of pitch sets and Schenkerian reductions. Theoretical abstractions and rote memorization tend to take students further away from the music itself, while musical transcriptions and technical analyses are scarcely more effective at getting at the energy that made the music so exciting to begin with.

In trying to make sure that I teach rock & roll for the same reasons that I love it, I find that I constantly walk a tightrope between the need to make my courses "serious" enough for a college classroom and fun enough to keep Keith Richards from gagging, should he happen to wander in. It's a hard balancing act, though I try to err on the side of irreverence and make no apologies for having strong personal tastes that are inevitably reflected in course material. My first concern is that students know and love the music—learning details *about* the music is important, but secondary. Even then, I try to focus on what they hear and on what made the artist unique, and tend to shy away from pointless guitar solo transcriptions or overly technical discussions of chord progressions, "rock lyrics as poetry," rock as "ritual dance music for a new tribe of disaffected youth," and the like. The music itself needs no justification and yields its own rewards as long as it is not forced into a strict analytic model or academicism that loses sight of the music's emotional power, spontaneity, and sheer fun. The strict "cultural studies" approach to rock music gaining currency in academic classes and journals can, with the best intentions, render an even greater disservice by focusing so exclusively on audience responses, ideological agendas, mind-numbing charts of lyrical references, and abstract, post-Marxist theories on the popular that tend to ignore the fact that these are *songs*, written, played, and sung by real people with guitars in their hands. This peculiar type of reverse discrimination tends to validate popular music, only to consign it to a cultural studies ghetto where it is still "only rock & roll," but now interesting as an assumed background "text" that gains importance when it is manifested as a function of youth, a product consumed in fascinating ways, a reflection of society, class structures, etc. These are all important issues, to be sure, but "Eight Days a Week" is just fine all by itself, too.

There are, of course, many rewarding approaches to rock/pop music possible within the framework of a university. Sociology, English, Cultural Studies, Telecommunications, Comparative Literature, and other departments—even Music departments—can all embrace rock & roll as a legitimate and compelling topic applicable to their interests. The fact that it is a popular subject and already an integral part of most students' lives should be cause for celebration rather than scorn. Isn't helping students make sense of their own lives, world, and culture one of the central aims of higher education?

While some still argue that rock will "cheapen" curricula and academic standards, there is a different and more valid concern coming from the opposite direction—that rock's ascent to the classroom is, at best, a hollow victory for such gloriously unacademic music. Whether or not rock "deserves" to be taken so seriously, it certainly never asked to be taken so seriously. At the 1990 Rock & Roll Hall of Fame ceremony, Kinks leader Ray Davies looked out at the sea of tuxedos and noted that rock & roll "has become respectable." Visibly shaken by the applause (applause?!) that greeted his remark, Davies quickly added "what a bummer."

Indeed, the last—and worst—thing anyone thought rock & roll could ever become was "respectable," yet here it is, crammed into tuxedos at awards ceremonies, embraced by middle-aged babyboomers, exploited by Madison Avenue as an effective marketing tool and fast achieving the ultimate stamp of legitimacy as a subject for college classes. How respectable can you get? Or, more to the point, how respectable can rock get before it loses the very urgency and rebellious spirit that made it so exciting to begin with? The Band's Robbie Robertson once said that "music should never be harmless," but isn't rock rendered exactly that when it is studied in a classroom and assigned as homework? You must address historical and musical details, but can students get emotionally involved with Little Richard while they're worrying about remembering who his sax players were or what year he recorded "Long Tall Sally" or whether it's a 12-bar blues?

Those questions continue to haunt me, as I'm sure they haunt many others trying to force "All along the Watchtower" into the Ivory Tower, though my misgivings about the classroom as a viable arena for rock have lessened over the years. When I was first hired, much to my surprise, to teach jazz and rock history at a junior college in Wisconsin in 1977, the thought of sticking rock in a classroom and assigning it as homework seemed absurd. I was quite comfortable with the musical schizophrenia that separated my classical training and composing from my love for rock & roll and feared that combining the two would cheapen both (the same sort of feeling I had later when I heard the Kronos Quartet playing "Purple Haze"). The rock music I loved still seemed too new to be "history," too emotionally personal to discuss coherently, and far too exciting and rebellious to be deemed respectable enough for a college class. In those disco-mad days, though, it seemed that rock might indeed be history, as in "dead." I quickly learned, for example, that my students had only the faintest knowledge that the recently deceased King of Rock & Roll had ever been anything but a running joke on late-night movies. Most had never heard of—much less heard—Buddy Holly, the Everly Brothers, Martha Reeves, Roy Orbison, or Smokey Robinson, and were quite surprised to learn that Linda Ronstadt wasn't the first to sing "That'll Be the Day," "When Will I Be Loved" and "Heatwave," not to mention "Blue Bayou" and "Tracks of My Tears." Not all of the students were of the "I hear Paul McCartney was in a band before Wings" variety, but enough had never heard "Great Balls of Fire" to make me think there was a point to teaching rock after all, if only to make sure they'd heard it.

There are still college students who have never listened to Jerry Lee Lewis, but, happily, far fewer these days. Yesterday's hits, formerly relegated to the Oldies bins and a few AM nostalgia stations, are now enshrined as Classic Rock—timeless works of the Old Masters who live on in CD reissues and reunion tours and carry the weight of their legacy like an elderly Stravinsky conducting the *Rite of Spring*. Free from the confines of MTV and specific video imprints, they live on as songs, suspended in time for each new listener to claim, define, and apply to his or her own life (unless they have already been rendered lifeless in California Raisins or Coke commercials). Even the newer artists tend to define their stance and claims to "authenticity" in terms of rock's glory days, many invoking their ancestors directly with reverent covers of old hits or with sounds, images, and fashions that evoke the aura of rock's noble and defiant past. For all the new stars, trends, and technologies that appeared in the 1980s, the decade seemed dominated by triumphant comebacks, rock anniveraries—of the Summer of Love, Woodstock, the Beatles hitting America—and one musical "revival" after another, ranging from the rockabilly revival that opened the decade to the psychedelic revival that closed it, with blues, heavy metal, folk, mainstream pop, roots rock, traditional country & western, and even punk and disco revivals thrown in along the way, as if the basic parameters within which rock works had all been explored and fixed by the end of the 1970s.

There were also, of course, plenty of new stars, visions, and voices to give rock's heritage a personal stamp, and plenty of rap groups and alternative bands to prove that it has not all been done or said. Most of my students, nonetheless, continue to list bands and albums from the 1960s as their personal favorites and seem quite fascinated by that decade (especially for a generation otherwise known for its historical amnesia); more than a few dress and act as if they'd just returned from Woodstock and none of them were alive when Woodstock took place! Classic rock is history to them, their Great Tradition, and the giggles at getting course credit for rock & roll, and the delight at "pulling one over on their parents" I encountered a decade ago, have been replaced by a genuine desire to learn about rock's heritage—the type of searching curiosity that should make even Allan Bloom feel heartened. The reaction of my students' parents has changed even more dramatically: I used to spend a good deal of time writing notes explaining that "Rock History" was indeed a real and worthwhile class; these days I spend more time fending off parents' requests for copies of my class listening tapes and nodding politely as they tell me how happy they are that their sons and daughters are being exposed to good music like the Beatles and Elvis rather than the junk they play on the radio. It's getting harder for rock to perform its most crucial function (driving parents crazy) now that Dad keeps yelling "Turn it up!" or "I used to love that song!" In any case, it's worth remembering that most current college students were first exposed to "classic" rock by their parents; and instead of rebelling against it, they found lyrics that still spoke to their lives and concerns, and a musical vitality undimmed by the decades. Although this might be a rather sad commentary on the music scene of today and the suffo-cating media stranglehold of the babyboomers and "classic rock," it also speaks well of rock's ability to retain its youth and resonance, and bolsters the arguments for rock as a musical form of lasting value that deserves attention, even in classrooms.

Rock & roll is here to stay, as they say, or said, thirty-three years ago (Danny and the Juniors, that is, Question #23, answer "b"). Its uniquely American roots in blues, rhythm & blues, boogie-woogie, country & western, pop, and gospel musics make it a fascinating melting pot that should be a great source of interest and pride. Still rightly claimed as "our music" by each new generation, rock's embodiment of the dreams, values, experience, and worldview of those generations also offers a vital focal point for discussions of recent times and culture. The current controversies surrounding rap and heavy metal prove that even its ability to challenge and threaten remains intact. It's heartening, in a way, to hear Tipper Gore and the Parents Music Resource Center (PMRC), the archbishop of New York, several state legislatures and other defenders of morals attacking rock & roll, and heartening for the same reasons to know that there are still plenty of people who think rock has no business in a college classroom. The day rock truly becomes respectable will be sad indeed, but it might be inevitable. We're close enough to it already to make poor Brian Jones roll in his grave: "Satisfaction" has become homework, his former bandmates are encased in the Hall of Fame, and by now he could have been a Distinguished Professor.

Notes

1   Milton Babbitt, lecture at Indiana University, 1987.
2   Allan Bloom, *The Closing of the American Mind: How Higher Education Has Failed Democracy and Impoverished the Souls of Today's Students* (New York, 1987), 79–80.
3   The history and fallacy of our obsession with the Great Tradition is presented convincingly in a paper by Austin B. Caswell, "How We Got into Canonicity and What It Has Done to Us: An American Music Historian's View of Music in Academia," forthcoming in the *Journal of Aesthetic Education*.

Paul Smith

Playing for England

Without a doubt, the biggest cultural event of the summer of 1990 in Britain was the one for which about half the population stayed at home every night over a period of about three weeks. That event was the World Cup soccer finals which were held in Italy and which, according to the British Broadcasting Corporation, were also represented on television in some way in every country of the world, producing a total television audience of about twenty-six billion people (with over half of that audience in Asia). The prelude to the visit of the England national soccer team to this year's finals was the occasion for a set of quite telling fears and hopes in the culture. The hopes centered around the sense in the media and on the streets that the team had a relatively good chance of getting to the final game, even if no one was foolhardy enough to predict that they would actually win the World Cup. Such hopes were finally not entirely disappointed since the team did reach the semifinal round and performed creditably enough. One reason that the expectations were not stronger was that most British football players had for several years been deprived of the useful experience of playing against European teams; that was because British club teams had been banned from the various European cup competitions in the wake of the 1985 Heysel disaster in Brussels, where British (specifically, Liverpool) football supporters were held to be responsible for thirty-nine deaths and hundreds of injuries, mostly to Italian supporters, during a disturbance in the stadium.

The Heysel disaster—undoubtedly the most lethal of many incidents involving British soccer fans over the last two or three decades—informed many of the fears that attended the popular media's preparation for the 1990 World Cup finals: that is, it was widely suspected that this tournament would become the site for England's renowned soccer hooligans to exercise their peculiar brand of warfare against the soccer supporters of other European nations and particularly against the host Italians. Elaborate arrangements were thus made to try to head off the possibilities of violence. The England team's first games were subject to a kind of quarantine by dint of their being located on the island of Sardinia. The island itself was turned into a paramilitary fortress by soldiers, uniformed police, undercover agents, and the appearance at least once of a brigade of Italy's special anti-terrorist forces. Back home in England the Conservative Minister of Sport, Colin Moynihan, gave his moral blessing to any steps, however repressive or unfair, that the Italian authorities might wish to take to counter the greatly feared English football supporter. Alcohol was banned on the island for the period; Italian immigration officers regularly refused entry to unsavory looking characters; police in Sardinia periodically arrested, imprisoned overnight, and then deported individuals and groups of Britons without the intervention of courts, and so on. The British Minister of Sport was subjected to some criticism at home for his condoning of this official activity; often the criticism came from his right wing in the form of a complaint that he was being hypocritical since he had proved himself unwilling to take such draconian measures against the supporters who are popularly presumed to terrorize the high streets of British towns every Saturday afternoon during the football season.

The Thatcher government made some slow attempts to curb and

repress the often dangerous presence and behavior of the football supporter, particularly in the wake of the Heysel Stadium event and after several other quite serious domestic disturbances around football games. A Home Office report in 1986 had laid a good part of the blame for hooliganism on the state of the football stadiums, most of which were designed and built between the turn of the century and World War II. The report also attempted to grasp the nature of hooliganism by appealing to some categories of sporting violence designed in the crassest and most positivistic American sociological tradition; but those kinds of explanations of football hooliganism were unable to lead the Home Office Committee to any very insightful conclusions. The Commission's final report proposed measures all aimed at the production of an American-style sports stadium and at audiences which, it is to be assumed, would squeeze out the hooligan element. Rather than fully grapple with the vexed question about what cultural meaning football hooliganism has within British society, the British government has suggested the gradual upgrading of football venues so that they become all-seating stadiums to be patronized only by good citizens who can qualify for a special football supporter's ID card. Those citizens would be protected by beefed-up policing: the police would have unlimited rights of search and widened powers of arrest, new criminal offenses would be put on the books for sports grounds, and alcohol sales would be severely restricted. These solutions all suggest, I think, that those who would attempt to regulate hooliganism and the everyday violence of British football grounds have little or no interest in seeing them as symptoms of subcultural resistance, or even of class *ressentiment*, but are rather more invested in thinking of them simply as criminal or pathological activities to be dealt with by the repressive state apparatuses.[1]

For the purposes of the World Cup finals, the British government's attempts to head off the much-expected violence and disruption actually took the form of an attempt to curtail the travel of known (that is, previously convicted) hooligans. The British police shared information with the European Interpol network and also assigned plainclothes policemen to travel with suspect groups of fans. In general, the level of cooperation among the security forces of the European nations was high during this period. The Dutch and German police, especially, worked hand in hand with the British and Italians, since the fans of those four nations have historically had especially troubled relations at footballing events, and each country has its hooligan problem. Yet it was still the British fan who was assumed to be the most potentially dangerous. In some ways this is not surprising, given the history of violence among football supporters and given, too, their sometimes very close identification with neo-fascist movements in Britain.

The often noticeably far rightist sentiments of some among the British football hooligans have their echoes and manifestations in the soccer cultures of other European nations, especially in Germany. But the British configuration is perhaps the clearest, thrown into sharp relief when the discourse of neo-fascism vies with—and all too easily resembles—the discourse of the Conservatives over issues of British nationalism and patriotism. By dint of this resemblance, football hooliganism can be read as a somewhat unwelcome alter ego of the Thatcherite regime. Thus when the Sports Minister mouthed his views about the virtues of repression against these animals who watch football, one could almost get the impression that the plan was to allow and even encourage a displacement of the soccer hooligan problem to another site where official repression could be undertaken under the auspices of the necessity of keeping this world-stage event safe and disturbance-free.

There are some grounds for thinking this: particularly, the summer of 1990 was also expected to be the moment of massive popular rebellion against Margaret Thatcher's newly activated poll tax. The poll tax (a name, incidentally, which Thatcher's government spokespersons were instructed not to use, Thatcher preferring the name "community charge") is a tax to replace the system of property taxes or "rates" that had funded local government programs throughout most of this century in Britain; whereas the rates had taxed households according to land and property values in a relatively progressive manner, the poll tax is a regressive tax that places a burden on every adult person at the same rate. It's fair to say, I think, that the poll tax was and still is a deeply unpopular, and at least divisive, tax. The first unmistakable sign of this was the huge demonstration in Trafalgar

Square on 31 March 1990 that greeted the changeover from rates to the poll tax. This demonstration was followed up by multiple events across the country during the summer.

The poll tax was also attacked at the level of the appeals court, where its legality was finally upheld. However, popular refusals to pay the tax led to a number of mass legal summonses in different parts of the country during the summer, in the course of every single one of which the courts found reasons not to convict nonpayers of the tax. The first major case of that sort on the Isle of Wight involved nearly four thousand summonses. Most of the delinquent taxpayers turned up at the court hearings along with many other opponents of the tax, and the normally orderly and placid procedure of local governmental business was massively disrupted. The court in this instance forced the local authority to withdraw the summonses on the grounds that reminders had been sent out by the notoriously inefficient second-class postage rate, leaving insufficient time between the reminders and the subsequent summonses.

This case and its somewhat factitious ruling set the tone for many later such cases, such as one in Newcastle where the local council withdrew its summonses because their documentation had not distinguished between monies owed for the tax itself and monies owed by way of penalty. By and large the courts seemed to prefer to leave local government with the problems of collection and enforcement, or simply with the prospect of depleted budgets, rather than to provoke more popular discontent and resistance than was already being manifested. Here, as in the exporting of the soccer hooligan problem to Italy, the government's effective action in relation to potential civic disturbance was to make a certain amount of noise and to rely upon various confirmatory rulings of the higher courts in deciding the general legality of the tax, but at the same time to refuse direct confrontation with the forces of resistance and malaise. The poll tax issue has not yet disappeared, even after the fall of Margaret Thatcher whose hobbyhorse the tax was widely assumed to be; but it seems that the new Prime Minister, John Major, in his first few months of office, has stepped back considerably from the hard Thatcher line on the poll tax and that its nature will be massively revised in the near future. In that sense the popular resistance to this tax might be said to have succeeded in its aim, and even to have helped unseat Thatcher herself.[2]

The important point, for me, about the stories of the poll tax and the apprehension about soccer violence in Italy is that they were both direct challenges to the ideologies and indeed the policies of law and order which the Thatcher government had highlighted during its time in office. By the summer of 1990 the somewhat facile options that the Conservatives had for ten or more years exercised or proposed in relation to questions of crime and civil disturbance had led to widespread media and public discussion of a possible, or indeed probable, summer of trouble. Prognoses of this sort turned out to be somewhat off the mark in the sense that neither soccer hooliganism nor poll tax resistance led to the kind of widespread or profound civic disturbance that might have been expected. Indeed, the fears of the law-and-order party were perhaps most vindicated in altogether different arenas. First of all, the summer of 1990 saw the IRA step up its bombing campaign in Britain and Europe; they scored a notable success with the bombing of the elite Conservative party club, the Carleton, in June, yet suffered the embarrassment of killing some Australian tourists, having mistaken them for British servicemen in Europe. Second, there was the announcement in late June of a quite remarkable rise in crime statistics. Notifiable offences reported to the police during the first quarter of 1990 showed an increase of 15 percent, the most precipitous such rise in over thirteen decades, and one that provoked the *Guardian* newspaper to talk about a veritable "tide of fear" crossing the country.[3] The party of law and order was reduced to pointing out that, in Thatcher's words, we "have to remember that violent crime in this country is on a very much lesser scale than in some other countries."[4]

It is in the context of this widespread apprehension about violence, civic disturbance, and popular *ressentiment*, and indeed in the context of the ultimate failure of those issues to actually confirm the worst fears of the media and the establishment, that I want to turn a bit more squarely to the pretext of this paper: "World in Motion," a single by the band New Order, and its place in the rock music scene during the summer of 1990.

A large sector of Britain's rock culture has historically been more attuned than the American or European rock cultures to the political conditions in which it operates—at least, I'd say that's been more consistently true in Britain than elsewhere, and thus there has been constructed a wide range of cultural practices and institutions by means of which rock music and its performance intervene in overtly politicized contexts. In relation to the poll tax opposition last summer, rock appeared to be playing a familiar kind of role, with many bands playing benefits for the numerous anti-poll tax organizations that were quickly set up in the early part of the year. Those interventions are not unexpected, of course; indeed they are almost de rigueur in a rock industry whose rhetoric of subcultural opposition and whose resistant display remain crucial affectations, and crucial marketing components. Furthermore, it is especially not surprising to see such interventions in this instance since the poll tax represents a new and increased taxation on the young, the working class, and the poor. Many young people, for instance, who as renters had been exempt from the old form of rates, or who were subsumed under household taxation and thus were paid for by parents, suddenly found themselves subject to an annual poll tax imposition. Thus a tax such as this one is in a sense the natural enemy of a large sector of rock music's constituency. To a certain extent, the rock music culture did respond to the challenge of the poll tax, which had also given a considerable fillip to a number of leftists political groups and organizations that, like several anarchist groups and the Socialist Workers party, were attached to the popular dismay.

One of the effects of Britain's preparing itself for a summer of thunder, for a massive outbreak of football violence and for the expression of popular dissent in terms of the poll tax, was the distraction of attention from some of the chronic problems that have been brought to a head in the last dozen years under Thatcher, particularly from problems of racial tension that have been of late the most likely site of civic disturbance in British life, and from the problems in the economy that were exacerbated by Thatcher's twin-headed policy of making Britain an American-style laissez-faire capitalist power and at the same time flirting with but never completely accepting the federalization of the European countries into the European Community.

Arguably the latter problems in the economy have, since the summer of 1990, brought the downfall of Thatcher, while the problems of
race and ethnicity were and continue to be elided under the Conservatives. But during the months of June and July 1990, the threat of
violence and civic disturbance was a consistent strand of discussion
in most of the popular newspapers, magazines, and on the television.
As it happens, the promised thunder was not to come—at least not
in the extreme forms that were promised. The football supporters
were relatively untroublesome, despite a couple of ugly incidents in
Sardinia and despite many of them being arrested and deported by
overzealous Italian police. And the poll tax agitations were somewhat
declawed by the courts' stepping back from judgment, as it were.
Instead of the summer of our discontent that various media were
promising, the summer became what the youth culture magazine,
The Face, was pleased to call "The Third Summer of Love." [5]
   The first "summer of love" had been in 1988 with the burgeoning
in the largely white youth culture in the English Midland cities (Birmingham, Manchester, and Liverpool in particular) of a revamped
1960s or hippy style and ideology in music, drugs, and dress. The hal-
lucinogen Ecstasy became the drug of choice, more or less replacing
LSD after that drug's revival in the early 1980s. At the same time, Acid
House music began its reign in the clubs, bearing a lot of similarity in
ethos to the hippy revival. Acid House, despite generally being taken
as an evolution from Chicago House music, owes a great deal to the
British reggae tradition, particularly to dub reggae, even while it has
transformed that tradition to become, in Simon Reynolds's words,
"close to the frigid, mechanical, supremely white perversion of funk
perpetrated by early eighties pioneers like D.A.F. and Cabaret Voltaire." [6] Acid is in that sense, according to Reynolds, a supremely
alienated form of black music, loosed from the various strands of
black musical traditions. Acid is similar to neo-psychedelia not so
much in rhythmic quality (it is almost frighteningly metronomic,
set strictly at somewhere between 125 and 135 beats per minute),
but in what Reynolds calls the encouragement of "perceptual drift,"
and what both he and Helena Blakemore see as the production of
transitory, ephemeral, and trance-like experience. [7]
   The melding of these two kinds of music became increasingly ap-

parent in 1989, the second "summer of love." The club scene was largely transported as a matter of course to illegal venues like warehouses and temporary, unlicensed clubs. Outside London, in Manchester, for instance, these illegal parties, or raves, became a point of attention for the police as the audiences became increasingly ethnically mixed and as blissing out on Ecstasy became epidemic. These first two "summers of love" had been in many ways the manifestation of a kind of passive resistance to the conditions of Thatcherite Britain, and an expression of alienation from that context; thus their manifestations had attracted the requisite amount of police and media disapproval. The "summer of love" in 1990, however, turned out somewhat differently. With the government and the police focusing on other potential problems, the drug scene and the illegal raves were more or less left alone. Although in the early spring the police had threatened various harrassment tactics, the restrictions on 1990 raves turned out to be mostly just a few bureaucratic ones.

This left the raves and festivals to develop according to their own logic. At the level of the music itself, Acid House consolidated its joining with the neo-psychedelic music of the Manchester and Liverpool bands. As Reynolds noted in 1988: "House has been bordering on the psychedelic for some time . . . with the spaciness of its dub effects, its despotic treatment of the voice and its interference with the normal ranking of instruments in the mix (encouraging 'perceptual drift')."[8] The marriage of the two modes readily gave preeminence to the more familiar and commercial melodiousness of neo-psychedelia, over the alienated trance qualities of Acid House. Thus the bands centered on Manchester, the so-called scallydelics like Stone Roses, Inspiral Carpets, or The Farm, settled into recording contracts and big sales. The independent music scene participated in a massive revival of 1960s hippy music and mixed it with the futurism of Acid House. Helena Blakemore has described Acid House itself as exactly this mixture of revival and futurism, productive of an air of "instant culture."[9] One could say that the marriage of Acid and scallydelia marks the appropriation of that instant culture by the music industry for the purpose of prolonging it enough for commodification.

At any rate, it was not a big step from what we might call this non-nostalgic revivalism in the music itself to the revival during the summer of 1960s-style outdoor rock festivals. Between May and September there were about a dozen rock festivals lasting a day or more, located at outdoor sites and arenas all across the country, all of them more or less unmolested by the police. One of the least invigorating of these was held in June at Knebworth. Cosponsored by the BBC's Radio One and America's MTV, it top-billed a handful of old rock stars like Paul McCartney, Elton John, and Cliff Richard as part of a media industry attempt to appropriate the festival fad. But even the independent festivals turned out to be by and large innocuous and blissed out affairs. The only one that involved any real antagonism between festivalgoers and the authorities was an abortive one that had been planned for the summer solstice at Stonehenge and that finally consisted of about three hundred ravers attended by seven hundred police whose aim was to keep the ancient stone monument safe from hooliganism and vandalism.

Apart from their ecstasied innocence, one of the most consistent features of these festivals was the way they demonstrated the full integration of a footballing motif into the styles, performances, and musics of the subculture. In particular, the clothing of the people drew upon what had been a steady rise in the fashionability of various kinds of designer sports clothing: among the multifarious track suits and football shirts adorned with club logos, the distinctive yellow and green strip of the Brazilian national team seemed particularly prominent. These, appended to ubiquitous wide-flared jeans, epitomized the juxtaposition of acid culture with the sports ethos. Inevitably the game itself was played during interludes, and at the Glastonbury Campaign for Nuclear Disarmament Festival one band even kicked footballs around on stage (I had last seen that done by Rod Stewart and the Faces in the late 1960s); the crowd duly broke out into a chant of "In-ger-lund."

There is something uncanny about a cross-fertilization of acid culture and football, particularly given the relation to violence that they might respectively be assumed to hold. Earlier in the year, the February issue of *i-D* magazine (their "Good Health" issue) had pointed out the contradiction in an article on Manchester youth culture. One young Mancunian is quoted thus: "We're not into wearing fucking daisies in our hair and all that walking around shouting 'karma fuck-ing peace man.' Fuck that. We like the violence, we like getting off our heads, we like the dancing, the sweat." *i-D*'s comment on this is to suggest simply that "the drippy peace and love optimism of the 60s has been replaced by a harder, more cynical sense of community and local pride based around your band, your area and your football team." One might also add, around your favorite drug: the commit-ment to hallucinogens among the bands and their followers has had, as *i-D* points out, "a massive catalytic effect on a whole generation of Thatcher-alienated youth."[10]

But the infatuation with football has had, I want to claim, a con-solatory or pacificatory effect—it marked a particular way of main-streaming the House and hippy subcultures, and at the same time constituted an argument against—and an assimilation of—the re-sistant energies of football subcultures. The alienation that appears to be at the root of all three of those subcultural styles is cancelled out by their confluence during that summer in the celebration of the World Cup finals.

Many rock bands capitalized on the World Cup mania during the summer. Perhaps the most amusing of such instances was the single "Touched by the Hand of La Cicciolina," by Pop Will Eat Itself, who urged that the trophy be presented after the final game by La Cicciolina, Italy's best-known porno star and member of parliament; the most irrelevant and irreverent was Saint Etienne's single, "The Official Saint Etienne World Cup Theme"—not official at all and a minimalist dub drone ornamented only by the repeated words, "Cool and deadly"; while perhaps the most banal was the band James an-nouncing its "World Cup Tour," carefully arranged so as not to clash with any soccer dates. For me the most interesting symptom of this infatuation (and perhaps even an effective cause in the infatuation) was the recording of the ritual "official theme song" for the England team by New Order. There has been a tradition, dating back to at least 1966, of marking any major football events involving the England team with a recording by the national squad of some dreadful pop ditty: titles like "Back Home" (1970) or "This Time We'll Get It Right" (1982) featured the whole squad cheerleading in unison. This time, in 1990, the officiating body of English soccer, the Football

Association, decided to get it right by having the theoreticians of subcultural dance modes, the band New Order, produce the official England theme song.

New Order has been perhaps one of the most important bands in British rock over the last decade or so. Beginning life as the legendary Joy Division and never entirely eradicating their origins in the minor key drone music of a certain moment in post-punk sensibility, New Order has become the best and the best-known purveyor of a highly polished but minimalist technobeat. Demonstrable forerunners of House, the band has both led the way in and absorbed the influences of the major trends in both dance music and rock in the last decade. Its significance is broader than the extent of its music alone, however. New Order has been for a decade the leading band for Britain's most fiercely independent and influential record label, Factory, and has used profits from sales to reinvest in the local Manchester community, including the establishment of Britain's most notorious club, La Hacienda. In these and other respects, New Order has been an exemplary independent band.

New Order's single for the Football Association is called "World in Motion," and the CD version is accompanied by three mixes, the "b-side," the "subbuteo mix" (named after the popular proprietary indoor game of table football), and the "no alla violenza" mix that very rapidly became the club favorite. In the lyrics of the single, New Order's refusal to make a football song is quite apparent, and the remarks of Barney Sumner, the lead singer, on this point signal the band's attitude:

> At one stage, the Football Association came to us and made it clear that the song really had to distance itself from hooliganism. Hence our line, 'Love's got the world in motion.' It's an anti-hooligan song. There's a deliberate ambiguity about the words which don't have to refer to football. I think you're right when you say that pop and football culture are nearer than they've been in years. And from our point of view, there's been a football element in our fans for about the last six years. Even so, there was no way I could have written the lyrics. I really couldn't write a football lyric.[11]

As it turns out, the credited lyricist for the song is Keith Allen, a Manchester comedian. His words constitute a deliberate admixture of two lyrical strands: of what is almost a mimicry of New Order's familiar love songs, and what would perhaps be more predictable in a football song. The footballing strand is marked at the very beginning by the voice of Kenneth Wolstenholme, a BBC sports commentator, long since retired, whose name is almost a byword in the culture for the somewhat fatuous and yet strangely endearing mode of football commentating that the British media consistently produce. His opening words recall the England team's one and only outright victory in the World Cup final in 1966, and they are overlaid with a typical New Order drum and synthesizer introduction announcing the song's melody.

Sumner's voice enters for two verses with lyrics of which the following give a taste: "Express yourself, create the space. You know you can win, don't give up the chase. Beat the man, take him on. You never give up. It's one on one." While these lyrics perhaps adequately address elements of the sport, the choruses have a little less obviously to do with football:

> It's one on one, you can't be wrong.
> When something's good, it's never gone.
> Love's got the world in motion
> and I know what we can do;
> love's got the world in motion
> and I can't believe it's true.

New Order apparently insisted on the phrase "Love's got the world in motion," rejecting the Football Association's preferred chorus, "We've got the world in motion." And the fact that the song became a sort of anthem in gay clubs by virtue of its exhortations to "express yourself . . . beat your man . . . take him on . . . it's one on one," and so on, probably made it even less approvable to that body. What the Football Association undoubtedly did approve of, however, was the introduction of the voice of England's premier black player, John Barnes, in a sort of rap sequence, and his mouthing of the phrases "we ain't no hooligans," and "with three lions on my chest we can't go wrong." But even between those lines Barnes clearly states that "this ain't no football song." [12]

All in all this is probably the least likely official football theme song ever recorded: denying its own status as a football song, introducing elements of subcultural love lyrics, and becoming a gay club hit, but also assuming the burden of combating football's major peripheral problem, hooliganism, the song is ultimately *unheimlich*, even despite its closing chorus that speaks of "playing for England; playing this song." It does not quite work as a pseudo-national anthem, and yet it effectively draws together several strands of British subcultural life and merges them into a peculiar cultural product where their elements of resistance leave few traces. The song's gesture of cancelling the resistant elements of its own context—the football and rock subcultures—was not sufficient to make it acceptable to the mainstream media. That is, although the single did well in the clubs and in the charts, it was not much heard in the mainstream media slots to which a different kind of song might have had access. Both the BBC and the independent television companies forewent the pleasure of having "Love's got the world in motion" going across the airwaves every night, and the BBC used as their World Cup theme another piece of music that quickly became a number one hit: Luciano Pavarotti singing his version of the "Nessun Dorma," an aria from *Turandot*.

In its way the well-known Puccini aria is just as *unheimlich* as the New Order song: one can only imagine that it was meant to be allegorized as the utterance of the footballing prince determined to name himself to the trophy/princess in the morning of his triumph. But the use of this operatic aria, in all its overdetermined Italianicity—which, of course, could be fully exploited in the running patter of the television anchormen—was in many ways appropriate in that it effected a kind of Europeanization of the cultural appurtenances of the World Cup. The World Cup finals was an event that, for all its audience in the South, and for all the playing success of the underdog team from the Cameroons, was ultimately dominated in competition by the countries of the North, and represented in economic terms a massive draining of capital and resources from South America, Africa, and Asia into the coffers of the sponsoring corporations, towns and cities, media networks, and advertising industries of Western Europe and the United States (the probable host nation in 1994 and whose team appeared in the finals in Italy for the first time in many years). The world in motion, to be sure: a motion whose nature is underlined by the fact that "World in Motion" represents the first time that New Order's label, Factory Records, has been distributed by the American corporation MCA (itself now taken over by the Japanese mega-corporation, Matsushita).

New Order cannot, of course, be held responsible for the workings of this kind of world in motion, any more than Pavarotti can. And yet the band's song, in its abortive attempt to represent a certain kind of populist nationalism, and in its annulment of the resistant energies of its own cultural context (football culture's violent antagonism, and neo-psychedelic subculture's alienation), can be understood as a symptom, or even as a symbol, of the ease with which subcultural forms and energies can be made to contribute to and participate in what we used to call the military-industrial complex, but which I think we really need to call the military-industrial-*sports* complex.

As I finish writing this article, in the United States in January 1991, the world has set itself in motion by way of a vicious military adventure which, we are told, is designed to help establish a "new world order." British and American airplanes, ships, and soldiers are in the process of demonstrating who truly owns the means of violence and to what ends. Their activities underscore the global nature of the context into which New Order, in their small way, intervened in the summer of 1990.

Notes

1   Home Office, *Committee of Inquiry into Crowd Safety and Control and Sports Grounds*, 1986. A group of British sociologists based at Leicester University have recently provided more insightful work than that of the American sociologist— one Jeffrey Goldstein—to whom the Committee had recourse; see Eric Dunning et al., *The Roots of Football Hooliganism: An Historical and Sociological Study* (Routledge, 1988) and Eric Dunning et al., *Football on Trial* (London, 1990). For a brief and conservative overview of the social history of football in Britain, see Tony Mason, "Football," in *Sport in Britain: A Social History*, ed. Tony Mason (Cambridge, 1989).

2   In late March 1991, the poll tax was finally laid to rest with Environment Secretary Michael Heseltine's words: "The public has not been persuaded that the poll
tax is fair" (*Manchester Guardian Weekly*, 31 March 1991, 4). Heseltine had been a
prominent antagonist to Thatcher for several years; his being named to the post-
Thatcher cabinet was an indication of John Major's desire to move away somewhat
from Thatcherite policies. The poll tax has been revised and local authority funds
will be collected by way of a mixture of taxes: an increase in value-added tax and
a new system of property taxation that seems considerably more progressive.

3   *Manchester Guardian Weekly*, 8 July 1990, 12.

4   *Manchester Guardian*, 29 June 1990, 1.

5   *The Face*, June 1990, front cover.

6   Simon Reynolds, *Blissed Out: Raptures of Rock* (London, 1990), 177.

7   Ibid., 178; and Helena Blakemore, "Acid—Burning a Hole in the Present," in *Readings in Popular Culture*, ed. Gary Day (New York, 1990), 18–25.

8   Reynolds, *Blissed Out*, 177.

9   Blakemore, "Acid," 20.

10   Mike Noon, "Freaky Dancing," *i-D*, February 1990, 46–48.

11   Quoted in Stuart Maconie, "Love Will Terrace Apart," *New Musical Express*, 19 May 1990, 16.

12   As far as Barnes himself is concerned, it's perhaps just as well that the usual vain-
gloriousness of such official songs was somewhat muted by the other elements
and the "deliberate ambiguity" of the song, since his own performances in the
finals were, not to put too fine a point on it, lackluster. As the strongest hope
for those observers who desired some exotically skilled player to counterbalance
the England team's preponderance of journeymen, Barnes had been set up as a
classic kind of token. In failing to reproduce the excitement and excellence of
his club form while playing for the England team, he became the target of barely
veiled racist commentary which charged him with disloyalty, unreliability, and
even laziness. During the course of the finals, his place in the expectations of
many soccer fans was easily taken by a white boy, relatively new to the team, Paul
Gascoigne.

David R. Shumway

Rock & Roll as a Cultural Practice

> When thinking about rock or "pop" music what is in question is not simply a well-established corpus of records, performances, groups or images. Unlike television, film or arguably theater, the forms of this music irreducibly involve an intersecting range of practices, without an obviously assured primary discourse or text. To take the gramophone disc as the "text" of rock music is to marginalize or dismiss a wide range of activities (such as domestic improvisation, or live performances by pub or club bands) which never accede to reproduction by way of the recording process; it is also to neglect the way in which rock's musical forms have importantly diffused through a variety of technical means other than gramophone recording—"live" performance itself, cassettes, television and film soundtrack, currently "promotional" videos.
> —Alan Durant, *Conditions of Music*

Rock & roll is elusive. It doesn't easily fit the models that we have for cultural objects. For example, there is no definition of rock & roll as a musical genre upon which most critics would agree.[1] To call something rock & roll is to distinguish it from other forms such as jazz, classical, or country, but to attribute nothing very definite to it. More significant, however, it is unclear just what an individual instance of rock & roll is, since neither records nor lyrics nor written music can be regarded as primary. There is no text in this genre. Or at least there is no text of the same order as a poem or a novel, which is to say that rock texts are elusive in more ways than those that poststructuralism has claimed for texts in general. Rock lyrics are no more or less unstable than other kinds of language. Rather, rock & roll as a discursive practice cannot be identified with any one of its many codes or products. We need a new way to conceive of the kind of cultural formation that rock & roll has become, since to call it music is to repress or neglect the other elements in which rock & roll is articulated.

Most people probably continue to think of rock & roll as a musical genre. While this popular conception requires no explicit definition, some critics have tried to give it one by resorting to a periodization of rock history.[2] By reserving the name "rock & roll" for music featuring the combination of rhythm & blues and country & western that emerged in the 1950s, these critics assert an original and genuine form of music. In naming the dominant music of the 1960s "rock," they identify another period and in the process distinguish what must inevitably appear as a lesser genre, diluted or bastardized in its relation to the original. But aside from writing these critics' tastes into history, such periodization relies on a monolithic conception, which is nonetheless only vaguely specified, of 1950s rock & roll. Not only does the mixing of two previous genres tell us too little, but it also describes only a handful of significant 1950s rockers: preeminently Elvis, but not, for example, Little Richard or Chuck Berry. The point is that rock & roll has always been a hodgepodge, and the music of the 1960s represents only a wider diversity of raw materials. Most important, the rock & roll/rock periodization represses the continuity of practices that has existed from the 1950s until today. The various activities associated with rock in the 1960s and later—radio programming, concerts, dances, festivals, etc.—all are impossible without the break in American popular culture that the emergence of rock & roll represents. The Woodstock festival itself is best considered an instance of rock & roll, and, therefore, all of the music performed at the festival, regardless of its formal diversity, is properly identified as rock & roll.

But if rock & roll is not a musical genre, what is it? My solution to this problem is to think of rock & roll as a historically specific cultural practice. Rock & roll is not the only form that could be described this way. Jazz, classical, country, and musical comedy could all be understood as cultural practices, and the rise of the recording industry has changed each of them. Classical critics may still claim that recordings recall the memory of live performances, but, to most listeners, the recording has become the most common experience of classical music. Jazz and country music have undergone a much greater transformation than classical as the result of recording, but both remain more rooted than rock in music that preceded recording. When F. Scott Fitzgerald dubbed the 1920s the "jazz age," he almost certainly did not have recorded music in mind, but then he had more than just music in mind. He understood jazz as a cultural practice. Like "rock & roll," the name "jazz" conflates music, dancing, and sex. Jazz meant not just a certain musical form, but the speakeasies where it was performed and the manners that went with them. Jazz as a cultural practice of the 1920s was largely dead by the 1930s, however, and the music in a certain sense followed suit. Jazz as a popular medium came to be adapted to the dominant tradition in Western music. By the 1930s, jazz was being performed by "orchestras" or big bands using music written or "arranged" in advance and principles any classically trained musician could comprehend.

Rock & roll had a different trajectory because it emerged in the context of the explosion of electronic media of the 1950s. Like jazz, rock's antecedents were folk forms, but they were transmuted in an entirely different way. Instead of being progressively tamed and assimilated, rock & roll took on a life of its own, not just as youth music, but as a way of life that youth lived, and, more important, were represented as living. Rock developed as it did not because of its special musical properties, but because of the conjuncture of particular social conditions and technological developments. As has often been asserted, the youth culture of the 1950s and later could not have happened without teenagers having become a significant market—

that is, without their having significant disposable funds. Having that money and an increased independence from family, teenagers began to identify themselves as a group, and they sought models by which to understand themselves as such. The media provided those models, which included the juvenile delinquent as "news" and as portrayed by James Dean and Marlon Brando in the movies. Businesses of all sorts were more than willing to provide the commodities teens would use to differentiate themselves from others. Rock & roll records were one of these commodities, along with blue jeans and motorcycle jackets. But rock & roll combined these two structures of identity. Stars were both models and objects to be possessed and fetishized: millions of dollars of Elvis paraphernalia were sold in 1956 alone.[3] In addition to cheaper, better recordings, television and films also disseminated rock & roll on a scale that far exceeded the jazz of Fitzgerald's era. Over four hundred rock & roll films were made between 1955 and 1986.[4]

As a cultural practice rock & roll includes, then, not just music, but the other forms and behavior associated with it; it also includes both performers and listeners. But it would be a mistake to reverse the usual hierarchy and simply substitute subjects for objects. Lawrence Grossberg acknowledges the elusiveness of the object when he asserts that "without claiming that the actual construction and sound of the songs are unimportant . . . one needs to argue that they cannot be directly interpreted to explain the effects of the music." His solution is to resort to the self-understanding of rock listeners ("the structure of their responses") in order to get at the music's meaning and function.[5] Such a strategy assumes that subjects, rather than having effects produced in them by a determining object, have consciousness of and control over the object. In treating rock & roll as a discursive practice, I mean to refuse the model that would give us this choice of object or subject. Rock is both a sign system—or perhaps an ensemble of such systems—and a practice: a form of semiosis and an activity in which performers and listeners engage. From the perspective of discursive practice, one does not ask questions about the "effects" of rock & roll on its audience, or of the way the audience understands its own experience of the form. Both questions assume a subject/object opposition, and they tend to lead to giving one side of that opposition dominance. To think simply of rock as having certain effects renders its audience mere objects, while to focus on the experience(s) of members of the audience or the "uses" to which they put the music is to remove them from discourse entirely. No discourse has mechanical effects, but no subject ever escapes discourse. To speak of performers and listeners practicing rock & roll avoids either implication.

The cultural practice of rock & roll entails more products and activities than can even be surveyed in so brief a space as this. Rather than attempt such a survey, I want to look at some examples of the nonmusical registers in which rock & roll is expressed, particularly the performers themselves, those who produce and are produced by rock & roll.

In the first place, it must be admitted that rock is not unique in its lack of a primary text or its combination of discourses. On the contrary, in many respects it recalls the way music was produced prior to the emergence of "classical music" as a secular form. The musical concert, for example, developed out of the prior use of musicians to accompany theatrical performances.[6] And even today, rock is hardly the only cultural form to combine several sign systems or discourses. Alan Durant, in the passage quoted as an epigraph for this essay, may overstate the case for the uniqueness of rock & roll. Film is precisely an instance of the combination of discourses, even if individual films are finally the primary texts. On the other hand, textual primacy in music and other performing arts has always been questionable, and it became radically more so with the advent of recordings which added a third "text" to those of score and performance.

In general, classical music is most identified with the score, music represented by a visual sign system and the work of an individual composer. That representation works as a norm or essence in terms of which any particular performance can be judged, and it functions as a stable object for critical and scholarly study. Performances obviously involve some degree of variation, but in general the performer is understood as serving the work, perhaps even serving as a medium for the genius of the composer. This stance is reflected in the highly conventionalized manner in which classical music is presented. The concert implies not only a single spatial relationship between audience and performers, but even the dress and behavior of each group, both of which reflect reverence for the object being presented. The most significant variation among performances thus becomes the virtuosity of the musicians. While such a quality must be vague to function as a general aesthetic category, it implies mastery of the music and expression of a unique ability, both of which reflect a tension between performer and composer. While virtuosos must master the music—be in control of it so as to be able to give it their own interpretation—they must also be mastered by it or risk appearing not to play the score correctly. While an individual style is necessary, the composer's "intentions" must also be expressed by the performer.

But not all forms usually understood to belong to the classical are the same. Perhaps the most interesting example for my purposes is opera. Polymorphously discursive, opera exists at one extreme of the formation that we call classical music, while at the other extreme are those compositional styles and techniques of presentation that tend toward mathematics and the disappearance of the performer. In no other genre is virtuosity so valued as it is in opera singing. Opera diverges, however, in many other respects from what is typical of the classical formation.

Rock & roll, of course, differs in many respects from classical music as a cultural practice: it does not, for example, value virtuosity. Although certain factions of the audience during the early 1970s did value virtuoso guitar in bands such as the Allman Brothers, the Grateful Dead, and the various Eric Clapton vehicles, this was an oddity in rock history. During most of its existence, rock & roll has been distinctly anti-virtuosic. Even in heavy metal, where guitar mastery is an important element, the technical ability of the player is not the focus. Nor is it even in the blues, although a stronger case could be made there. Unlike the concert soloist, the guitar playing of rock performers is only one aspect of their performance. Rock performers are never merely musicians. They are to a greater or lesser extent also actors playing characters they have invented. Rock audiences do not come to appreciate nor merely to listen to the music being performed; they come to participate in an event and to establish some kind of relationship with those characters. That is why rock audiences usually sing along, shout, whistle, stomp, and clap, regarding it as much their right to be heard as the performer's.

Virtuosity aside, however, rock & roll and opera have much in common. This statement may seem shocking at first, especially since rock & roll and opera seem to have nothing in common *musically*. Some rock & roll—art rock, such as that produced by the Moody Blues or Emerson, Lake and Palmer by explicit allusion, and music by the Who or Bruce Springsteen—does share some musical properties with opera, but that is not the point of my comparison. Rather, the central similarity between rock & roll and opera is that both are practices which are most often identified as music, but which are not purely musical: they communicate through a variety of different sign systems of which music is only one. Both rock and opera are heavily dependent upon lyrics, but they also entail narrative, as well as the costumes, staging, acting, and other elements of theatrical performance. Other similarities between rock and opera reside in the cultural role each has taken on: in the way, for example, each tends to make stars of its performers, something rare in the instrumental side of classical music. Luciano Pavarotti has his share of passionate "groupies" who will press up against the stage with a fevered excitement we've come to expect from the rock & roll fan, but not from the middle-aged woman in pearls and high heels. In the nineteenth century opera was a form of popular culture that engaged strong passions and produced deep loyalties that occasionally resulted in riots over performances; sometimes opera was explicitly identified with radical politics, just as rock was in the 1960s. In noting these similarities, I am not attempting to raise the prestige of a mass form by depicting it in the reflected glow of an elite one, but rather, to shift metaphors, to compare two cultural practices that are both "impure" forms. As much as one could claim that rock & roll aspires to the condition of opera—and it has done so explicitly in *Tommy*—one could also assert that contemporary opera staging and performance aspire to the condition of rock video.

But I want to say more than merely that rock & roll is an impure musical form; it is not even mainly a musical form. One strong piece of evidence for this has been the conspicuous failure of rock criticism to develop even the most rudimentary musicological discourse. In its place there is a rough but ready-to-hand taxonomy of styles, including soul, funk, punk, and heavy metal. In general, these styles carry conventional meanings that are rarely questioned, and they are defined as much by extramusical features as musical ones. Of these extramusical features, we might begin with lyrics, which can be regarded as a defining feature of rock & roll (purely instrumental performers, such as the Ventures, being mere curiosities). Yet in spite of the ubiquity of lyrics and the fact that they do seem to receive the lion's share of attention in most rock criticism, it has long been a widely shared aesthetic principle that lyrics are not the most significant aspect of the genre. Records such as R.E.M.'s *Murmur* were praised because most of the lyrics could not be understood. Sociological studies have claimed to show that rock lyrics are routinely ignored by many listeners. Rock & roll lyrics may function mainly as "music," just as scat singing does in jazz, or as foreign-language lyrics do in the experience of opera either on stage or record.

In the United States, opera is almost exclusively sung in languages that the majority of the audience does not understand. Furthermore, when opera is sung in English, people routinely complain that they cannot understand the lyrics anyway. But neither in opera nor in rock & roll are the lyrics merely an expression of music. In each case they contribute to the meaning of the performance even if their meanings are not immediately understood. Even if the listener does not know what the words "Celeste Aida" mean when the tenor sings them, the opera *Aida* is still understood as a narrative. Similarly, while most listeners to "Radio Free Europe" haven't any idea what the song is about, they have already come to understand the meaning of R.E.M. as distinct from all other bands and performers of rock & roll.

An opera has a clearly distinguishable primary "text," the libretto and score, even though it includes both verbal and musical "discourses." This text can be interpreted in performance by different companies, but it can also be interpreted by critics apart from any particular performance. When Durant argues of rock that it has "no single primary discourse or text," he points out that to take the record as the primary "text" is to "neglect the way in which rock's musical forms have importantly diffused through a variety of technical means," including concerts, films, and videos.[7] Opera may be reproduced in any of these media, but it continues to be identified as what the composer and librettist wrote. Rock & roll on film or video is not merely reproduced, but translated. If the video presents a narrative, for example, it is seldom a narrative the song actually tells. There are "rock & roll films," any number of American International pictures, for example, where the presence of the music is much less significant than the teenage subject matter. *Blackboard Jungle* contained only one rock song, Bill Haley and the Comets' "Rock around the Clock," but the film helped to define the culture's conception of dangerous youth and to make rock & roll a part of that definition. This conception, and the attitudes and behaviors that illustrate it, do as much to define rock & roll as a distinct cultural practice as any musical elements or products.

Technologies such as film, television, and video have usually been regarded as marginal to or merely supportive of the rock performer's work as a maker of records. Grossberg describes them as mere "apparatus" for the music.[8] But the career of the King of rock & roll himself throws this conception into doubt. Elvis Presley is usually assumed to have embodied, if not produced, the beginning of rock & roll when he made a recording at Sam Phillips's studio to give to his mother. In this and his subsequent recordings for Phillips's Sun Records, Elvis brought together the formal elements that have most often been taken to define rock & roll music. The regional popularity of these records led RCA to sign Elvis to a contract that would allow national distribution. But Elvis first reached a national audience on television, and a strong case can be made that the visual aspects of these performances were as significant in defining rock & roll as were the formal features of his music.

What was most remarkable about Elvis on television was the dancing or gyrating that he did while he performed. His first TV appearances, on the *Dorsey Brothers' Show*, included some of his dancing, but, perhaps because the shows were seen by relatively small audiences or because Elvis's dancing was photographed from above, these appearances produced no significant reaction. In his first appearance on the *Milton Berle Show*, however, Elvis's dancing was both more extreme and went on not only during the instrumental break but during the entire last half of the performance of "Hound Dog." The reaction of both professional critics and of self-appointed guardians of morality was swift and harsh. The public outcry nearly caused NBC to cancel Elvis's next scheduled TV appearance, on the *Steve Allen Show*. Rather than cancel the show, the network devised a plan to contain Elvis. Allen dressed him up in tails and had him sing "Hound Dog" to a live basset hound. Later in the same year, Elvis was restrained by court order from making any offensive gyrations on stage in Jacksonville, Florida. Early in 1957, in what was Elvis's third appearance on the *Ed Sullivan Show*, Sullivan insisted that Elvis be photographed only from the waist up.[9]

Why did Elvis's dancing cause such outcry? In the history of mass culture, Elvis is the first male star to display his body as an overt sexual object. While most male movie stars have doubtless been portrayed as sexually desirable, their bodies have not been the locus of the attraction. Rudolph Valentino and James Dean were exceptions to this rule and precursors of Elvis, their bodies being displayed at moments in their films as "adored objects," the actors themselves becoming objects of worship by cults of (mostly female) fans.[10] But movie narratives and editing presented Valentino and Dean as active subjects from whose point of view the audience experienced the story, while Elvis as a singer and dancer was a more passive object of the audience's gaze. Contemporary commentators made it clear that it was his overt sexuality that shocked them, and they hinted at their awareness that it was also a violation of gender codes. Elvis's performance was discussed in terms usually applied to striptease: "bumping and grinding." By the time of the *Berle Show* performance, he had already been given the nickname "the pelvis," a name which, of course, means what it doesn't say. But because I want to differentiate Elvis from later male stars, I want to insist that the phallus is not fetishized in Elvis's dancing. Elvis's costume, which always included a jacket, hid, rather than displayed, his genitals. Elvis's motions imitate intercourse, and his performance should be read as a public display of "sex." Elvis thus put the "sex," which the name rock & roll described, explicitly into his performance. But in calling attention to himself as sexual—that is, in presenting himself as an object of sexual incitement or excitation—he violated not just conventional morality but more importantly the taboo against male sexual display. In violating this taboo, Elvis became, like most women but unlike most men, sexualized. As Frigga Haug and her collaborators have illustrated, women are routinely sexualized as the result of their socialization under patriarchy. Various parts of women's bodies—hair, legs, breasts—become loci of sexualization; women's fashion always calls attention to these features that are presented for the male gaze, and thus mark the woman as a sexual object.[11] The transvestism of later rock stars may be read as their taking on the markers of the sexualized gender.

The television and newsreel photographs of Elvis introduce another dimension of his sexualization. According to one narrative, Elvis made his "pelvic gyrations" a regular part of his act after girls screamed and applauded in the small southern clubs and schools where he played before he became a national act. Photos of one of these early performances already show young women in various states of rapture watching Elvis perform.[12] When Elvis is featured on major national TV programs, the audience becomes part of the show. In the Berle performance, the film cuts between shots of Elvis and shots of the audience, not as a large mass of indistinguishable faces, but of particular faces whose response tells us of the excitement the performer is generating. But this editing also reinforces Elvis as the object of the gaze. It is not just an audience, of which each viewer is a member, that is watching Elvis; television or newsreel viewers experience Elvis as the object of the gaze of the (almost exclusively female) individuals who scream, faint, and otherwise enact ecstasy. This representation of Elvis is formally equivalent to the shot/reverse shot editing that structures the gaze in narrative cinema. It becomes a standard trope of the representation of rock, and will be repeated numerous times during the British invasion of the 1960s. These pictures showed other fans how to respond appropriately to rock acts, while at the same time they created a new representation of male sexuality.

During the 1950s the representation of rock & roll on television might have been the way that the practice was visually experienced by most of its adherents. During the 1960s, however, the rock concert became television's rival. The current form of the rock concert became "routinized" in the 1970s under the influence of Frank Barsalona, a promoter who wanted to assure attendance by " 'guaranteeing' a good night out." [13] The concert as a form had long been standardized by classical and pop predecessors of rock & roll, but rock concert performances also derive from a nonconcert tradition, the performance in clubs by jazz and r&b musicians. The audience plays a distinctly different role in each of these forms. In the (nonoperatic) classical concert, the audience is passive and focused on the stage; in a club, the musicians may or may not be the center of the audience's attention. This decentering of the musicians increases the audience's role in the event. Not only do patrons typically dance, but they usually eat, drink, and talk during the performance. Rock concert patrons display both concert and club behavior and have added some of their own. On the other hand, the theatrical elements of the concert, reduced to the barest minimum in classical performances, are considerably revived in rock concerts. One could argue that rock & roll is fundamentally a theatrical medium and that its characteristic forms of presentation imply a hidden narrative structure. If this assertion holds, music videos can then be understood not as promotional devices essentially extraneous to rock & roll, but as a logical development of the aesthetic character of the form.

Classical musicians, even soloists, do not attempt to stand out in front of their music. Violinists or pianists known for their emotionally demonstrative playing are quite subtle by rock standards. One might argue that the main thing we expect of rock artists on stage is that they emote. Such emotion is displayed only partly through vocalization; just as important are facial expressions, which, even though they get lost in big halls and stadia, are often magnified in video displays or concert films. Bodily gestures and dancing have clearly long been a part of rock performances; more recently, elaborately choreographed videos have led audiences to expect the same on stage. The well-known result has been that some performers have chosen to lipsynch to recorded music so as to be able to perform elaborate dances and movements. With a performance such as Madonna's recent "Blond Ambition" show, it is hard to know whether one is dealing with a concert at all and not theater pure and simple. But not all rockers perform theatrically. At the other extreme, bands like the Grateful Dead just stand there and play. But a Dead show is something else entirely from a classical concert. Relying on the audience's familiarity with their music, the Dead achieve, or at least give the impression of achieving, a much more subtle form of communication. In fact, Dead concerts seem less like shows than rituals, including a standard repertory of music, a community of devoted followers, and even a pacing that strikes one as liturgical.

In analyzing several of the registers or codes that make up the practice of rock & roll, we are, I think, led to treat performers as texts, perhaps even the primary texts of the form. But by suggesting that performers might be the most important of the many objects produced by rock & roll, I do not mean to advance an auteur theory. In one sense, such a theory is unnecessary because rock stars since Elvis have always had auteur status regardless of who writes their songs. In another place, I have suggested that bands or individual performers be thought of as "performing units" as a way to call attention to their artificiality—that is, to the distinction between actual individuals such as Mick Jagger or Bill Wyman and the roles they play in the Rolling Stones.[14] What makes performing units different from artists is that the former are represented by a great variety of products, their involvement in the production of which varies widely. A band or singer is identified not just with particular recordings, but with music and lyrics, album covers, dress, films, videos, performing style, and concert staging. And whatever the involvement of the performer in producing these objects and behaviors, they remain as much collaborative productions as are feature films. To make a record or mount a tour, a performer typically needs a veritable army of collaborators, including producers, session musicians, promoters, and roadies. Since the performer is what gets represented on record and on stage, the performing unit is as much what is produced as any of the signs or products with which it is associated.

Consider the Monkees, a group created by the entertainment industry as the subjects of a situation comedy, who made a number of successful singles in the 1960s and in whose records there was a revival of interest in the late 1980s. The point is not merely that it is possible to invent a rock band out of whole cloth and market it like soap or automobiles, but that it was done with so little resistance. The Monkees were not all that different from most other new rock bands that the entertainment industry tried to sell, except that they had their own television program, a sales opportunity no other new band has enjoyed. But the acceptance of their records suggests that the audience was not put off by the knowledge that the band consisted of actors playing musicians, perhaps because the audience already comprehended rock stars as actors of a sort. Nevertheless, the Monkees succeeded only because a sense of authenticity was manufactured for them, not only—and paradoxically—by means of fictional lives their television show gave them, but also by the usual methods: interviews and biographies presented in fan magazines and other media. Thus the Monkees came to seem to be playing themselves.

If the term "performing unit" seems awkward, if not silly, it is precisely because rock & roll assumes the fiction that its stars are who they appear to be. We do not take John Lennon or Bob Dylan to be playing a role. We don't take a classical soloist to be playing a role either, but we also don't read much personality in his performance. We may perceive opera stars' personalities in all of the roles they play, but a rock star like Mick Jagger always plays Mick Jagger even when he acts another role in a narrative film. "Lennon," "Dylan," and "Jagger," however, are roles that, unlike those in opera or film, exist in no libretto or script. Rock stars do not transform or animate the creation of another; they make themselves up as they go along.

Yet these roles are not as original as they may at first seem. Even the most individualized and personally expressive performers are at best collaborators in their own creation. Dylan, for example, asks us to believe that styles of music as diverse as folk, rock, country, and gospel are all genuine instances of self-expression. Along with these styles, Dylan has assumed a series of personae, different social roles. He is perhaps best-known as the prophet of such diverse messages as "Blowin' in the Wind" and "You Gotta Serve Somebody,"' but he has also played the aesthete (*Highway 61 Revisited* and *Blonde on Blonde*), the down-home balladeer (*John Wesley Harding* and *Nashville Skyline*) and the confessional poet (*Blood on the Tracks*). Each of these new roles that Dylan has taken up has been written in advance, not with the goal of marketing Bob Dylan, but as part of a preexisting

cultural system. Thus Dylan's initial role as folksinger was a conscious imitation of Woody Guthrie, which was clearly marked when
Robert Zimmerman renamed himself Bob Dylan.[15] Similarly, Mick
Jagger's much more consistent persona derives from the blues tradition, and perhaps most directly from Robert Johnson—not, of course,
the real one, but the legendary Robert Johnson who was supposed to
have made a pact with the devil.

Whatever we call rock performers and however much we insist
on their constructedness, we cannot get away from the problem of
authenticity. To understand this point is to see the flaw in the often-
articulated position that the singer-songwriters of the 1970s (like
James Taylor or Joni Mitchell) represent in their claim to individual
expression a deviation from genuine rock & roll. In fact, the most
successful rock stars had always been presented as "real people." The
illusion that we could know the real Elvis, McCartney, or even the
real Monkees was fostered by such superficial means as fan magazine
interviews or facts on the back of bubble-gum cards, but it was also
implicit in Elvis's insistence on his own style of recording the songs of
others, and explicit in those performers who wrote their own songs.
The appearance of artistic authenticity distinguishes rock & roll from
Tin-Pan-Alley-style pop music which exhibits no desire to conceal its
own craft and thus comes off as obviously constructed. Rock conceals
its constructedness.

Performers such as Springsteen and Dylan are often contrasted with
David Bowie and others who call attention to rock as a set of conventions rather than claim authentic self-expression. According to
Simon Frith, Springsteen is a "rock naturalist," his music aiming at
the appearance of natural expression. Elsewhere Frith shows in some
detail how Springsteen's authenticity is constructed, how Springsteen
plays in his professional life a person he is not in real life.[16] But it's
not clear to me that Bowie or others who emphasize the fictionality
of their roles ever fail to make claims to authenticity. Authenticity is
not dispensed with just because a performance is not understood as
self-expression. The different roles Bowie has adopted call attention
to the fact of his performance or his playing those roles, but they do
nothing to diminish, and they may in fact heighten, the sense that
there is a real Bowie behind them. Bryan Ferry's insincerity, his patent

artificiality define him just as much as Dylan's advertised sincerity. The fact is that performers are constructs whether they lay claim to natural or conventional expression, but claiming convention does not dispense with the expectation of authenticity. The performer who exposes convention claims to be the more real because he does so.

To treat performers as the primary texts of rock & roll is not to stabilize rock meanings by reference to the intentions of singers, song-writers, or musicians. It is rather to suggest that the various codes and media in which rock & roll finds expression all contribute to the production of the performer. While a record, a video, or a film may rely on only some of these elements, the performing unit is finally the result of all of them. And yet even this text should not be allowed a simple primacy or centrality. For while the audience of a performing unit doubtless contributes to its production, we also need to consider how the audience is positioned by various performances, as well as how it practices rock & roll in general. Treating performers as texts is a useful strategy for dealing with an obscure object of intellectual desire. We should be careful not to imagine that we have captured that object.

In that spirit, it must be added that treating rock & roll as a cultural practice is not a means to an exhaustive or total understanding of the phenomenon. We should not be tempted to reify a useful analytic tool and thereby make it into an actual, unified object existing autonomously, out there. Even considered as a cultural practice, rock & roll is still a group of related but often contradictory products, activities, styles, and forms.

Notes

1   Alan Durant, *Conditions of Music* (Albany, 1984), 167.
2   Dave Marsh, *Born to Run: The Springsteen Story* (Garden City, N.Y., 1979).
3   Alan and Susan Raymond (producers), *Elvis '56* (Media Home Entertainment, Los Angeles, 1987).
4   Linda J. Sandahl, *Rock Films: A Viewer's Guide to Three Decades of Musicals, Concerts, Documentaries and Soundtracks, 1955–1986* (New York, 1987).
5   Lawrence Grossberg, "Teaching the Popular," in *Theory in the Classroom*, ed. Cary Nelson (Urbana, 1986), 181, 189.
6   Durant, *Conditions of Music*, 9.
7   Ibid., 169, 168.

8   Grossberg, "Teaching the Popular," 190.

9   Alan and Susan Raymond, producers, *Elvis '56*.

10 Jon Savage, "The Enemy Within: Sex, Rock, and Identity," in *Facing the Music*, ed. Simon Frith (New York, 1988), 131–72; and Miriam Hansen, "Pleasure, Ambivalence, Identification: Valentino and Female Spectatorship," *Cinema Journal* 25 (Summer 1986): 6–32.

11 Frigga Haug et al., *Female Sexualization: A Collective Work of Memory*, trans. Erica Carter (London, 1987).

12 Alan and Susan Raymond, producers, *Elvis '56*.

13 Simon Frith, *Sound Effects: Youth, Leisure, and the Politics of Rock 'n' Roll* (New York, 1981), 136–37.

14 David R. Shumway, "Reading Rock'n'Roll in the Classroom: A Critical Pedagogy," in *Critical Pedagogy, the State, and Cultural Struggle*, ed. Henry A. Giroux and Peter McClaren (Albany, 1989), 231–32.

15 Ibid., 232–34.

16 Simon Frith, *Music for Pleasure* (New York, 1988), 94–101.

Robert B. Ray

Tracking

The Tin Pan Alley songs that have become
what we know as "standards" typically derived from a specific songwriting process: the
composer, responsible for the music, settled
first on a melody and second on a harmonic
accompaniment, consisting at this stage of
usually no more than instructions regarding
the chords that would inflect the vocal line
in a particular way. The lyricist, presented
with the completed music, would then set
words to it, and the result would be something like "My Romance" (Rogers and Hart),
"Someone to Watch over Me" (George and Ira
Gershwin), or "Stardust" (Hoagy Carmichael
and Mitchell Parish). Occasionally, of course,
these jobs might be performed by the same
person: George M. Cohan, Irving Berlin, and
Cole Porter wrote their own lyrics, although
Berlin relied on professional harmonizers to
write down chord progressions he could only
hear. At times, the order of this process was
reversed: while Larry Hart always required
Richard Rogers's music to get started, Oscar
Hammerstein preferred going first, writing

lyrics (to a dummy melody's scansion) that Rogers would subsequently orchestrate. In general, however, the standard pattern became the norm, persisting into the rock & roll era. Lieber and Stoller, Goffin and King, and even Jagger and Richards worked in this way, and in doing so, they confirmed the traditional definitions of "the song" and "songwriting."

The metaphysics of this method have become obvious only in retrospect: the division of labor, the priority of music over words, the telos of an AABA song—these aspects of traditional songwriting issue from a culture whose worldview Derrida has labeled "logocentric."[1] Recently, however, new ways of writing songs have begun to challenge the standard procedure. For both *Graceland* and *The Rhythm of the Saints*, Paul Simon built songs up from rhythm tracks—some found, others recorded with no particular song, or even *kind* of song, in mind. "I waited for the melodies and words to emerge from the tracks," Simon has said about *The Rhythm of the Saints*, but this emergence, unaided by teleology, often had to proceed by trial and error.[2] Having recorded one unaccompanied drum track, Simon worked to "find" a song by trying out genres (New Orleans rhythm & blues, gospel) before settling on doo-wop for what became "The Obvious Child."

Rap composing, of course, is the prototype for this songwriting procedure. Concentrating on rhythm (to the extent of eliminating the vocal melody line), working almost entirely with found music (sampled and recontextualized into new combinations), rap, in one writer's words, "is the scavenger of the music business."[3] In another sense, it represents the pop analogue to a similar activity, one that also turns on knowledge of a tradition which can be reactivated by quotation for new purposes: scholarship. With his 19,000-record collection, Akai S900 sampler, and Ensoniq EPS sequencer (tools for effecting infinite recombinations), Public Enemy's Hank Shocklee seems less like the aural "shoplifter"[4] he has been compared to than the specialist scholar whose impulses, Walter Benjamin observed, lie proximate to those of the collector.[5] As Susan Buck-Morss points out, the collector represented for Benjamin someone "who assembles things that have been set out of circulation and are meaningless as use values," an apt description of rap composition.[6] Think, for example, of the backing track to De La Soul's "Eye Know," an aural montage of fragments, including the whistling from Otis Redding's "Dock of the Bay" and a horn phrase from Steely Dan's "Peg."

For Benjamin, the scholar and collector resembled still another type that he called "the ponderer," "the man who already had the resolution to great problems, but has forgotten them. . . . The thinking of the ponderer stands therefore in the sign of remembering":

> The memory of the ponderer holds sway over the disordered mass of dead knowledge. Human knowledge is piecework to it in a particularly pregnant sense: namely as the heaping up of arbitrarily cut up pieces, out of which one puts together a puzzle. . . . The allegoricist reaches now here, now there, into the chaotic depths that his knowledge places at his disposal, grabs an item out, holds it next to another, and sees whether they fit: that meaning to this image, or this image to that meaning. *The result never lets itself be predicted*; for there is no natural mediation between the two.[7]

The result never lets itself be predicted—in this element of surprise lies the great advantage of the ponderer's method. Indeed, the terms of Benjamin's description anticipate communication theory, with its redefinition of information as precisely a function of unpredictability.[8] By this account, then, the initial difficulty of Public Enemy's records issued from the "informational density" of aural collages like "Fight the Power," with its seventeen different samples in the first ten seconds. This move is not without risks: it increases information by minimizing the redundancy on which easy reception depends. It wins its bet when it tells us something new.

Scholarship, collecting, pondering, information theory—these activities may seem heady company for rap songwriting. Benjamin, however, has taught us to detect the similarities between occupations normally regarded as unrelated, and having done so, we might begin to see in contemporary songwriting suggestions for a new writing practice. What if academics were to write essays the way Paul Simon now composes songs? Given the predictability of so much contemporary criticism, this question seems worth taking up.[9] Hence the form of this essay. I decided to begin with "sampling," building up individual tracks (the essay's rhythm?) by appropriating familiar information, while keeping open the purpose to which it might ultimately be put. I hope that as in rap, while the contents of the individual tracks may sometimes sound familiar, the final mix may be less so.

This essay is composed of six different tracks (two more than the Beatles had at their disposal), conceived at different occasions (as recorded parts might be), and brought together only in the final mix, which you are reading. Just as any modern mixing board allows you to "solo" any given track (to hear it alone, isolated from the others), and just as such soloing is typically the first step in mixing, I will begin here by running down the contents of my individual tracks, so that you can see (or hear) the parts before they dissolve into the blend.

―――――

Track One. During the past two years, a group at the University of Florida has participated in something called the Institute for European and Comparative Studies (recently renamed the Florida Research Ensemble, to suggest our interest in music and collaborative work), one of many such institutes whose cropping up suggests the increasingly widespread desire for interdisciplinary approaches to subjects perhaps not comprehended by traditional departments—subjects, for example, like rock & roll. Our institute organized itself around a single topic, the orality/literacy opposition described by Walter Ong, Jack Goody, Jacques Derrida, and others. What has interested us is the notion of writing as a *technology* whose advent and development have dramatically altered human consciousness. As both Ong and Goody demonstrate, a person surrounded by writing thinks differently from someone without it, and he will do so even if he himself cannot write.[10] Abstract definitions, critical analysis, particular logics of ordering—these things that we take for granted in fact depend on the presence of writing and its various apparati: lists, indexes, alphabetization, charts, paragraphs. Without writing, the kind of thinking dependent on those categories does not exist.

Here is an example, first described by A. R. Luria, and summarized by Ong: given a set of drawings of four objects (a hammer, a saw, a log, and a hatchet), subjects were asked to point to the one dissimilar from the rest. While literate subjects will inevitably exclude log, the one item not a tool, illiterate subjects see the problem differently, not in terms of abstract categories, but in terms of practical situations involving use. As Ong observes: "If you are a workman with tools and see a log, you think of applying the tool to it, not of keeping the tool away from what it was made for—in some weird intellectual game." Thus, one peasant replies:

> "They're all alike. The saw will saw the log and the hatchet will chop it into small pieces. If one of these has to go, I'd throw out the hatchet. It doesn't do as good a job as a saw." Told that the hammer, saw, and hatchet are all tools, he discounts the categorical class and persists in situational thinking: "Yes, but even if we have tools, we still need wood—otherwise we can't build anything."[11]

Even more important than this example is Ong's conclusion that were he living in a fully alphabetic culture, the peasant would respond differently, would understand the concept of "tool"—and would do so even if he himself did not read or write. For my purposes here, I don't intend to develop further the orality/literacy distinction, except to point out the obvious parallel to performance/recording, and to suggest that like writing, recording changes consciousness, and that people surrounded by records will develop different attitudes toward music, and will do so even if they do not know how to make records themselves.[12]

Track Two. The debates over sampling have called attention to the rapid development in recording technology and the attendant reconceptualization of the recording process. Recording itself has been possible only since 1877, when Edison invented it; writing, of course, is much older, invented by the Sumerians around 3500 B.C. As Ong reminds us, almost everything we take for granted about writing took centuries to arrive: the alphabet itself, for example, appeared 2,000 years after the Sumerians' script, and paper was first manufactured in Europe only in the twelfth century. Other familiar uses of writing, Ong points out, arise still later, like the personal diary, which remained virtually unknown until the seventeenth century.

Recording, by contrast, almost certainly because of writing's existence, has developed more quickly. Nevertheless, most of the major changes have occurred in the last twenty-five years. Before the mid-1960s, most engineers and producers, especially those working with jazz and classical artists, regarded their job as capturing a live sound, as simply recording (reproducing) the sound the musicians made while playing together in a room built for its ideal acoustic properties. Again and again, we hear producers such as John Hammond lamenting the difficulties of catching something like the sound of the 1930s Count Basie Band in full flight. In the 1960s, Glenn Gould scandalized the classical community by openly acknowledging that his recorded performances consisted of multiple takes joined by inaudible splices. The Beatles made such things famous, with "Strawberry Fields" resulting from two takes, played at different tempos and in different keys, spliced together and matched by speeding up one and slowing down the other. Simon and Garfunkel's "Bridge over Troubled Water" made the punch-in respectable with the revelation that Garfunkel's vocal had been pieced together from dozens of takes, often of a single word or phrase.

In the 1980s, these procedures began to seem primitive. For those musicians still playing in studios (many had been replaced by drum machines and synthesizers), the punch-in (or "drop") became so routine that songs were rarely played all the way through. Recording came more and more to resemble cinematic acting, as mixing (the analogue to editing) *constructed* a performance out of fragments often played on different days (and even in different places: the phenomenon known as "flying in" a part became standard, whereby a musician is sent a multitrack take, to which he adds his part before returning it).[13] And then the explosion of computer-aided recording: MIDI (musical instrument digital interface, the linking together of multiple instruments through a digital signal), sequencing, sampling. The effect of this technology has been increasingly to remove recording from performance, to create sounds that cannot be readily reproduced in live situations. In semiotic terms, a record, like a movie, has become a sign without a referent: behind *Casablanca* or "Fight the Power" lies no single, "real" event which has been transcribed and reproduced. Instead, there are only fragments of behavior, snatches of sound: a turn of the head filmed one Monday for a sequence completed a month later, a drum beat sampled for mixing with a radio announcement. In 1967, situationist leader Guy Debord warned that in "societies where modern conditions of production prevail, all of life presents itself as an immense accumulation of *spectacles*. Everything that was directly lived has moved away into a representation."[14] For film and music, we can amend this last sentence: "Everything that was directly *performed* has moved away into a *construction*, a recording composed of performance's surviving fragments.

═════

Track Three. It would have been surprising if these developments in recording had *not* begun to affect live performances. If, as Ong points out, the existence of writing modifies the way we speak, we would expect that the existence of recorded music would affect the way people play. And of course it does. From the start, jazz musicians played differently for having heard Louis Armstrong's records.[15]

But I have in mind here less records' influence on musical styles than their impact on protocols of performing, an influence which begins with the rise of the microphone, first for singers (replacing the megaphone, used anachronistically by Rudy Vallee), then for orchestral or band sections too quiet to compete with louder instruments. The microphone's redefinition of popular singing, immediately audible in the shift from Jolson's stentorian bravura to Crosby's quiet intimacy, is the first dramatic result of performance's admission of recording technology. This development flourished in rock, first with the spread of the electric guitar and bass, then with sound reinforcement systems (P.A.'s), which by the late 1970s had spawned electronic drums, triggered by hitting the acoustic set. Inevitably, this "contamination" of the live by the recorded has resulted in the actual replacement of the live, as Madonna, Janet Jackson, New Order, Milli Vanilli, and almost every rap group perform to taped music and/or lip-synch to prerecorded vocals. If we want to understand why so many people are upset about this trend, why state legislators in New York and New Jersey have proposed regulating the use of recorded music in live concerts, we need to look at the next track.

═════

Track Four. If Ong's observations about orality and literacy account for recording's increasing power to shape performance in its own image, it is Derrida's demonstration of Western culture's historical preference for speech over writing that explains why this process has been so resisted. For, surely, recording amounts to simply another means of writing, and thus it becomes regarded as secondary or supplemental to performance. Indeed, many of the objections raised to the new recording technologies (especially to sampling) reiterate precisely the Platonic objections to writing made in the *Phaedrus*, the dialogue so carefully remarked upon by Derrida.[16] Writing, Plato argued, by providing mankind with an artificial method of storing knowledge, eroded our real powers of memory. Sampling and sequencing, go the current complaints, make musicians unnecessary: you can make records now entirely by recombining bits and pieces sampled from other records; you don't have to play a musical instrument at all.[17]

We can detect here the historical complaint against every new technology and every avant-garde movement that embraces it: the new technology makes things too easy. What previously was possible for only a few (storing large amounts of information, producing a figurative representation of a person or object, making a record) becomes possible for many with, respectively, writing, photography, and sampling. Plato dismissed writing as *artificial* memory. This characterization issued from his own anxious, prescient intuition of all technology's fundamental *automatism*, its potential to continue producing long after the control exacted by human consciousness has been relinquished. For Plato, the ghost in the machine was language that survived not only its author, but also every context of its own enunciation. In the twentieth century that fear has persisted, finding representation in the movies' fatal robots (*Blade Runner*), Frankensteinian monsters devouring assembly lines (*Modern Times*), and computers-run-amok (*2001*). But the rock community has developed an alternative attitude toward its technology's independence. After the Velvet Underground and Jimi Hendrix, concerts frequently ended with guitarists leaving their instruments onstage for the self-sustaining feedback that would accompany the audience's departure. At the other end, the Who began opening shows with "Baba O'Riley's" programmed synthesizer pattern, set to continue throughout the song. Were these strategies part of a ritual, whose basis was precisely that loss of self which Plato feared? Or were they simply a sanguine (and loud) promise of future songs, future shows?

Disciplines such as film studies and the history of science have shown us that, far from being disinterested, technology follows the route of ideology. Western culture's animus toward writing, therefore, would help to explain why, in a culture of headlong change, recording technology has taken such a relatively long time to develop. If one conceives of live performance as the privileged instance, and of recording as only a supplemental means of capturing it, then such things as multitrack tape recorders, reverberation and delay units, compressors, pitch controllers, harmonizers and doublers, sequencers and samplers, will all seem less important, and their invention and implementation will have to wait.

≡≡≡≡

Track Five. I should reveal here something about my own interest in what I am writing about. Since 1982, I have been an active member of a rock band armed with a strange name, for which, I hasten to add, I am not responsible: the Vulgar Boatmen. In fact, as I write, I have just emerged from a two-week session for a second record, during which many of the technologies I have mentioned were used. I will give only one example. For one song, our drummer happened by accident upon an unusual and pleasing snare drum sound. I won't go into details, but only mention that achieving this sound involved a kind of juggling act, holding the drum between the legs so that one foot rested against the lower drum head (slightly muffling the snares) while striking the other head with a combination of cross-sticking and taped brush. Well, it seemed worth it at the time. A week later, however, in mixing, he discovered that for all of its appealing sound, the snare was poorly played (perhaps because it was so difficult to hold), often falling so far behind the beat that any sense of pulse was lost. How to fix it? The drummer started by honoring speech and performance: he wanted to replay the part from start to finish. But five hours' work convinced him that a sound he had achieved by accident could not be reproduced by calculation. He then chose to sample one snare hit (which, after all, he had produced himself) and replay the part by simply triggering this sampled sound in the appropriate, and now properly timed, places.

This process has come to seem normal. What nevertheless still seems strange about the Vulgar Boatmen, especially to the rock press, which never fails to mention this fact when writing about us, is that there are two sets of Vulgar Boatmen, one in Florida that records and one in Indianapolis that tours. Only one person, the Indianapolis leader, regularly participates in both groups, since he also works on all recordings. While this arrangement derived from practical circumstances (I have a job which prevents my touring, I have a family, my idea of a tour resembles Brian Eno's: I stay in one place and the audience comes to see me), I now realize that having two bands of Vulgar Boatmen enacts the performance/recording dichotomy at the heart of so many debates about contemporary rock & roll. Warhol signaled his acceptance of technology's automatism by calling his studio The Factory, by basing his serial paintings on found photographs, by sending other men to fulfill his speaking engagements. Having cloned ourselves once, the Vulgar Boatmen might become available for franchising—a Vulgar Boatmen in every town, always accompanied by a sign: 6,352 records sold.

≡≡≡

Track Six. In a recent issue of the MLA's journal *Profession*, Marianna Torgovnick calls for an "experimental critical writing," but admits that she does not yet know how to produce it.[18] For the past few years, my own courses have asked students to do such experimenting, and I have worked from the assumption, proposed by my colleague Gregory Ulmer, that the avant-garde arts might provide ideal models for different kinds of writing.[19] My own project has been to start with a group of films, the Andy Hardy movies, that beg for the kind of ideological, semiotic, psychoanalytic criticism current in cultural studies, but then to prohibit students from taking that conventional approach. Instead, I have asked them to extrapolate from such models as surrealist games, Derrida's signature experiments (in *Signsponge* and *Glas*), Julian Barnes's *Flaubert's Parrot* (a hybrid text, part novel, part biography, part criticism), Benjamin's *Arcades Project* (a never-finished collage of found material on nineteenth-century Paris), Godard's films and television programs, Barthes's autobiography (with its alphabetized fragments).[20] Six months ago, when I first thought about this essay, I assumed that recording might provide yet another model for experiments with critical writing, which has traditionally resembled simply transcriptions of spoken lectures. What kind of academic writing, I asked myself, would result from the alphabetic equivalents of studio effects like reverberation, delay, sampling, flanging, phase-shifting, doubling, equalization, compression? But just as mixing or editing can often produce a different song or movie than one expected, so mixing these tracks here has led me to a different conclusion and to three final propositions.

Final Mix. (1) What distinguishes rock & roll from all the music that precedes it—especially classical, Tin Pan Alley, and jazz—is its elevation of the record to primary status. While classical and jazz recordings for the most part aimed only at approximating live performances, regarded as the significant event, many of rock's most important musicians, beginning with Elvis, made records before ever appearing in public. In fact, the performances that began rock & roll, Elvis's Sun recordings, could not be reproduced in any live situation except a very small and empty (to permit reverberation) room, since Elvis's acoustic guitar and Bill Black's acoustic bass simply could not be heard. (Having grown up in Memphis, I know. I attended several early Elvis performances.) Thus, any complaints against Madonna or Janet Jackson for not starting as live performers ignore rock's history.

(2) Derrida and others have alerted us to postmodernism's defining condition: the triumph of an opposition's previously suppressed term. At the end of the twentieth century, we live in a world in which we almost always encounter a representation of something (the *Mona Lisa*, Mikhail Gorbachev, Bruce Springsteen) before we encounter the thing itself. Where once records hoped only to provide a souvenir of a live performance, concerts now exist to promote records, and to do so they use technology to reproduce as much of the recorded sound, and associated imagery, as possible. In embracing this state of affairs and the technology that has created it, rock affirms its postmodernism.

In rejecting this situation, in clinging to speech/performance as the authentic site of musical presence, jazz clings to previous traditions, especially those of modernism.

(3) As I have said, I began preparation for this essay by thinking of recording (not songwriting) as a model for academic writing. But I now realize that the relationship is the reverse. For writing, as the more advanced technology, has been the example for recording. What, after all, is sampling except quotation, which writers do all the time? What are punch-ins except revisions? What are multitracks but columns? I would argue, however, that *academic* writing, a particularly retrograde subspecialty, continues to make very little use of the technology's resources, and that it might begin to notice how much more willingly recording engineers, producers, and musicians have begun to experiment with what is possible.

Notes

1   The term "AABA song" refers to the Tin Pan Alley norm of chorus/chorus/bridge/chorus. Show tunes typically began with a "verse," an introductory section that occurred only once. While maintaining the AABA form, rock & roll dropped the verse, except in such rare cases as the Lennon-McCartney "Do You Want to Know a Secret?" with its opening "You'll never know how much I really love you / You'll never know how much I really care." This move, and the inclusion of Broadway's "Till There Was You" on their first American LP, suggests how much the Lennon-McCartney team owed to Tin Pan Alley.

2   Quoted in Stephen Holden's "Paul Simon's Journey to Brazil and Beyond," *New York Times*, 14 October 1990.

3   Public Enemy's Hank Shocklee, quoted in "Ebony and Ivory," an interview/conversation between Paul Simon and Hank Shocklee, *Spin*, January 1991, 84.

4   Mark Dery, "Public Enemy: Confrontation," *Keyboard*, September 1990, 84: "Rap, by definition, is political music. Fabricated from stolen snatches of prerecorded music by smash-and-grab producers who frequently thumb their noses at copyright laws, it is the musical equivalent of shoplifting." Despite this remark, Dery's article displays considerable sympathy for rap in general and Shocklee in particular.

5   See Walter Benjamin, "Eduard Fuchs, Collector and Historian," in *One-Way Street and Other Writings*, trans. Edmund Jephcott and Kingsley Shorter (London, 1979), 349–86.

6   Susan Buck-Morss, *The Dialectics of Seeing: Walter Benjamin and the Arcades Project* (Cambridge, Mass., 1989), 241.

7   Quoted by Buck-Morss in *Dialectics of Seeing*, 240–41; emphasis mine.

8 "The more probable (banal) the message, the less information it conveys": Gregory L. Ulmer, *Applied Grammatology* (Baltimore, 1985), 308.

9 Meaghan Morris puts the matter bluntly: "I get the feeling that somewhere in some English publisher's vault there is a master disk from which thousands of versions of the same article . . . are being run off under different names with minor variations" ("Banality in Cultural Studies," in *Logics of Television: Essays in Cultural Criticism*, ed. Patricia Mellencamp [Bloomington, 1990], 21).

While the *Wall Street Journal* has denounced this tendency as indicative of American academics' overwhelming leftism (see "Politically Correct," *Wall Street Journal*, 26 November 1990), it in fact signals precisely the opposite: a commitment to capitalism and business-as-usual. Since at least the eighteenth century, ideas (like any product) have been subject to commodification. But what marks contemporary intellectual life is the intense speed with which even the most critical positions can become the newest way to make a living. With the chronic oversupply of Ph.D.'s enabling the humblest colleges to link promotion, tenure, and now hiring itself to publication, more and more people are producing more and more books and articles. Because these people are often working on deadlines (at my university, assistant professors have only five years before the tenure decision), they inevitably gravitate to hot areas, those methodologies and topics that insure publication. As a result, cultural criticism, more than ever before, is now subject to the boom-and-bust cycles that have always haunted capitalism. This development has real effects: at any given moment, everyone seems to be writing about the same thing—and then, no one is. Morris cites a Japanese media analyst's coolness toward a collection containing several essays on Foucault: "Ah Foucault . . . I'm very sorry, but there's no boom" ("Banality in Cultural Studies," *Discourse* 10 [Spring–Summer 1988]: 5—this essay is a slightly different version of the one cited above). Again the pop analogy seems appropriate: a hit parade of critical ideas that changes every month.

10 See Walter Ong's *Orality and Literacy* (London, 1982) for a summary of research on this topic. Jack Goody's books are more specific, but equally interesting. See especially his *The Domestication of the Savage Mind* (Cambridge, 1977) and *The Logic of Writing and the Organization of Society* (Cambridge, 1986).

11 Ong, *Orality and Literacy*, 51.

12 The pioneer in extending this argument to music was Glenn Gould. In his famous 1966 essay "The Prospects of Recording," Gould stated flatly that "[w]e must be prepared to accept the fact that, for better or worse, recording will forever alter our notions about what is appropriate to the performance of music" (*The Glenn Gould Reader*, ed. Tim Page [New York, 1984], 337). In particular, Gould maintained that the advent of tape splicing, by means of which perfect performances could be constructed in the studio, created for live performances audience expectations impossible to satisfy. In this context, classical performances became what Gould called "the last blood sport," something like a high-wire act where the audience waits breathlessly for the fall.

Significantly, Gould argued that this development cut both ways. On the one hand, it encouraged conservatism among performers, afraid to take on new or difficult pieces for audiences grown unaccustomed to, and ultimately intolerant of, mistakes of any kind. On the other hand, recordings create active listeners who themselves could, by taking charge of their own editing, develop utterly nonconformist attitudes toward music and its history. If rap recording seems the result of this latter development, the spread of lip-syncing and tapes in "live" performance appears to issue from the former. All discussions about contemporary music and its technology should begin with Gould's warning that "[t]he technology of electronic forms makes it highly improbable that we will move in any direction but one of even greater intensity and complexity" (Page, ed., *Glenn Gould Reader*, 352).

13   Glenn Gould was quick to spot the obvious analogy between the recording process and filmmaking: "[O]ne should be free to 'shoot' a Beethoven sonata or a Bach fugue in or out of sequence, intercut almost without restriction, apply postproduction techniques as required, and . . . the composer, the performer, and above all the listener will be better served thereby" (Page, ed., *Glenn Gould Reader*, 359).

14   Guy Debord, *The Society of the Spectacle* (Detroit, 1977), sec. 1.

15   In his interesting book *The Recording Angel: Explorations in Phonography* (New York, 1987), Evan Eisenberg proposes that "[r]ecords and radio were the proximate cause of the Jazz Age. . . . [R]ecords not only disseminated jazz, but inseminated it—. . . . [I]n some ways they created what we call jazz" (143–44). To avoid paying royalties, groups like King Oliver's Creole Jazz Band and Armstrong's Hot Five replaced published songs with on-the-spot improvisations whose recording granted them a permanence they would otherwise never have had.

16   Jacques Derrida, "Plato's Pharmacy," in *Dissemination*, trans. Barbara Johnson (Chicago, 1981), 61–171.

17   Public Enemy's Hank Shocklee has made explicit the implications of sampling and sequencing:

> We don't *like* musicians. We don't *respect* musicians. . . . In dealing with rap, you have to be innocent and ignorant of music. Trained musicians are not ignorant of music, and they cannot be innocent to it. They understand it, and that's what keeps them from dealing with things out of the ordinary. . . . [Public Enemy is] a musician's *nightmare*. (*Keyboard*, September 1990, 82–83)

Another Shocklee remark indicates what's at stake: "You get a person who says, 'I don't have time to study an instrument.' Rappers sample" (*Spin*, January 1991, 61).

18   Marianna Torgovnick, "Experimental Critical Writing," *Profession* 90 (1990): 25–27.

19   Gregory L. Ulmer, *Teletheory: Grammatology in the Age of Video* (New York, 1989), 18–19.

20   For a preliminary report on this project, see my "The Avant Garde Finds Andy Hardy," in *Modernity and Mass Culture*, ed. Patrick Brantlinger and James Naremore (Bloomington, 1991).

Mark Dery

Signposts on the Road to Nowhere:
Laurie Anderson's Crisis of Meaning

The world is disappearing. Oliver Wendell Holmes augured this surreal state of affairs in "The Stereoscope and the Stereograph," his 1859 essay on what was then a newly arrived technological marvel: photography. "Form is henceforth divorced from matter," he declared. "In fact, matter as a visible object is of no great use any longer, except as the mould on which form is shaped." Jean Baudrillard, in his 1975 essay, "The Precession of Simulacra," posited the notion that the world as we know it is a hyperreality of simulacra, a hall of mirrors where the original is lost in an infinite regress of reflections. And Bryan Fawcett argued, in *The Public Eye: A Deliberation on the Disappearance of the World*, that mass media images of desire-commodified, strategically deployed by Madison Avenue, constitute the better part of reality for all who view the world through the cathode-ray tube.

The assertion that reality is undergoing a gradual process of dematerialization is evidenced, literally as well as metaphorically, by events in every corner of the cultural arena. Cosmologists, for example, now believe that the universe is comprised, in large part, of an invisible mass called "dark matter." Jaron Lanier, founder of VPL Research, Inc., is spearheading the development of "virtual reality," a computer-based technology that allows cybernauts equipped with motion-sensing Datagloves and televisual goggles called EyePhones to roam digital dreamscapes. On *This Week with David Brinkley*, NPR reporter Cokie Roberts observed that death by joystick in the Persian Gulf, viewed through bomber nose-cone cameras, seemed like a video game. And our commodity culture, once based on manufactured goods, now trades in intangibles: brand names, junk bonds, cultural heroes, celluloid myths. "We sell fabulous merchandise at very high prices," confided a Disney executive in a December 1990 *Fortune* cover story titled "Pop Culture: America's Hottest Export Goes Boom!" "But what we really sell is the Disney characters—warmth and honesty and family."

One result of this inversion of the time-honored primacy of original over reproduction has been what German cultural theorists call *Sinnkrise*, a "crisis of meaning." In "The Semiotics of Semiotics," in the anthology *On Signs*, Wlad Godzich details the multiform manifestations of this crisis: "The great explanatory systems of the West are felt to be inadequate, if not obsolete, whether they be of a social-democratic, Marxist or educated-liberal variety. The master narratives are dying for lack of credibility . . . and nothing is taking their place."

The crisis of meaning crystallizes in the art of Laurie Anderson. A performance artist cum pop star, Anderson makes virtual vaudeville for a world of pure simulacra. When Roland Barthes defined semiosis, in *Elements of Semiology*, as "images, gestures, musical sounds, objects, and the complex associations of all these," he could have been describing a Laurie Anderson performance. Her brand of cybercabaret is a synesthesiac's dream, a giddy headrush of song and soliloquy counterpointed by still and moving images.

Of course, her art hasn't always been one of push-button presto chango. Formally trained—she graduated magna cum laude in art history from Barnard College in 1969, and took an MFA in sculpture

from Columbia University in 1972—she began as a post-conceptual-
ist, meditating, then as now, on our mediated society. She sculpted
newsprint pulp into post-Gutenberg fetishes, cut newspapers into
ribbons and wove them into latticed, Mondrian-like collages. Early
performances such as *For Instants* (1976) constituted chapters in a
fictionalized autobiography: Hunched under an umbrella in an imaginary downpour or pretending to row a boat across a gallery floor,
she told droll, beguiling stories about growing up in well-to-do Glenn
Ellyn, Illinois, the daughter of a paint manufacturer; hitchhiking to
the North Pole; and living in Chiapas, Mexico, with the last remaining Mayan tribe "as a spy for [her] anthropologist brother."

In time, she moved away from the elitist sensibility native to
white-walled Soho galleries, a hermetic aesthetic she would later lampoon in her 1989 song cycle, *Empty Places*, where she suggested that
would-be performance art stars obtain housecats—"preferably rather
limp ones"—and make them act out the words to Stephen Foster's
"Swanee." In place of such self-important silliness, she offered unabashedly accessible fare that borrowed equally from high and mass
culture.

In 1979, art Brahmin Holly Solomon commissioned a work for her
husband's birthday, and Anderson produced *Americans on the Move*,
a blend of sights, sounds, and special effects that would later become
United States. As Janet Kardon notes in *Laurie Anderson—Works from
1969 to 1983*: "Up to this time, Anderson seems to have identified
herself primarily as a sculptor; molding a space with her own pres-
cence could be construed as an extension of a sculptor's activity.
This changed [at the Carnegie Hall performance of *Americans on the
Move*, where she] . . . commanded the stage, with attendant musicians as visible counterpoints to her persona and the instrumentation
more strongly identified with rock music." Two years later, "O Super-
man," the nuclear mantra from her *Gesamtkunstwerk, United States*,
had been released on an independent label and was climbing the
British pop charts; shortly thereafter, she signed a record contract
with Warner Bros. Anderson's departure from the world of performance art, a high modernist tradition strongly rooted in Dada's absurdist cabaret, the geometric dances of the Bauhaus, and the Diony-
sian happenings of the 1960s, was nearly complete.

United States, Parts I–IV (1983), was a watershed in her development. A six-hour symphony for slides, shadow play, semiotics, and semiconductors, it is the equivalent of Marshall McLuhan's *The Medium Is the Massage* set to music. Thematically divided into four sections—transportation, politics, money, and love—it is a sometimes jocular, often jaundiced look at America, seen through the wide eyes of a rooster-coifed waif, a new wave incarnation of Chaplin's Tramp. Throughout, the operant mode is avant-vaudeville: glib, darkly funny "bits" are delivered with a nightclub comedian's sense of timing, bookended by visual and instrumental interludes. Harpo Marx-ist theatrics—Anderson "singing" by means of a tiny pillow speaker concealed in her mouth, rapping out a percussion solo on her contact-miked skull, or pantomiming bowling to the taped accompaniment of a ball rumbling down a lane and knocking over pins—are a far cry from Joseph Beuys's alchemical rituals, the Kipper Kids' Three Stooges version of the Theater of Cruelty, and other 1970s performance art; they are closer in style to the pratfalls and pie-in-the-face antics of a music hall showman. The parallel can be seen in *United States'* score as well, where the honking klaxons, slide whistles, and kazoos of vaudeville sound effects men resound in Anderson's squeaking baby gavels, quacking toy saxophones, chattering percussion, and electronic wolf howls. Her trademark tape-bow violin (an ordinary violin rigged with an audio playback head and played with a bow whose horsehair has been replaced by prerecorded tape) seems more like a ventriloquist's dummy than a musical instrument when it speaks with a human voice. Even her use of pitch-shifters and digital delays to create alter egos—a stern, eat-your-peas authoritarian, a naive hayseed—is distinctly vaudevillian.

Razzle-dazzle routines, equal parts talk show, MTV, and Mister Wizard, play in Peoria; performance art like that documented by Bruce Nauman in *Bouncing Balls* (1969), a nine-minute movie of the artist playing with his testicles, filmed close-up and in slow motion, does not. Performance art, which flared in the 1970s, fizzled in the 1980s; its few remaining practitioners—Karen Finley is perhaps the best known among them—want desperately to communicate with their audiences. In a sense, then, Laurie Anderson and the populist ethos she embodies have triumphed. As she only half-facetiously confides, in "Yankee See," "I was out in L.A. recently on music business, and I was . . . filling them in on some of my goals / And I said: Listen, I've got a vision / I see myself as part of a long tradition of American humor / You know—Bugs Bunny, Daffy Duck, Porky Pig, Elmer Fudd, Roadrunner, Yosemite Sam / And they said: Well, actually, we had something a little more adult in mind / And I said: O.K.! O.K.! Listen, I can adapt!" And adapt she has. Having recorded five albums for a major label, released *Home of the Brave*, a $165 million concert film, and even written a jingle for Reebok, she is well on her way to becoming the "Bob Hope kind of person" to whom she once compared herself. Still, there's that nagging question of the crisis of meaning.

It is a question that has dogged her down through the years, as the following siftings from her clip file indicate. Debra Rae Cohen, writing in a June 1982 issue of *Village Voice*, sniffed, "Laurie Anderson's aphoristic recitations and elliptical lyrics add up to less and less the longer she stays on stage." In the March 1984 issue of *Artforum*, Thomas McEvilley excoriated the artist for her tendency to dish up moldy chestnuts, time and again:

> Over the years, Anderson has recycled the same texts, and [her retrospective exhibition] followed her lead—I saw one language "bit" in five different places, the dates ranging from 1972 to 1983. The result is to make a slender body of work look fat. If the texts were deeper or sharper one would not mind their constant repackaging, and could be more appreciative of the cleverness of the packaging, but they are, after all, just the rather lightweight, caught-in-a-loop, hip posturing familiar from *United States* (where many of the old texts resurfaced).

John Piccarella wrote, in a January 1985 *Village Voice* article, that the "criticism most often leveled at Anderson's work is that it has the hollow ring of signs without referents." "She's not a thinker," asserted Gregory Sandow, in an April 1986 *Village Voice*. "Along with Dylan Thomas, she might say, 'I'm never very hot on meaning; it's the sound [and in her case the look] of meaning that I like.'" And Erika Munk, in her October 1989 *Village Voice* review of *Empty Places*, observed that the performance rendered "absence, lack, loneliness in ways much more distressing than Laurie Anderson intends. Perhaps it can never be said often enough that referring to an event or person or idea isn't always throwing a stone into a vast pond of meaning so we can contemplate the ripples. Mostly it's just picking an idea up and dropping it, thump. [E]ven when [Anderson] does an extended riff, she does no more than lay the subject out for our inspection."

Laurie Anderson's art is information anxiety incarnate, fashioned from the white noise of postmodernity—sound bites, photo ops, advertising jingles, TV themes, pop songs, slang, and doublespeak. Implying everything, signifying nothing, it generates much heat, little light. In *White Noise*, Don DeLillo's harrowing chronicle of one man's descent into the media maelstrom, brand names, bromides, and buzzwords worm their way into the narrator's innermost thoughts, "the coded messages and endless repetitions . . . like mantras." So in Anderson, where singsong wordplay—"Talkshow, Uplink, Update, Phaselock, Downtime, Hotline," "Stop the press, beat the clock, rock the cradle, and rule the world"—is substituted for substance. "Say Hello" and "Lighting Out for the Territories," the routines that bookend *United States*, are revealing. "You can read the signs," assures Anderson. "You've been on this road before." Again, as the last strains fade and the piece draws to a close, she purrs, "You can read the signs. . . . You can do this in your sleep." But it is a semiotician's nightmare, a road to nowhere dotted with signs pointing only at each other. Endlessly traveling, never arriving, she—and we who accompany her as her audience—is a Kerouac who has mistaken a treadmill for the road, a Huckleberry Finn lighting out for territories he will never find.

The following interview was conducted on 11 June 1989 in Charleston, South Carolina, minutes after Anderson's performance of *Empty Places*, the multimedia theater piece that closed that year's Spoleto Festival.

Anderson, it should be noted, is an incandescent presence. Her smooth skin has a milky translucency to it, as if her features were sculpted out of quartz, and her large, intelligent eyes give her gaze a powerfully mesmeric quality. Quizzical eyebrows and an elfin grin, topped off by a mussed, moussed new wave do and a wardrobe that runs to rumpled, outsized men's suitcoats and frumpy sneakers, make her resemble a cross between Marcel Marceau's Mister Bip and the gamine in Chaplin's *City Lights*. Although she will soon turn 44, she possesses an uncanny, Peter Pan-ish ability to look forever child-like. Speaking in the cool, exquisitely modulated tones of a classical radio announcer, she pauses often, choosing her words with care as she snaps the filter off yet another Marlboro. Poised, professional, and intensely private, she is adept at the art of amiable obfuscation. Questions that probe a little too close to the bone, ideologically or biographically, are deflected, invariably, with an anecdote, often one that has been honed to perfection through repetition. Like Pee-Wee Herman, Ronald Reagan, and Michael Jackson, she is *always* in character: her onstage and offstage personae are virtually inseparable. She seems, in fact, to view her interviews as scaled-down versions of her performances. Her tone, like that used in concert, is an unlikely mingling of childlike awe and postmodern irony; her sentences are interrupted by the same arbitrary caesuras that mark time in her onstage monologues. The overall impression is that of an Audio-Animatronic minikin hosting a Disney recreation of the New York art world. Perhaps one of her characters said it best in "Language is a Virus," from *Home of the Brave*:

> And he said: Hey!
> Are you talking to me?
> Or are you just practicing
> For one of those performances of yours?

MARK DERY: You begin *Empty Places* with a first-person anecdote about falling into a New York sewer. What was it like down there? Big gators splashing around?

LAURIE ANDERSON: No gators, although after I'd fallen in somebody gave me a book called *Underneath New York* that says there have reportedly been some gator sightings, but I don't know, the whole thing sounds a little sketchy. The sewer was very stinky; that was the main thing. And the other thing was, after I fell in, a lot of people were passing by and I was trying to pull myself out—I was right in front of my agent's door—and I kept poking my head out and saying, "Could you, uh, ring that doorbell for me?" And they kept saying, "Wait a second—what route did *you* take?"

MARK DERY: That story, which ends up with you in a hospital emergency room, surrounded by homeless people, strikes me as the linchpin of the show; it rattles the audience in a way that none of the other monologues do. It seems like a turning point for you, the beginning of something new and gritty, something with real bite.

LAURIE ANDERSON: Well, there's lots of first-person narrative in *Empty Places*, and they're all based on something. I think when you put a date on it, the way I did with this particular piece, it somehow seems more real. You see, I'm not sure I understand people's reactions to this piece.

MARK DERY: Is it somehow perhaps more resonant, more jagged-edged than the rest of the show?

LAURIE ANDERSON: It's an unadorned story about pain and it doesn't have any imaginary items in it like hosts of angels mowing your lawn. I had hoped to have the whole performance feel more raw and by the time it's finished, it probably will feel more jagged. I think, by the time it's performed in New York [at the Brooklyn Academy of Music, 3–15 October 1989], a third of it will probably be different.

MARK DERY: In a sense, you predicted this piece in an interview with Charles Amirkhanian in *The Guests Go in to Supper* when you said, "The next thing that I do will be a solo work, just a couple of hand puppets, strip it down."

LAURIE ANDERSON: In fact, it's quite a relief for me not to be working with a band. I'm no good at rounding people up and talking to them on the phone about rehearsal times, and I'm not a good band leader, I don't give people enough to do. I say, "Well, here's this tape and it goes, 'Ugh-glug-glug,'" and they're going, "Ohhh, *great*, that sounds like fun.'" Sometimes, I've used them as soloists, which is my only solution to the whole problem, but I found that I still had to pay a lot of attention to the band, not just before the show, rehearsing, but during the performance as well. Band rapport is not one of my strong points [affects Miles Davis-style jazz cool growl], "Hey, like, you know, dude, I'll trade licks with the bass player." I'm more interested in making contact with the audience. That, as far as I'm concerned, is where the show is going on; it's not happening on the stage. I've never liked that kind of onstage banter and goofing around. I'm not that kind of musician or person.

MARK DERY: I expected *Empty Places* to be Laurie Anderson fiddling avant-folk tunes around the digital campfire. Instead, you're still swaddling the voice in digital harmonizer, silhouetting your live playing against taped backing tracks. You've said you like to frighten yourself; wouldn't it have been more frightening to go out there for an hour and just . . . play fiddle?

LAURIE ANDERSON: You know, I'm not sure how interesting that would be, given my fiddle playing. I did do a European tour this year, in Berlin and Paris, that was quite stripped-down. There was just a little bit of video in it, but hardly anything else; that was the closest I've come to doing something as pared down as I could. I enjoyed that a lot, and I learned something from doing it, but I also learned that I really like to use images.

MARK DERY: I'm curious about the process whereby you choose what image will be linked to a given lyric. I sense a tension in your work between your stated desire not to be didactic and the obvious need to have content of some sort, especially in a narrative context. Critics have lobbed bombs at you for counterpointing lyrics that are more or less strings of non sequiturs with seemingly unrelated, iconic images. For example, one song in *Empty Places*, about a dream, is accompanied by a visual subtext—slides of rumpled bedsheets, whose meaning is obvious enough, and a sequence featuring an umbrella. There's nothing more cloddish than asking an artist what the umbrella means, but what does the umbrella mean?

LAURIE ANDERSON: Well, I wanted to make something that was just a very pristine sort of thing and I had a whole sequence of umbrellas opening and closing for another song and they ended up being too illustrative for that song. I wanted to get a few white images that could suggest what I was talking about, which was dream imagery that just gets intercut with itself so that it becomes increasingly irrational. More than anything else, I was organizing the images in the same way that things get organized in your dreamworld. I wanted to suggest just a little bit of motion, you know, an umbrella opening and closing.

MARK DERY: Tell me the difference—and I'm entirely willing to believe there is one—between one of your pieces, where you're reciting a monologue or singing a song framed by seemingly unrelated slides or filmic images, and MTV, where one encounters the gratuitous surrealism of tubas flying through windows, this Joe Six-Pack version of René Magritte. What separates your performances from an assemblage of dreamlike images that really don't add up to anything?

LAURIE ANDERSON: The things that work the best in my work, visually, are things that connect rhythmically and also thematically to what's happening in the text. I mean, I work in many different ways. In the case of a song like "Coolsville" (*Strange Angels*), which is accompanied in *Empty Places* by these digitized people moving by, I had this film I'd shot in Japan and digitized. I really liked watching their faces and so I wrote a song based on that film. It came from just rolling the film for a few days, watching it.

MARK DERY: "Coolsville" seems to be a conflation of an adolescent girl looking at the ideal man, a cross between James Dean and the Marlboro Man, and Americans looking at the Japanese.

LAURIE ANDERSON: It's not really about the Japanese, although they understand what I'm doing very well. They get it. I think they appreciate that electronics work; they like to see buttons. But I have no interest in spending much time in Japan; I have much more interest in spooking around here, seeing what's going on. To me, being in Charleston is almost as foreign as being in Japan, certainly more so than being in Tokyo, which seems very similar to New York, as far as the art world goes.

MARK DERY: Much of your work is a meditation on America; if there were anything intrinsically American about your work, what would it be?

LAURIE ANDERSON: One of the digitally harmonized voices, this guy who's definitely a midwestern, cornpone-type guy, an incredibly naive, cheerful yokel willing to tackle any topic that comes his way. He's the ultimate shoe salesman.

MARK DERY: To return, for a moment, to this idea of discursive, nonlinear structure in your work. You admire Pynchon and Joyce, but in the writing of each, every image serves, arguably, to advance the plot, whereas in your work there's a sense of interchangeability—one slide can work as well as the next. What would Pynchon or Joyce have to say about *Empty Places*, I wonder?

LAURIE ANDERSON: I don't think one slide works as well as the next. I've tried it, believe me.

MARK DERY: So each slide that we're seeing is the best possible slide to illustrate that lyric?

LAURIE ANDERSON: Well, I wouldn't say that either. In some cases, that's true; in other cases, I'm quite aware that the visuals need some chopping. You see, I don't really know until I get the visuals up on the screen what they're going to feel like, because they don't look the same on paper, obviously; you throw it up on the wall and you say, "Whoops, that's not it at all," it feels flat or it suggests something completely different. So the sooner I start shooting and recording, the better; I tend to get off the paper pretty fast.

MARK DERY: Shifting gears again: Your work has always managed to be puckish and haunting, but now, for the first time, it has a razor-edged, angry quality. Does this come out of nowhere, or has it always been there, lurking in the shadows?

LAURIE ANDERSON: Where would you say that is?

MARK DERY: Certainly in *Empty Places*'s feminist numbers, songs such as "Beautiful Red Dress." Are you angrier than you were in the past?

LAURIE ANDERSON: Probably, yeah.

MARK DERY: What's making you angry these days?

LAURIE ANDERSON: Oh, that the feminist movement doesn't seem to have made much difference at all. There's been a tiny bit of progress, but what does that really mean to the woman on the street? Not a hell of a lot. That's why I talked about the discrepancy between what men and women earn in that song; it really comes down to money for a lot of women.

MARK DERY: How do you feel about the ascent of neo-folkie feminists such as Tracy Chapman, Michelle Shocked?

LAURIE ANDERSON: It's great. I love one person/one instrument things; I think that's really exciting, and both of those people do that very, very well. I never really loved folk singing, though, except for Bob Dylan, who was wordy. And raunchy. I guess I wish the girls in pop music would get a little bit raunchier.

MARK DERY: But you're not raunchy.

LAURIE ANDERSON: I'd like to try to get raunchier! This is advice for myself as well.

MARK DERY: It seems to bother people that sex rarely intrudes on the world portrayed by your work.

LAURIE ANDERSON: Oh, but it does! I think it figures incredibly prominently!

MARK DERY: By its absence, maybe.

LAURIE ANDERSON: I wouldn't say that at all. One of the longest songs in *Empty Places* is "Red Dress," and I don't know how someone could say that has nothing to do with sex. As far as I'm concerned, sexual stereotyping is built into this particular work.

MARK DERY: In that song, you create invisible backing vocalists by singing through digital harmonizers. But they're more than a chorus; they have personalities.

LAURIE ANDERSON: They are personalities, and their biggest role in this particular show is in "Red Dress," as "the girls." They sometimes sing in chorus with the shoe salesman-type voice, and sometimes with me, it depends. "Red Dress" is a diatribe, and in it, the girls have a plan. It's not fleshed out, but they know they're gonna save themselves, somehow.

MARK DERY: From—?

LAURIE ANDERSON: Things too numerous to mention. There's one verse in the song that runs, "Well they say women shouldn't be / the president / 'Cause we go crazy from time to time / Well push my button baby here I come / Yeah look out baby / I'm at high tide." The idea of using that crazy sexual energy to be creative and not to be exiled into the swamp intrigues me. I mean, when you talk about, for example, the human condition, who are you talking about? Your little six-year-old brother? A seventy-five-year-old woman? No, you're talking about a man. It sounds preachy to say this, but if more women made history or wrote history books, when you discussed the human condition, you'd discuss a certain kind of biological insanity and that, to me, would be extremely interesting—to respect that, to celebrate its crazy energy. Because it's *very* crazy and all women know and understand that and yet it's not considered a part of the human condition, but rather some sort of aberration.

Glenda Jackson in *Strange Interlude* is an image that really haunts me. It's one of the most wonderful little monologues ever, where she's going on about if God were a woman, talking about how you basically have this guy who supposedly created the world, created it and is very proud of it, letting you know how quickly he did it—Seven days, pretty good, huh? So you come into a situation of pride and leave it into one of judgment, because he's also going to judge you for what you've done in this life. She wonders how things would be different if the universe had been born in the absolute agony of the female experience, instead of pride, and if we left the world to return to a fetal state. That maleness is so deeply ingrained in our culture.

MARK DERY: We were talking earlier about anger, about the ragged edges in *Empty Places*. I was wondering, on that note, how the gang rape of the Central Park jogger affected you.

LAURIE ANDERSON: Oh, I think it affected everyone the same way—filled them with rage and real fear. Lots of teenagers are confused, but girls don't gang up and go out and try to kill someone; they just don't do it. It's not that I blame these kids, because I know you have to be macho to live in projects; I'm just saying that the whole culture is built on that "Don't be a wimp" ethos and to prove that, sometimes you have to kill someone. To me, that's pretty insane!

MARK DERY: It's interesting to note, in light of your abhorrence of the ingrained maleness in our culture, that phallocentricity, that you often adopt a male narratorial voice. It seems rare that you address your audience in a feminine guise that isn't a caricature of femininity—the teenage girl dreaming of Frank Sinatra in "Smoke Rings" [*Home of the Brave*], for example.

LAURIE ANDERSON: I don't exactly disagree that most of my work adopts that stance because when I use my own voice I speak as myself. It's true, I don't wear puffy sleeves or miniskirts. I talk like who I am, which is first, an artist, and second, a New Yorker, and third, a woman. I don't see myself as a woman first.

MARK DERY: Perhaps that's why it was so startling to see you in a backless dress and elbow gloves for "Langue D'Amour," in *Home of the Brave*.

LAURIE ANDERSON: I was telling a story from *the* woman's point of view; it was Eve's story and also the snake's story, so I was a kind of combination woman and snake, with these black gloves. It probably is harder to use a harmonizer to give you a male voice if you wear a dress during a concert; it still is more usual to see women in pants than men in skirts. Too bad, because skirts are really comfortable.

MARK DERY: Men, in your work, are usually George Orwell-meets-Tennessee Williams "Big Daddy" archetypes—scientists, government officials, and other authority figures. They're never lovers, intimates, equals in romantic, sexual settings.

LAURIE ANDERSON: I'm interested in authority figures. There's lots of really wonderful, tender love songs written so I don't often do that, myself; it's a genre that I think is pretty well covered.

MARK DERY: "Beautiful Red Dress," with its references to full moons and high fevers, crackles with what strikes me as lesbian energy. In *Empty Places*, it's accompanied by a visual subtext of tiled walls that suggest a bathroom. Do you have any interest in addressing the gay audience?

LAURIE ANDERSON: Only obliquely, I suppose. I think I've found a place for lots of people in *Empty Places*. There's a story about gay men having a bake sale to greet these sailors. I hadn't thought of "Beautiful Red Dress" as specifically gay but I suppose it is. I'd thought of it more as something odd going on with language.

MARK DERY: Feeling this rage, as an artist, you reach inside yourself for an anecdote to illustrate it. In the case of *Empty Places*, you pulled out a story about picketing the Playboy bunnies in 1972, a story that goes back to a 1981 interview with Rob LeFrenais, editor of *Performance* magazine. What prompted you to reach that far back into the past as opposed to generating something new, a story you hadn't told before?

LAURIE ANDERSON: Trying to make a lecture into a show very, very, very fast. I've been doing these lectures for a long time, all over the place. It's the kind of situation where I really want to cut down on the didacticism and make it punchier, although I do like a lot of talking in my shows. At the same time, I'm doing more singing now than ever before, although I'm not sure about the ratio because what was called talking in the past was often very soft, singsong things that I considered songs. To me, "Walking and Falling" [*Big Science*] is a song. The ratio of speech to singing in a song like "Coolsville" is about half and half. I'm very aware of the fact that I'm not really a singer and yet it's very hard to go back and forth between singing and talking unless the song is written specifically that way.

MARK DERY: You've been taking singing lessons, haven't you?

LAURIE ANDERSON: Yeah, with Joan Lader. She's a wonderful teacher, in all kinds of ways. Her approach is based on a lot of physical exercises and ways to visualize sound. She's worked with a huge range of people, all of whom are very dedicated students of hers, ranging from Yoko Ono to Roberta Flack to Sting to Ryuichi Sakamoto to an opera singer who's lost his voice to a secretary who worked for three lawyers and every day one of them gave her different instructions and one day she just . . . couldn't talk. Joan helped her to learn to talk again. She really respects the ways in which speech and singing are connected.

MARK DERY: Why the decision, on your part, to learn to sing?

LAURIE ANDERSON: I was shamed into it. I was doing a vocal on a song that required some back-up vocalists and they did their part and it was really wonderful and then I was supposed to do the lead vocal and I thought, Wait a second, I haven't even thought about how to sing this and besides, I don't know how to sing! I had this choice of croaking along like I usually do or half-talking, half-singing. So I thought, Well, I can do one of these things, neither of which will really work in the case of this song, or I can learn to sing. And then I said, Hey, learn to sing! I've wanted to get a new instrument—that would really be fun! So I just started working with Joan and it's really been so interesting. It's a very emotional experience to find where your spoken words become song.

MARK DERY: I can really hear that in the half-sobbed, unabashedly emotional quality of "My Eyes." It's light-years away from the metallic, android inflections of some of your earliest performances. Do you want to have more of an emotional impact on your audiences these days?

LAURIE ANDERSON: Yes, absolutely. On the other hand, I've always felt that. People sometimes think that this is some kind of tech show *about* something. To me, it's completely sensual; it's about things you see and hear rather than ideas you're going to write down. Some things need to be expressed that way, rather than just, Here's what it is. Art can be more flexible than that.

MARK DERY: On a tangent: you've studied Wittgenstein and "The Dream Before" [*Strange Angels*] is dedicated to the Marxist theorist Walter Benjamin. In the eighties, literary philosophers and cultural theorists such as Jean Baudrillard and Jacques Derrida had a profound impact on the art world. Can their imprint be read in your work?

LAURIE ANDERSON: No, absolutely not. I don't really get it when visual artists start talking about Derrida.

MARK DERY: It seems that ideas, in some way, don't interest you as much as the forms they take.

LAURIE ANDERSON: I'm not a writer, and I think that writers, for the most part, are more interested in that sort of thing. Then again, I don't know if I'd call myself a visual artist, either. I like images, but I haven't done any of the things that visual artists do, like have exhibitions. My visual sense only crops up in a very secondary way, although I had a lot of fun drawing bluebirds for the animated sequence in *Empty Places*. I was going to hire somebody to draw some bluebirds and then I thought, Why not do it myself? I bet that would be fun! I also like it when things look kind of crude. I wanted to set up a contrast in the piece between the hysterical cheerfulness of the bluebirds near a picket fence, this happy, wacky nature setting, and then just cut to a void—the bluebirds of lugubriousness.

MARK DERY: Almost like the hyperreal birds in *Blue Velvet*.

LAURIE ANDERSON: Oh yeah, it's definitely an homage to David Lynch. Anytime you see a white picket fence, you go, "David Lynch!" I like him because his work is about the underbelly, what's under the lawn.

MARK DERY: Lynch, like David Byrne and yourself, is someone who has moved from the underground to the mainstream. In *Empty Places*, there are two routines where you lampoon the avant-garde. In one, you position stupid pet tricks as cutting-edge performance art, and in another you suggest that anyone who can tease out the meanings in "Yankee Doodle's" absurdist lyrics is ready to decipher avant-garde art. Do I detect a thinly veiled snideness there?

LAURIE ANDERSON: Absolutely! The avant-garde gave up on me awhile ago. At first it hurt, and then I thought, Wait a minute—they're being totally consistent. One of the things about the avant-garde is that it has to be very self-protective, otherwise it won't survive. It has to be a situation of, Hey, hey, hey, we in here in the avant-garde know what those poor suckers out there don't know. So as soon as I did something for the poor suckers outside who didn't know but nonetheless got it, I could no longer be considered part of that group. But then you do something here, in Charleston, South Carolina, something you think is a fairly accessible performance, and it's considered *very* avant-garde, so it depends on the context. I try to be both traditional and avant-garde. You can't always be working outside of traditions, because then what are your materials? I mean, there are certain things that I've gotten good at doing, and at the same time there are certain things that I want to break down, among them expectations. In a way, that's the whole point. Even something as simple as handing out sketchpads to audience members before the show, as I did this afternoon, can rattle peoples' expectations. In that sense, I think that I am an avant-garde artist. But I'm not sure what that means. Members of the avant-garde still come to things that I do and I still go to things that they do. I'm not that interested in what people say about the disappearance of the avant-garde. Somebody's always going to be sneaking around, breaking new rules. I find that very exciting. There are plenty of rules and taboos yet to be broken, and somebody's gotta do it. I'll do my part.

Michael Jarrett

Concerning the Progress of Rock & Roll

Histories of popular music routinely employ a model derived from nineteenth-century physical science in order to describe the process of popularization. What semioticians call conventionalization is most often characterized as a cultural equivalent of the second law of thermodynamics. Energy tends toward a state of equilibrium; "innovative, unconventional codes gradually become adopted by the majority."[1] John Fiske, in *Introduction to Communication Studies*, uses this entropy model to explain the "broad cultural acceptance" of jazz (presumably during the Swing Era). Dick Hebdige, in *Subculture: The Meaning of Style*, a now classic study of "punk" culture, relies on it too. What Simon Frith and Andrew Goodwin call a theory of "progress by attrition" is, perhaps, *the* foundational myth of popular music.[2] It lies at the heart of all distinctions that attempt to delineate a boundary between the authentic and the commercial, in whatever guise that may take: rock vs. pop, black vs. white, modern vs. postmodern, art vs. commerce.

Conventionalization, though, like its counterpart in physics, is in itself neither negative nor positive, neither good nor bad. It just *is*— or so the discourse of communication theory would have us believe. A good description, this theory seems to at least tacitly argue, merely indicates—it does not seek to establish a norm. If we perceive conventionalization or popularization as a "lowering of quality because it involves appealing to the 'lowest common denominator,' " writes Fiske following Basil Bernstein,

> we should be aware that it [such a judgment] is made from within a particular value-system, one that values elaborated, narrowcast codes and the expression of individual differences. A value-system that rates highly the reinforcement of cultural ties and restricted, broadcast codes will find the metaphor of the lowest common denominator offensive, elitist and inaccurate.[3]

All the same, descriptions of conventionalization typically, perhaps always, employ a rhetoric of degeneration. They chart it as a downward course, a semiotic diaspora, and rely on readers decoding such a journey Platonically, as a deviation from the Good. Hence, popularization receives a plot—tragedy—and thereby the very notion of the authentic (pure code) is erected as something opposed to the conventional (popularized code).

Any reader familiar with the literature of deconstruction will recognize this "logocentric" opposition (founded on a notion of "presence"). It is yet another version of the opposition that pits *original* against *copy*. But demonstrating the untenability of the authentic/conventional (pure/popular) opposition is not my desire. I do not care to recapitulate what has become the most standard sort of deconstructive reading.[4] Instead, I want to reread (then misread) the rhetoric of degeneration that informs the history of popular music. My first example is a brief tragicomic history of jazz, but it could be read allegorically as the "progress" of rock & roll. Hebdige writes:

> As the music fed into mainstream popular culture during the 20s and 30s, it tended to become bowdlerized, drained of surplus eroticism, and any hint of anger or recrimination blown along the "hot" lines was delicately refined into inoffensive night club sound. White swing represents the climax of this process:

innocuous, generally unobtrusive, possessing a broad appeal, it was a laundered product which contained none of the subversive connotations of its original black sources. These suppressed meanings were, however, triumphantly reaffirmed in be-bop, and by the mid-50s a new, younger white audience began to see itself reflected darkly in the dangerous, uneven surfaces of contemporary *avant-garde*, despite the fact that the musicians responsible for the New York sound deliberately sought to restrict white identification by producing a jazz which was difficult to listen to and even more difficult to imitate.[5]

Hot jazz turns to swing, bop turns cool, eroticism becomes lassitude, black bleaches to white, the dirty gets laundered, and the uneven is worn smooth: the structure of this apocalyptic sequence reproduces itself any number of times in accounts of American popular music since World War II. To pick several examples, it is the story of how Arthur Crudup's "That's All Right" (a hit for Elvis Presley, 1956) became "Sugar Shack" (Jimmy Gilmer, 1963) and, then, "I Want to Hold Your Hand" (the Beatles, 1964), or how 1960s rock became 1970s disco before its fundamental values were reaffirmed in late-1970s punk (only to transform into the techno-dance music of the 1980s). It is also the structure of Elvis Presley's career: from 1956–1958 (hot as Memphis asphalt) to 1959–1967 (bland as grits) to 1968 (meaner than a hornet).[6]

This model of conventionalization—an aesthetic version of entropy as heat-death—adequately accounts for the degradation of a code imagined as original. It feels ontologically stable because it explains popularization: the process whereby "authentic" music (a narrowcast code) is translated into "commercial" music (a broadcast code) for the purpose of selling music to a wide audience. And it sounds (politically) correct because it explains what Andrew Ross calls "the everyday, plagiaristic, commerce between white ['commercial'] and black ['authentic'] musics"; it conceptualizes the history of American popular music as a series of unilateral, commercially driven energy exchanges that everywhere bespeak "a racist history of exploitation exclusively weighted to dominant white interests."[7] Like all received models, this one has its attractions.

It also has real failings. As Ross points out, the formula "commercialized music = whitened music" simply will not hold. Since "commercial and contractual relations enter into *all* realms of musical entertainment, or at least wherever music is performed in order to make a living," there can be "no tidy coincidence" between "discourse about color ('whitened' music)" and "discourse about commercialization ('alienated' music)." To subscribe to such an equation

> is to imagine a very mechanical process indeed, whereby a music, which is authentically black, constitutes an initial raw material which is then appropriated and reduced in cultural force and meaning by contact with a white industry. Accordingly, music is never "made," and only ever exploited, in this process of industrialization.[8]

The biggest failure of the heat-death model of conventionalization is this: it cannot account for innovation. By picturing the history of popular music as a downward spiral of "progress" by attrition, it fails to explain how so-called authentic music arises. More specifically, it continues to rely on the thinly disguised metaphysical assumption that genius visits select musicians, or (the more contemporary view) that the rock & roll muse does not strike so much as she resides within a "tradition." Serious musicians, through searching (one's "soul" or one's "roots"), locate her; listeners, on the other hand, find "authenticity" when they tune in to the exotic (Delta blues or world music), the esoteric ("alternative" music), or the canonical ("classic" rock).

We need a better theory. I nominate one that extends the possibilities suggested by the old theory of conventionalization. It would exploit the potential energy of decay (decomposition), and in providing an account of innovation in rock & roll, it would suggest a paradigm of invention that could be generalized for every type of writing (for all fields of knowledge). In other words, I want to sketch out a theory that, without denying "degeneration," would insist that something is gained through conventionalization. Before initiating that project, however, I want to emphasize the overlap of "authentic" and "commercial" music. Only by unsettling this opposition can we begin to rethink a cultural model of conventionalization predicated on heat-death.

Our experience of twentieth-century popular culture is defined by what Frith calls "the contrast between music-as-expression and music-as-commodity." He writes: "[H]owever much we may use and enjoy its products, we retain a sense that the music industry is a bad thing—bad for music, bad for us."[9] For me (a white, male, and, now, middle-aged music consumer), "music-as-expression" has always meant African-American music. It was "authentic," a genuine outpouring of real feeling (quality is a function of closeness to the blues). I have long regarded commercialization as corruption: an "essential human activity" colonized.[10] I dote over artists such as Aretha Franklin, James Brown, Otis Redding, Chuck Berry, Muddy Waters, Al Green, Sly and the Family Stone, and Parliament because, simply put, there "ain't nothing like the real thing, baby"; I love Bob Dylan, the Rolling Stones, the Velvet Underground, Talking Heads, Elvis Costello, and Roxy Music because they are—I tell myself— "ironic." But there are two problems with this belief:

(1) It is romantic and, ultimately, racist. Like Rousseau's *Confessions* (and, later, Lévi-Strauss's *Tristes Tropiques*), it imagines non-European peoples "as the index to a hidden good Nature, as a native soil recovered, of a 'zero degree' with reference to which one could outline the structure, the growth, and above all the degradation of our society and our culture." It is, Jacques Derrida notes, enabled by remorse—the "remorse that produces anthropology."[11]

(2) It supposes, as Frith points out, "that music is the starting point of the industrial process—the raw material over which everyone fights—when it is, in fact, the final product."[12] Certainly white people exploited, and continue to exploit, black people. That point needs to be admitted. But it is also important to realize that "authentic" African-American music was an effect of industrialization.

In its early years, radio fostered and relied upon live music, bands with members who could play endless variations of recognizable tunes (the Ellington and Basie orchestras), as well as bands with a staff of arrangers (the orchestras of Benny Goodman and Tommy Dorsey). Later, after the discovery of magnetic tape (one of the spoils of World War II), radio fostered and relied upon the recording industry. To oversimplify, the history of rock is a consequence of the development of recording technology (and, to some extent, television and video), just as the history of jazz is a consequence of radio (and, to some extent, a nightclub scene made possible by the invention of the electric light). Stated differently, radio was the prosthesis of jazz, just as magnetic tape was the prosthesis of rock & roll.[13]

We must also remember that the music industry organizes itself around certain naturalized oppositions. It has a discourse. It speaks. Industrialization, through institutions such as radio, music publishing and licensing, and recording, sanctioned the antithesis that holds that "authentic" music is something distinct from "commercial" music. We consumers, in turn, inherit—organize our thinking by means of—this and other antitheses. When I state, with all sincerity, that "white people exploited, and continue to exploit, black people," I am articulating a central tenet of the music industry. It literally banks on—makes money off—my belief. The assumption that bad (commercial) things happen to "authentic" music is sufficient to generate the real/fake distinction that has become musical common sense.[14] It creates a consumer who understands the history of rock as a series of authentic moments that deteriorated into conventionalized moments, transforming the music into a field of "commercial" imitations of some real thing, and it prompts histories organized around the proper names of acknowledged innovators.

There is, however, an alternative way of looking at the history of popular music and conceptualizing conventionalization that involves an investigation of decomposition as an image capable not only of organizing information, but of generating a formula for the discovery or invention process. Nathaniel Mackey opened up the possibilities of this image when, in his epistolary novel, *Bedouin Hornbook*, he wrote: "There must be some way, I'm convinced, to invest in the ever so slight suggestion of 'compost' I continue to get from the word compose."[15] Brian Eno, a recording artist best known for his production work with David Bowie, U2, and Talking Heads, took it further when he responded to an interviewer's statement: "I would think you'd have mixed feelings about new artists doing something that really isn't new art." He said:

> If you think of culture as a great big garden, it has to have its compost as well. And lots of people are doing things that

are . . . not dramatic or radical or not even particularly interesting; they're just digestive processes. It's places where a number of little things are being combined and tried out. It's like members of a population. We're all little different turns of the same genetic dice. If you think about music in that way, it makes it much easier to accept that there might be lots of things you might not want to hear again. They happen and they pass and they become the compost for something else to grow from [laughs]. Gardening is such a good lesson for all sorts of things.[16]

Even though he has claimed, "I now disagree with nearly everything he said," Eno must have been thinking about composer John Cage when he read gardening as an analogy for musical production.[17] During this interview, Cage—an expert on fungi (and founder of the New York Mycological Society)—was seated in the room with Eno.

In *Silence*, Cage wrote: "I have come to the conclusion that much can be learned about music by devoting oneself to the mushroom."[18] But, one might ask, why mushrooms? Cage remarks, with a wink, that it is because the secondhand bookshops in which he purchases "'field companions' on fungi" are "in some rare cases next door to shops selling dog-eared sheets of music." His "logic" alerts us to the obvious conclusion that anything mushrooms have to teach us about music is the result of a fortuitous allegory (an accident of signification). Whether mushrooms speak the truth about rock & roll, tell the *real story* of the way pop music progresses, is completely beside the point. What, then, is the lesson of mushrooms? Simply this: all the Baptist ministers I heard pontificating against pop music while I was growing up were right. Rock & roll is a mushroom, a fungus in the garden of culture. ("My records are parasites on the music business," says Eno.)[19] But given my conception of fungi—greatly influenced by deconstruction, the "parasitical economy" of grammatology, and the "logic of disintegration" advanced by Theodor Adorno and Walter Benjamin—the ministers' accusations were not nearly as damaging as they were intended to be.[20] In practice, I responded to ministerial admonitions much as David Arora, author of *Mushrooms Demystified*, responded to his parents' admonitions to "stay away from mushrooms." They "inspired me to get closer."[21] As Gregory Ulmer notes, the lesson taught by mushrooms or, more properly, fungi, since a mushroom is the reproductive structure (fruiting body) of a fungus, is *symbiosis*. The kind of fungi hunted and eaten by Cage ("the fleshy, fruity, 'higher' fungi, Boletus, Morels, and the like") are "not parasites, but *saprophytes* (any organism that lives on dead organic matter)." They exist in a "mutually beneficial relationship with their hosts (the green plants and trees which supply the organic 'food')."[22] Writes Arora: "They are nature's recyclers." In feeding on dead matter, they "reduce complex organic compounds to simpler building blocks, thereby enabling plants to reuse them."[23] The saprophyte—which is to say, rock & roll—feeds off the decay of tradition. It treats culture as a compost pile.

To understand what this means we need only note that "something becomes an object of knowledge . . . only as it . . . is made to disintegrate."[24] Popularization does to ideas what decay does to organic materials. It turns them into compost so that they can be transformed into something new. What makes Eno especially interesting is that he has turned this process into a compositional methodology. In the liner notes to *Ambient 4/On Land*, he describes his interest in treating "found sound"—"pieces of chain and sticks and stones," "recordings of rooks, frogs and insects," and also the "complete body" of his "earlier work"—as a "completely plastic and malleable material":

> As a result, some earlier pieces I worked on became digested by later ones, which in turn became digested again. This technique is like composting: converting what would otherwise have been waste into nourishment.[25]

Although it is difficult to hear any relationship between his static soundscapes and, say, the music of Madonna or Bruce Springsteen, much less bands such as Sonic Youth, the Mekons, or Hüsker Dü, Eno's method makes explicit the normal functioning of rock & roll.

Conventionalization is the compost from which innovation grows: which is to say, it not only enables popularization, it fosters artistic renewal by generating conditions that allow for aberrant readings. To show how this happens, I want to rewrite, in a highly schematic form, Hebdige's history of jazz which I cited early in this essay. Like him, I begin with "white swing."

Conventionalization. Restricted (broadcast) codes seek to become elaborated (narrowcast) codes. White swing was less a monolithic style of music, than a variety of "popular" musics vying for a "cut" of the market, each seeking to promote itself as a privileged mode of expression.[26]

Aberration. Attempts to sell music to a mass audience—to make it fit a variety of conventions or cultural experiences—promote homogeneity (replication of conventions) as well as heterogeneity (aberrant readings of conventions).[27] On the levels of production and distribution, conventionalization prompts both experimentation and standardization; on the level of consumption, it allows aberrant decodings ("the rule, not the exception, with mass media messages," writes Fiske recalling Umberto Eco).[28] Musical innovators are aberrant readers; Charlie Parker ("Bird") "misinterpreted" the basic materials of swing.

Disputation. Boppers (followers of Bird) vs. Moldy Figs (followers of Bunk Johnson—traditional jazz). Conflicts between groups (competing systems of discourse) arise over which musics are and are not innovative, legitimate, authentic, original, etc. They most often take the form of contests or disputes which, as Jean-François Lyotard puts it, cannot "be resolved for lack of a rule of judgment applicable to both arguments."[29]

Ratification. Bebop, modern jazz, wins the day. A perceived innovation gains legitimacy by soliciting, gaining, or, in some cases, inventing institutional support. It is retroactively read back as "genuinely" innovative (canonized as a "pure code") by the institution that brings it into language. That, however, does not mean that other (suppressed) musical forms cease to exist; they have merely lost their position of power.

This process repeats itself (with a difference) when the validated "pure code," motivated by an institution's attempt to maintain pre-eminence or hegemony, gets conventionalized (turned into a broadcast code) and, subsequently, read aberrantly. In jazz, this happened when bebop was conventionalized as hard-bop (a style almost as diverse as "white swing"), then read aberrantly by Ornette Coleman.

The origins of rock also followed this pattern. In one version of its story, black rhythm & blues (a heteroglot style that had secularized black gospel) was aberrantly read by Little Richard and Elvis

Presley, and, following a dispute with what, for lack of a better term, might be called "classic pop" (recall Frank Sinatra and Mitch Miller's denunciations of the new style), it was institutionalized as rock & roll. But because it is, like film, a "technologically dependent, capital-intensive, commercial, collaborative medium regulated by the government and financially linked to mass audiences," rock subsequently progressed in a more complicated fashion than jazz (which was performance-dependent).[30] In elevating recording above performance, rock created a condition of perpetual conventionalization and, thus, a condition where aberrant readings are always, at least theoretically, the rule for both players and listeners (since practicing amateurs are still numerous in rock, these roles remain scarcely differentiated). That is why, to choose but one example, Prince was rock's exemplary artist of the 1980s. By treating rock history as a compost pile—one suspects that he heard George Clinton before he heard Jimi Hendrix or Little Richard—Prince signified that rock history, as a linear succession of styles supplanting one another, had ceased to exist (which is far from saying that rock is dead). He alerted everyone listening to the fact that rock's past was now always available in synchronic form. "Eventually," John Cage had written in 1954, "everything will be happening at once."[31]

Scene: Tower Records, South Street, Philadelphia. Mr X walks up to the sales counter and presents a clerk with a major credit card and a compact disc—Elvis's *The Sun Sessions.*
CLERK: Elvis Presley, huh?
MR X: Yeah.
CLERK: I don't know, man. If I wanted to hear good Dean Martin, I think I'd just buy the real thing.

In every case, the rock musician perceived as innovative is one who has creatively misread the popularized or conventionalized version of the compost pile produced by a previously recognized innovation. Steering a course between repetition (redundancy) and incomprehensibility (entropy), he or she has parlayed an aberrant or perverse reading of the past into an authorized reading for the present. Elvis Presley's "misreading" of Dean Martin (a conventionalized version of the saloon singer) makes a good example of this. Marion Keisker, the office manager of Sam Phillips's Sun Records studio in Memphis, remembers that Elvis, during his first audition, relied so heavily on Dean Martin material that she thought "Elvis had decided '. . . if he was going to sound like anybody, it was going to be Dean Martin.'" Guitarist Chris Spedding, picking up on this clue (left unexplored in Jerry Hopkins's biography, *Elvis*), argues that many of Elvis's "actions previously dismissed (or considered perverse when they could not be ignored)" are explained by his admiration for the actor-singer who was, during the mid-1950s, "*the* most bankable of matinee idols." Comparing Martin's big hit of 1955, "Memories Are Made of This," with "the song Elvis always said was *his* favorite cut, 'Don't Be Cruel,' a hit in the summer of the following year," Spedding notes:

> Now, apart from the fact that Elvis borrowed that descending-bass-run-followed-by-guitar-chord ending from Martin's arrangement, other common elements are that sexy, wobbly, almost hiccuping baritone vocal—not yet identifiably "rock" until Elvis made it so—and Martin's novel use of a four-piece gospel-type vocal group which we may now assume inspired Elvis to introduce the Jordanaires on *his* cut, effectively integrating them into a unique blend with his own lead vocal, thus establishing another rock archetype.[32]

The joke is, Elvis's music was a poor imitation of Dean Martin's, and that, strangely enough, has something—maybe everything—to do with why his music is so much better than Martin's ("fifty million Elvis fans can't be wrong"). Elvis's method (whether conscious or not makes absolutely no difference), not just the noise he made, is the essence of rock & roll. Simply notice that one can organize the entire history of rock & roll as a series of four revolutionary moments when something new grew out of critical misreadings of available materials: musical compost. Elvis and Little Richard (mid-1950s) perversely read rhythm & blues and country & western music; Bob Dylan and the Beatles (mid-1960s) perversely read early rock & roll and American folk music; the Sex Pistols and the Clash (mid-1970s) perversely read art-pop and reggae; Public Enemy and De La Soul (late-1980s) perversely read pop's basic material object—the record.

≡≡≡≡

A French professor of mine once informed me that Barthes's *S/Z* was grossly overrated. He said, "If you want to read *good* criticism on Balzac, don't read Roland Barthes." He was, of course, correct, but he had missed the whole point of contemporary experimental criticism. He not only failed to see that what counts as "good" criticism is now up for grabs, but that innovation (or what rhetoricians call invention) means learning how to read aberrantly, how to generate imminently co-optable misreadings. In *S/Z*, Barthes treated Balzac's novella "Sarrasine" as a compost pile, something from which he could fashion another text of his own. Like a rock musician, he treated his basic materials—and surely you thought of this well before I wrote it—like *shit*. Manure is etymologically linked to maneuver: *manouvrer*, Old French for working with the hands, cultivating.

What some people find objectionable about both contemporary theory and contemporary music is a supposed lack of respect for the very institutions that make intellectual and musical labor possible (entrepreneurial capitalism, the university, the technology of the book or record). Undoubtedly, many are mystified by the "provocative manner, attention to surfaces, aestheticized disposition, and oppositional hedonism" that characterize much theory and music.[33] What, they must wonder, accounts for such rampant questioning of authority, such suspiciousness of things settled long ago? One possibility is that we are seeing what Robert Ray labels "a later manifestation of dandyism." Barthes writes: "[I]n a given historical situation— of pessimism and rejection—it is the intellectual class as a whole which, if it does not become militant, is virtually a dandy."[34]

The dandy, Baudelaire observed, "appears above all in periods of transition," which makes me suspect that the nearly simultaneous rise of rock & roll and poststructuralism (an umbrella term designating semiotic, psychoanalytic, feminist, and ideological methodologies) is symptomatic of a paradigm shift, a fundamental change in the way we approach the materials of the past (the object of study).[35] I shall not elaborate upon this claim except to underscore what others have already said. Criticism and popular culture are now being "transformed in the same way that literature and the arts were transformed by the avant-garde movements in the early decades of this century. The break with 'mimesis,' with the values and assumptions of 'realism,' which revolutionized the modernist arts, is now underway."[36] This is what differentiates rock & roll and poststructuralism from classical music and formalism (close readings of texts): they entail a shift from *reading* (an interpretive method or "hermeneutics" founded, paradoxically, on replicating the ineffable) to *writing* (an inventive method or "euretics," playing upon surfaces). Or stated differently and, perhaps, hyperbolically, teaching people to analyze means teaching them to *reread*; teaching people to invent means teaching them to *misread*. Misreading is the essence of creativity, a skill which our educational institutions have, for the most part, neglected to teach. Most students know how to reread poorly, how to misread not at all.

And that is why poststructuralism and rock & roll are important. Both have taken responsibility for exploring means of invention. Both have discovered a few powerful, transferrable ways to misread. I should warn you that what follows is—in the manner of much rock and theory—a bit self-indulgent. In addition to listing and briefly describing four means of misreading, I have taken the opportunity to recommend four exemplary experimental essays and four great records.

(1) Doin' It to Death: the lesson of *repetition*. Cage wrote: "We know two ways to unfocus attention: symmetry is one of them; the other is the over-all where each small part is a sample of what you find elsewhere." Mechanical reproduction, notes Walter Benjamin in his landmark essay, repudiates the values invested in words such as "art" and "authenticity."[37]

> READ: Jacques Derrida, "Dissemination," *Dissemination*.
> LISTEN: *Parliament's Greatest Hits* (Casablanca, 1984).

(2) If I Were a Black Man: the lesson of *simulation*. The "rapp" was "a counterfeit coin, worth about half a farthing, which passed current for a halfpenny in Ireland in the 18th century, owing to the scarcity of genuine money" (*OED*). When Malcolm McLaren, the

situationist who packaged the Sex Pistols, was sued for "appropriating" others' music to make his own album, *Duck Rock*, he said: "All I can say is that accusations of plagiarism don't bother me. As far as I'm concerned it's all I'm useful for."

READ: Robert Smithson, "A Tour of the Monuments of Passaic, New Jersey," in *The Writings of Robert Smithson*.
LISTEN: Gang of Four, *A Brief History of the Twentieth Century* (Warner Bros., 1980).

(3) Cut & Mix: the lesson of *bricolage*. "The process of bricolage involves carefully and precisely ordering, classifying and arranging into structures the *minutiae*, the detritus, of the physical world. It is a 'science of the concrete' (as opposed to our 'civilised' science of the 'abstract')."[38]

READ: Gregory Ulmer, "Derrida at the Little Bighorn," in *Teletheory: Grammatology in the Age of Video*.
LISTEN: Beastie Boys, *Paul's Boutique* (Capitol, 1989).

(4) Bring the Noise: the lesson of the *parasite*. In French, "parasite" means (a) to inhabit another (as a demon possesses a body), (b) to make noise or static, and (c) to take without giving. Writes Simon Reynolds: "[T]he power of pop lies not in its meaning but its noise, not in its import but its force."[39]

READ: Gilles Deleuze and Félix Guattari, "1730: Becoming-Intense, Becoming-Animal, Becoming-Imperceptible . . . ," in *A Thousand Plateaus: Capitalism and Schizophrenia*.
LISTEN: Sonic Youth, *Goo* (Geffen, 1990).

Notes

1   "Entropy" received its formulation in 1885, when Rudolph Clausius coined the word and stated the first two laws of thermodynamics. See also John Fiske, *Introduction to Communication Studies* (New York, 1982), 87.
2   *On Record: Rock, Pop, and the Written Word*, ed. Simon Frith and Andrew Goodwin (New York, 1990), ix.
3   Fiske, *Communication Studies*, 87.
4   Suffice it to say, anyone searching for an essay demonstrating the impossibility

of the original/copy (speech/writing) opposition will find it in Jacques Derrida, "Plato's Pharmacy," *Dissemination*, trans. Barbara Johnson (Chicago, 1981).

5 Dick Hebdige, *Subculture: The Meaning of Style* (London, 1979), 46–47.

6 Simon Frith summarizes the rock era thus: "[B]orn around 1956 with Elvis Presley, peaking around 1967 with *Sgt. Pepper*, dying around 1976 with the Sex Pistols" (Simon Frith, "Introduction: Everything Counts," in *Music for Pleasure: Essays in the Sociology of Pop* [New York, 1988], 11).

7 Andrew Ross, *No Respect: Intellectuals & Popular Culture* (New York, 1989), 68.

8 Ibid., 69–70.

9 Simon Frith, "The Industrialization of Music," in *Music for Pleasure*, 11.

10 Ibid., 12.

11 Jacques Derrida, *Of Grammatology*, trans. Gayatri Chakravorty Spivak (Baltimore, 1976), 114–15.

12 Frith, "Industrialization of Music," 12.

13 My formula reworks one coined by Gregory Ulmer: "Video is the prosthesis of inventive or euretic thinking, just as literacy is the prosthesis of hermeneutics" (Gregory L. Ulmer, *Teletheory: Grammatology in the Age of Video* [New York, 1989], 42).

14 Frith, "Playing with Real Feeling," in *Music for Pleasure*, 57.

15 Nathaniel Mackey, *Bedouin Hornbook* (Lexington, 1986), 78–79.

16 Rob Tannenbaum, "A Meeting of Sound Minds, John Cage + Brian Eno," *Musician*, September 1985, 72.

17 Ibid., 66.

18 John Cage, *Silence* (Middletown, Conn., 1961), 274.

19 Ted Greenwald, "The Wayward Art Rocker Rediscovers Songs," *Creem*, February–March 1991, 39.

20 "Parasitical economy" is Derrida's phrase to describe writing *with* a text, what he has called the "affirmative" component of deconstruction. Cited in Gregory L. Ulmer, "The Object of Post-Criticism," in *The Anti-Aesthetic: Essays on Postmodern Culture*, ed. Hal Foster (Port Townsend, Wash., 1983), 100, 106.

21 I am citing David Arora's dedication to his *Mushrooms Demystified: A Comprehensive Guide to the Fleshy Fungi* (Berkeley, 1986).

22 Ulmer, "Object of Post-Criticism," 105.

23 Arora, *Mushrooms Demystified*, 6.

24 Ulmer, "Object of Post-Criticism," 97.

25 Liner notes to Brian Eno, *Ambient 4/On Land*, Editions EG, EEGCD 20, 1982.

26 Jim Collins, *Uncommon Cultures: Popular Culture and Post-Modernism* (New York, 1989), 2, 70.

27 Fiske, *Communication Studies*, 87.

28 Ibid., 81.

29 Jean-François Lyotard, *The Differend: Phrases in Dispute*, trans. Georges Van Den Abbeele (Minneapolis, 1988), xi.

30 Robert B. Ray, *A Certain Tendency of the Hollywood Cinema, 1930–1980* (Princeton, 1985), 6.

31   Cage, *Silence*, 187.

32   Chris Spedding, "Elvis & Dino," *Musician*, February 1990, 129–30.

33   Robert B. Ray, "The A B C of Visual Theory," *Visible Language* 22 (1988): 428.

34   Roland Barthes, *Roland Barthes*, trans. Richard Howard (New York, 1977), 106.

35   Cited in Ray, "A B C of Theory," 428.

36   Ulmer, "Object of Post-Criticism," 83.

37   Cage, *Silence*, 100; and Walter Benjamin, "The Work of Art in the Age of Mechanical Reproduction," in *Film Theory and Criticism*, ed. Gerald Mast and Marshall Cohen, trans. Harry Zohn (New York, 1985), 680–81.

38   Terence Hawkes, *Structuralism and Semiotics* (Berkeley, 1977), 51.

39   Michel Serres, *The Parasite*, trans. Lawrence R. Schehr (Baltimore, 1982), 7; and Simon Reynolds, *Blissed Out: The Raptures of Rock* (London, 1990), 10.

Paul Evans

Los Angeles, 1999

The bad rappers shot out of Compton as
every light in L.A. blew a fuse. Darkness
thundered over sweet California. Most everywhere the power was cut, but the B-boys had
batteries (good stuff, alkaline), and boom-
box rhyme kept on coming, classic—N.W.A,
Roxanne Shante, Run-D.M.C., Public Enemy.

MC Rudy at the tigerskin steering wheel,
switching stations out of sheer nervousness,
turned the fat radio knobs to pump up the
noise, three Kools smoking simultaneous in
his fresh mouth and yet him still chug-
ging malt liquor and huffing sly through a
def bullhorn: "Partytime, mothers, dance to
the death!"

The radio was blasting: he'd tuned in to
WLUV—some wild guitar shit, wordless, perfect.

Scorching the slick freeway, the crew got
spooked by the drive-by shooting under the
popped-out arc light—chromed Uzi barrel
from a hot Mercedes, wildstyle L.A. midnight fire.

DJ Johnny packed the crack, big junkie

tears shining his caved cheeks, and the ice pipe, too, flared cold brilliant in his shaking hand. Taiwan pipe, top quality. Johnny's man
Rudy had a fine Japanese beeper: supposed to radio him news from
fly Latifa. But the good girl was gone, she was nowhere tonight: nothing but loss and fried airwaves.

Johnny's ghetto bandanna jehovah witness mother was peeping,
watching from the smashed-window high rise, she was singing blue
gospel, and the boys of her life were high, large, and loose—riding
blind-night reckless to some lush ocean.

Heaven is a lot like here, only harder. Higher, deeper, sweeter, more.

High on the smog-baked hills, Sweet Jane was coming down. He stuck
his wet pink tongue through the O of the Hollywood sign, candy
red lips howling at the moon. He was a dancer, the baddest of the
bad—he had the night sweats, the bright purple ghost lesions, the
speed and holiness of terminal AIDS. KS, PCP, AIDS, the fucking
alphabet. Killer queen, sweet transvestite, pretty flamingo, Jane had
loved everybody in Beverly Hills—(everybody had whispered: Here
she comes, she's a femme fatale)—and now he was running on fire
through the night.

A strayed beauty from the long-ago, ended American farmland (insecticide? drought? napalm?—whatever), he'd been in town only a
month. But, oh baby, oh, what a glorious month. Triumph at the
tea dances, he'd been resurrected in the grand reopening death-wish
glory holes (after a while, with the plague so rampant as to lose
even the gallows-thrill of danger, the sex shoppes had flourished—
coupons, vacation giveaways, heavy-rotation promotion). Toast of
the town, he'd been burning.

Now, at the corner, his tinsel flapping the shadows of torched boutiques, he was panicked. Like silent movie star Theda Bara, popping
her eyes out big, her hot mouth open at the oncoming train. Somewhere near, a radio was playing, sending out signals: dangerous guitars. He clicked his red heels together, like some ditz Dorothy trying
to beam herself back home. But he wasn't in Kansas anymore. He
was another lost angel. He was a fallen-fast lady in the city of night.

Heaven is when you've had it up to here. Heaven is you ain't seen
nothing yet.

A beautiful girl from Illinois was crying in Los Angeles. Her dear curls fell down the left side of her face, her big brown eyes took your breath away. Brown-eyed girl in the city of dreams (Buddy Holly girl: every song sung on the radio sings about her). She was crying since she'd lost her baby sister at the mall—she'd searched Burger King, the Gap, Victoria's Secret—and now she had nowhere to run. Something weird had happened: for just a second someone had commandeered the Muzak speakers—for an instant, screaming guitars had poured down on the heads of the baffled shoppers. She fell out of the mall and—nowhere to hide—she kept on going.

Heaven holds her darling hand in his. Heaven just will not let go.

Down in the valley, stupid Gary trashed his guitar. With the power cut, it was useless. Something'd been strange with the amp anyway— hissing, sputtering, garbled messages like backwards tape. Weird. Awesome—probably some twisted interference with radio waves. In the momentary silence, he heard the allnight sprinkler watering the lawn outdoors, the spray of water fanning silver in the starlight beautiful green dreaming suburbs.

Moonshine glistened on Gary's skullfuck tattoo. He had the Megadeth T-shirt. One night the band had let him buy them liquor—white Russians and shooter specials at the Roxy uptown. Heavy metal. Now he put down his fingers, bleeding, from the fractured guitar. Dad was boozing on the sofa, Mom was lost in HBO.

Gary lay down, breathless, in his darkened room. Around the walls were signs and symbols. In the flickering gleam of the stereo the faked stucco glowed like a temple—half-lit icons: Ozzy Osbourne swallowing a dead bird, Jimi Hendrix igniting his guitar, Marc Bolan strutting a cloak full of eagles. Hieroglyphics off the cover of Zeppelin *IV*— runic, inscrutable magic.

He tuned in the radio, and just when some guitars faded, the radio guy was weeping. Vast, uncontrollable sobs. The radio guy was freaking, for once, for real.

The room vibrated. The amp in Gary's hot head vibrated. The radio guy cried—silver tears upon the airwaves.

Grabbing up the mousse and hair-spray, stupid Gary was out the window, his hightops just missing the head of the family dog. Gary on the lam. Go, Gary, Go.

Heaven is a kick in the teeth. Heaven is the volume cranked up to 10.

In the barrio, Father Diego was trembling. The lights had failed in the middle of mass. Ringing the statue of tender Mary Mother of God, candles blazed all the brighter. The airless, dark church was bare but for widows, rare and pathetic as saints. Rattling the stained-glass windows, low-riders, outside, rumbled the carnival streets. A mariachi band played, drunken, blasted, far-off, off-key.

Just before mass, Father Diego had stumbled. He'd been praying too long, his head was a fester. High stress in the hurt barrio: his hands were stained with tobacco like worn stigmata. From deep in his cassock—a pocket poking angrily against his martyred chest—he dug out, frantically, his pills.

But right at the sermon, he'd still coughed up blood. And then smiled back at the women to reassure. The smile hung lame, nobody believed it. He went on talking, his mouth crammed with the appalling fierce honey of the taste of Jesus.

Then it happened. Eerie. Pin-drop silence in the dark palm-tree barrio. The priest and the women, candle-lit: looking at each other— and flashing on the pain inside, throbbing like a bloody cut.

Diego ripped off his cloak, his shoes, his glasses, and he walked on out of there.

Heaven hurts like hell. Heaven is every angel crying.

His thirtieth mug (around the rim, it said, "You don't have to be crazy to work here, but it helps") of jetblack triple-strength coffee. Why not have the stuff IV'ed? He would if he could. Ditto nicotine. One quick, tubal rush: mainline into the hungry bloodstream. But then he'd have to forgo the subtle, quick crackle of fire as he drew the taste deeply in, the sharp Alpine rush of menthol, the heady dragon-clouds of Belair smoke.

Solo Jones inhaled again as he readied up another CD, another bulletin from his percolating soul—one more private fuck-the-programmer's-playlist song for his people. Smoke tumbled over the DJ's worry-streaked beard—an almost ironic beatnik goatee, it punctuated his chin, the exclamation point of some language so hip, so baffling, that even he sometimes could not decode it.

Solo Jones, lonely spook in his tower. The radio tower for WLUV was Babel-massive: 30,000 watts of power—somehow, tonight, its power was spared (the rappers, Sweet Jane, stupid Gary and half the misfits of strange L.A. were listening). Like the tower, Solo was high and mythic: his wraparound Ray Charles allnight orphic shades, his slow creeping cancer with the long shelf-life (alternately cradled and kicked, like a pet), his paychecks swallowed by five alimonies, the prophet had been on the air since fossil-stiff prehistory—Zoot Sims, sweet mean hurt-eyed Sinatra, Monk, Trane, St. Louie Armstrong babbling blissful "What a Wonderful World."

More than that, he'd been around since the New Beginning—when all the crooners' mouths had filled with dust, and the words ran out, and the new singers were nothing but a moaning and a cry. Johnny Ray. Little Richard. Ronnie Spector. He'd witnessed while the cocktail lounge exploded—redneck jigaboo cretin wiseguys hurling the piano through the plate-glass window—and the wired guitar screamed back. Sweet Gene Vincent, crippled and whirling. Eddie Cochran. Pickled in pain, Solo could hardly ever rise up and walk. He hadn't done daylight in fourteen seasons. With his voice as oiled and pleading as a phone-booth jerkoff's, through forty years of ratings wars, all he had had to do was talk.

And tonight he couldn't even get it up for that.

He'd been the first to receive the news. It came in fluttering fresh off the AP wire—reporting some sort of quake heading California homeward, some monster cipher on the Richter scale, seismic disturbance, galvanic, earth-shaking.

Solo's mama hadn't raised no fool. He deciphered the wire. Translated, interpreted the thing. Read it for what it really was. The goddam writing on the wall.

And now, with his show's producer tearing his hair out (dumb kid fresh from matchbook broadcast night school), Solo leaned into his microphone and cried. He cried with the news of the end of the world.

Heaven comes when you least expect it. Between commercials. In the middle of drive-time bullshit everyday what.

Her hand trembling the wood of her guitar, Loretta May Brown had the green DT's. Green. Seizing somehow for some control, she color-coded her shakes—depending on their force and kind. Green wasn't too bad. It came off Evan Williams Kentucky Whisky—every ounce charcoal-filtered. It wasn't the sharp blue pain she got from vodka, or the deep purple crash off Lord Calvert gin. It wasn't harsh red (J&B), or the brassy throb of Dewar's. Green was smooth and a little pathetic, because it traveled in high trucks from sad Kentucky. From Loretta's own weedy shattered defensive South—sweating ex-husbands loaded it up from smoky warehouses and headed 18-wheelers out from Louisville at dawn, so hot even then that heat wrinkled the fouled air. Evan Williams burned like home in her mouth—like home with Daddy, the crushing Bible, the flaying strap, and with Mama, diet pills, black eyes and thirty piled-up, smeared mail-order catalogs full of hope. How could Loretta May not have wandered? Sometimes, even now, 4 A.M., she could taste it—the recalling, so sweet on her tongue, of the moment of leaving: the screen door slamming, the low trumpeting of flies, and her strong, beautiful legs freed toward the road to the West.

Heaven: just fifty miles farther. Heaven: the next exit, road narrows, turn left.

Baby Catherine wailed. Twenty flights up, in Memorial Hospital, pink and impossibly perfect, one hour and eighteen minutes old, she was the first baby born at the end of the world. No dumb college for Baby Catherine, no sad job for this little sister, no stale gum to chew, no telephone calls, no clothes to buy, no drugs, no therapy, no endless search for love, the search so hard it's like stepping on razors, like bashing your head again and again and again on rock. None of that noise, and Baby knew it. She saw love coming on strong in fireball fury, in a deep and sudden kiss. Just love and love only at the end of the world.

   In the maternity ward, the doctor wheeled around, just as the lights shut off. He couldn't believe it: a newborn, laughing. Baby Catherine, laughing with the power of perfect love.

Heaven is a baby, nothing more. Heaven is skin so terribly soft.

Black water lapping his chest, the lifeguard dived through the trashed Pacific. Well-hung, broad-shouldered, he had a body that would not quit and, beautiful beast, my God was he dense. His brain, lovely like a teeny, bumpy pebble, you could hear it rolling in his gorgeous head. He was diving sleeker than a dolphin, but dolphins could speak better English.

Beachboy blonde in the toxic water, he felt the twentieth-century ocean pour through him, in one ear and out the other, but he had known this: how to save the drowning girl the day before, when, sun-struck, she'd wandered out into the deep end, and he'd cradled her panicked, spitting head, and he'd known how, too, to giggle alone at night in the waves, the infested ocean tumbling him—frugging, twisting, doing the pony—and then turning him loose.

Tonight, he stuck his dumb head out of the water—what were all these headlights, brighter than stars, coming at him? Whose were these footsteps heading toward the beach, far off still, but building to thunder?

Twenty miles to the east, the studios were over. The lights were dead, big cameras teetered for a second in the windstorm, then crashed and exploded in Hollywood. The ghosts of movie stars lit out seaward—red-jacket James Dean burning in his silver Porsche, Marilyn with her lipstick smeared by pills.

And, even deeper, buried in the hills that were vineyards, hidden behind the stone that was banks, malls, and condos, the animal thighs of Navajos and Apaches woke up. Ancient passions sniffed the trashed air. The bones bent, flared up, turned freshly supple, fires started in crumbling femurs, a claw of hand reached upward. The broken hearts quivered, nearly started to pump.

And soon, in the night, even the rocks on hills trembled slightly. Wind blew the high grass. Dirt grew damp, freshened. And even stones were eager.

Their headlights smoking through the smogged starlight, the bad rappers had never seen an ocean. Now, with it hissing around their hubcaps, they couldn't believe how hard it rocked. MC Rudy felt it pounding like a bass in his chest, he breathed like a baby for the first time in fifteen years, he smiled, and the moon got blinded by his gold teeth.

They'd come to the ocean because the radio told them to. That skinny hipster Solo maniac Jones had said the tide was high, the moon was full, everything everywhere would soon be over. And MC Rudy couldn't wait. Twenty years in the game, and he was blasted—exhausted, burned out, over with. Maybe the water would do it—hurl his head away. He scooped up water in his leaking cap. He drank it down, no matter the taste. And he turned to DJ Johnny, who'd gone crazy: diving again and again into the water—plunging, flashing like a knife.

Stupid Gary got down in the surf, his shaking hands doing air-guitar. He couldn't believe the ocean. It was like those movies they showed on the walls of rehab where all of a sudden some switch gets turned and life is fine, and you're breathing fresh air somewhere corny like maybe a farm, and a nice, pretty girl falls in love with you because you're for once clean and sober and you don't grunt and gasp and weep anymore—you talk like a human. The ocean was what you always wanted from the night: everybody just fucking leaving you alone, and the stars, and "Stairway to Heaven."

Gary was knee-deep in the ocean, then the water was high around his chest. He was not drowning but playing. Reaching down deep in the waves toward the guitar of his mind, he rose his hand in the starry, wet air. Power chords. Electric warrior. The amp in his head played the sounds of surf. Crash 'n' burn. Love so fine like crash 'n' burn.

The WLUV switchboard was going berserk, total nonlinear, all systems freaked. Every asshole and his brother phoning in. Complainers. Sob sisters. Whiners.

"Where's that dickhead DJ get off spreading panic? First that damn guitar, turned up so loud it nearly wrecked my speakers. Then him crying. Jesus Christ. I mean, talk about irresponsible."

"What's he mean, 'The end of the world'? I've got children, you know, and that kind of prank, well, it's just not funny."

Parents. The ratfuck FCC. Mothers Against Drunk Driving. Advertisers. Radio call-in psychologists. Buttinskis. The dream police. They all wanted the show shut down—N-O-W, now! Solo Jones—how dare he?

The spineless fuckwad station manager patched in a few anxious-listener calls to Solo (let *him* finesse the disaster: he's the freak who sparked it). The station manager gorged on Maalox, chewed his nails over the wife back home at the complex (was she bundling the kids into the back of the Volvo, packing the Mace and getting ready to head mad out to the water? was she tuned into WLUV and going crazy?). And he bitched at himself for ever quitting the gig at the gameshow and crossing over to Solo and this low-wage, bullshit thing called ART. He patched in a few more calls to Solo: Why doesn't the bonkers primadonna pick up?

But Solo Jones was gone. Out of it. Into his private moonglow tortured nirvana. Couldn't be bothered with telephone calls. Fuck 'em, raw. He knew who was calling, anyway. They'd been calling since the fifties. Nine-to-fivers. Joykillers. People who vote, mow the lawn, eat right. The enemy. And, tonight of all nights, he couldn't deal with them.

They'd never heard the music. Forget tonight's disaster. They'd never even listened when, for forty years, he'd played the songs.

Of course, he'd never played the songs for *them*. He'd put the needle down in the grooves, sent out the whispered dedications, breathed life into the airwaves—for the lonely. Only the lonely. He'd poured the music into the sweet sleeping ear of the American child, high and lost somewhere in the whitewood house. Driven it deep into the wet, famished lover, crazy in the sweated sheets. Coiled it around the anticipant fist. Fed it through the radio hidden under the pillow and clutched at desperate as death.

And tonight he was gone past even the music. Past even the shuddering, gasping guitars. Enraptured, inspired, weak at the knees, he needed to program the sounds beneath the sounds. Over the airwaves, he needed to send out what he knew quavered under every liberating, banging drum, under every bended string of all the outlaw guitars (Keith Richards, sliding his skull ring over the fret-board; Jimmy Page, gypsying a blues over the hills and far away). He needed to call to holy prefab fantasy California with moans beyond songs (beyond even the black-leather, skinny-muscled, loving-kindness of The Clash, beyond Joan Jett rocking for every voiceless, choked sister). Solo Jones needed to fill up the airwaves with weeping.

And into the mentholated, coffeed microphone, he wept.

In the cheap, turquoise sadness of her motel room, 20,000 miles from Nashville (where she'd first tried and failed to "break into the business"), Loretta May Brown got a grip on her guitar. Forlorn, blasted, its dynamo collapsed, L.A. poured in through the window, through the silly pink drapes, and it flooded Loretta. She'd come here because he'd told her to—Hank Williams, in one of her many 4 A.M. visions that could not be mistrusted: they hurt too much. Hank had pulled over, liquored, sweet, elegant and skeletal in his high hat and pale, punished body, he'd pulled over to the ditch in the road in his Cadillac, just as he'd done forty-six years before, a ghost heading north through softening snow on chloral hydrate and whiskey, five hundred songs in his nodding head.

And he'd told Loretta that L.A. now was where it's at. Country music was no longer bankrupt, greeting-card farms and pissed grasslands: it was "Steel and glass, baby. Sand and broken dreams and that nuked-up sun that, sugar, it don't ever set."

Hank had been right, naturally. Not that she'd ever doubted. Ever since she'd turned off the cactus freeway, the feeling had been right. Here was the heart of the country. City of night. Brilliant, beautiful, and sadder than she'd ever seen.

Nightclub to nightclub, bar to bar, motel to motel and bed to bed, she'd chased that sadness, tried to find the words and music to set it to.

Tonight, she picked up her guitar and she tried again. And right before she touched the strings, she was startled deep by the sudden silence. All L.A. for a moment: silent. Cars would start on the blacktop below, gunfire would ricochet, a baby would cry, some radio, far off, sounded like weeping. But then, for tense stretches so long they seemed like breath held back impossibly suspenseful, there would be silence.

And then she was singing. The one word, "lonesome." Over and over, again and again. It was the right word. The only word.

The song flowed out of her. Far from Kentucky, free and open in her lonesome motel room, free and open and final as an opened vein.

Saltwater over his bruised mascara, Sweet Jane shone like the silver surfer. His farmland eyes had never found such fantasy—this fierce current, rippling under moonglow, strong as muscle and glimmering soft. He'd become water inside the water: the heavy, burning demand of his body finally freed up and emptied. He lowered his pain into the cool, diseased ocean, and melted like one, long, sweet, inexhaustible coming. Littered with trash, the waves pounded like opera, but the sounds were simpler—a cheap song on the radio, lullaby from the forgiving father, a calling from some deep at last wherever that felt like home.

Climbing out of the burning Porsche, his plowboy boot darkening in the wet sand, James Dean drew his antique comb through his wild hair. Silver, ragged, it had grown in the grave and he was having trouble piling it high atop his cool skull. But the sea wind was fine, and soon James Dean was dancing, jittery at first, knock-kneed, but then fluid—and then his bones of hands were reaching, holding hot Marilyn high on the waves. Her white wet dress, mildewed and torn but still gorgeous, was whipping over the foam, and she and her plush mouth were laughing now—and it wasn't the stagy kittenish purr anymore, but the sudden light laugh of a woman.

Father Diego held the warm, saving hand of the beautiful girl from Illinois whose sister had found her (the girls had kissed too warm in the parking lot outside the mall, shocking everyone). They were gazing serenely out into the ocean, and the old women from his church had followed him, and they were deep waltzing in the water, feeling it gentle on the hems of their widow's nineteenth-century dresses, on their lace mantillas, their rosaries, and their old bones.

They were all gathered on the beach with the lifeguard—and he was wondering where'd they'd all come from so fast, and why, and what was happening.

What time is it? Finally, thought Solo Jones, as he checked the hour, it'd be dark enough to sneak a look outside. Exhausted from weeping, he glanced back again at his watch, and for a second turned almost nostalgic. He'd flashed on one of the old scars there, above the wrist. Track marks, retired, not quite faded. These days, he thought, nobody tied up anymore. An image flooded his mind—the gleaming old works, untouched for fifteen years: the needle and the spoon, almost medieval, an ancient long castaway sacrament, like some obscure Indian sweatlodge medicine-man trip, where they'd hang from spikes for some dream of purity and pain.

He infused more coffee, nearly ate another cigarette. In the cramped space above the shining radio control-room dials, he could just reach, creakily, the window. Tentative, he scratched at the aluminum foil— he'd pasted it up over the sunlight glass years ago, an old ghoul's vampire-paranoia trick he'd learned from Lenny Bruce, when the scalded cat was shaking and nearly gone, nearly exited fully into his final shaman funk. Solo Jones pierced the foil, and his tender tired oracular eyes peered out.

Movies near the sputtering end of the twentieth century had loved the scene. The cameras, fawning, had lingered long, creamed like a peeper. The lights of L.A. spread out twinkling. How'd it go? "Like diamonds."

But not tonight. Coal black, the night. Pure, like painted black. Only the moonlight through the chemical air. The wind blew the high grass. A few stars—stars that had been around since Sputnik, since Elvis first sang—fell on the eager stones. Just like Lennon sang, "Just like starting over."

Up in the hospital, Baby Catherine laughed in the dark. The end of the world was easy. It came around four in the morning, on a Tuesday, in Los Angeles, California. In the candle-lit delivery room —all the staff frenzied, rushing like ghosts in their gowns, prop- ping the newborn near the window, hoping for the gift of blasting, saving moonlight. Stuck there, not quite sightless, she beamed beyond thought down on L.A. Who knows what music sang, what signals fired and collided in her pure head?

Solo Jones breathed into his microphone. And even through the torn- foil window he heard his breath breathing back. A million radios— ghetto blasters, transistors, temporary shit, the people's radios. And, over to the west, he finally did see lights. Headlights. A caravan. Headlights of transitory pilgrim nowhere American cars, metal heaps of movement and the dreamer's impulse, all of them ghosting through the night. Led by his tears on the radio. December's children, the tribe of loss. Ahead of them: the ocean. Behind them: memory.

He looked over at the buildings across from the station. Dark, silent—banks, hotels, the hospital. But, from a room, he saw eyes staring back. Perfect, universal just-born eyes. Gypsy, unwhipped, freedom, universal eyes. They shone from a head so tiny it was entirely eyes. And they looked without blinking right into him.

Navajo and Apache, bare on the backs of bone horses, their ruined flag hair whipping in the wind—the wind, too, sweet on their dry and ancient teeth—were taking over L.A. Taking it back. A vapor and a riot through the dark, car-jam streets, they were drums and screaming and risen. Beneath their hooves, the stones sang. Riders released, they were rolling thunder.

Solo Jones shut the fuck up. His cigarette dangled in his old, rhythmic hand. Power drained from the radio tower. He'd stopped crying, stopped gasping, too. He sat back in the dark room, with the open microphone. It reached inside him and picked up his beat. Pounding like a drum. Purely rhythm. Fierce, hard, and lovely.

The ocean was singing—rock & roll. It was the waves doing what they wanted. It was nobody telling anybody anything. It was the whip of the world, dropping down useless.

Heaven is what nobody believes in. Heaven is nothing but the naked heart.

Martha Nell Smith

Sexual Mobilities in Bruce Springsteen: Performance as Commentary

> This guy, call him Bruce—no, he's not a queer, thank God, sir—will be a national hero.
> —Jefferson Morley

> I'm always somebody who has a lot of ambiguous feelings about, not necessarily what I want to *do*, but the style that I want to do it in.

> . . . But the world will never be simple again, if it ever was. The world is nothing but complex, and if you do not learn to interpret its complexities, you're going to be on the river without a paddle.

> Human politics. I think that people on their own can do a lot. I guess that's what I'm tryin' to figure out now: where do the aesthetic issues that you write about intersect with some sort of concrete action, some direct involvement, in the communities that your audience comes from?
> —Bruce Springsteen [1]

Had Allen Ginsberg written *Howl* in the 1980s, he could not have begun:

> I saw the best minds of my generation
>   destroyed by
>   madness, starving hysterical naked,

>   dragging themselves through the negro streets at dawn
>   looking for an angry fix.

At the advent of the twenty-first century, another New Jersey poet, one of the most provocative minds of our generation, Bruce Springsteen, disputes such a claim. Rising from the decadent ashes of rock & roll in the mid-1970s, "the Boss" sent us greetings from Asbury Park, told us about the wild, the innocent, and the E Street shuffle, and asked if we were born to run before, like Hester Prynne, he began to explore that darkness on the edge of town. In the worlds created by Springsteen, the edge of town teems with dangerous possibility: in "Driving out of Darlington County," a storyteller sees his buddy Wayne chained to the bumper of a state trooper's Ford; balladeer and "Highway Patrolman" Joe Roberts pulls to the side of the road to let his "no good" brother Franky escape the legal consequences of a barroom brawl; a heterosexual couple watches their happy illusion of knowing one another so very well begin to dissolve—"is that you baby," "is that me baby"—as their brilliant disguises and cold bed belie the promises of the altar; lives are on the line and "dreams are found and lost" in that darkness on the borderlines.[2] But Springsteen's dark is not simply despair, nor does it serve as cover for a Rolling Stones-like decadence, with the rocker nihilistically resigning himself to the belief that all is finally spectacle and money. As rock & roll critic Dave Marsh has pointed out, in performance Springsteen's medley of "Born to Run" and the Stones's "Street Fighting Man" empties Mick Jagger's question—"What can a poor boy do / 'Cept sing in a rock and roll band?"—of its "cynical irony."[3] Springsteen overflows not only with a riotous sense of the importance of having fun, but also with compassion and with the unfashionable faith that, working together, people really can make this a better world. Whether readers invoke Nancy Chodorow, Carol Gilligan, or Bob Dylan, just like a woman Springsteen makes love to his audience and pleads for connection, not for the romance of each to his or her own independent existence.[4]

For my purposes in analyzing the work of one of this particular moment's most challenging rock performers, the important questions concern what Springsteen's conflicting and ambiguous sexual expressions on stage and in music videos represent. What do the gestures of this performing self suggest and how might that be significant? His performances of the late 1970s often found him kissing and even humping the Big Man, Clarence Clemons, while the 1985 "Glory Days" music video foregrounds his elaborate homoerotic dances with Miami Steve Van Zandt. Even his album covers stage performances readily construed as homoerotic and/or ambiguously sexual: the shaggy bearded young man nestled among the boys in the band on the back cover of *The Wild, the Innocent & the E Street Shuffle*, or affectionately draped and smiling over Clemons's shoulder as the listener unfolds the jacket for *Born to Run*. The feminine earnest face in front of the blinds and peering at us from both sides of the *Darkness on the Edge of Town* package supplants the scruffy portrait inside the jackets of *Greetings from Asbury Park* and *Born to Run* and on front of *The Wild, the Innocent*, but still appears most comfortable smack dab in the middle of all the boys on *The River*'s inside record sleeves and in the photomontages for the songbook designed to accompany the five-record package, *Bruce Springsteen & the E Street Band Live, 1975–1985*. No face at all is necessary for the flirtatious pose foregrounding the New Jersey native's posterior as he, sending up *Patton* on *Born in the U.S.A.*, stands before the red and white stripes of the American flag, red baseball cap tucked in right back pocket. Hands in pockets, leaning against a creamy convertible, Springsteen appears both manly and boyish, simultaneously hetero- and homoerotically seductive in the portraits on *Tunnel of Love*.

In the 1990s, however, a scrutiny of Springsteen's video portrayals is more appropriate than study of his poses on album covers for any critique proposing to analyze some import of his social commentary. For one thing, album covers have been miniaturized to CD inserts, one-quarter the size of the soon-to-be extinct cardboard sleeves for LPs. More important, as visual rock-related productions, music videos have much wider currency and more far-reaching influence than album covers. In fact, MTV, VH-1 (Video Hits One), and TNN (The Nashville Network)—"24-hour, nonstop, commercial cable channel[s], beamed via satellite across the United States"—as well as video anthologies and singles for rent or to buy, and regular sixty-minute music videoplay programs like *Friday Night Videos*,

Music Video Connection, Night Flight, and *Midnight Love* have dramatically altered ways in which Americans receive popular music.[5] A viewer/listener of music videos may attend to the productions intently enough to study them or may see/hear them in the most casual fashion—as flickering/melody-making background in a bar or living room, or glimpsed in a department store display. Likewise, as they do with radio, the vast majority of Americans have some contact with music videos, even if only involuntarily. Unlike radio, music videos project televised images, and few in academe, government, or the media would bother to contest the commonplace that televised portrayals of any event or circumstance—wars, assassinations, poverties, political campaigns, space shuttle mission failures, rock & roll songs—are potently compelling in degree and in a multitude of ways that we have hardly begun to discern, much less understand.

Record companies believe the slickly produced sights and sounds have a significant impact on consumer spending, while various rock performers like Springsteen believe that videos are vehicles for extending artistic expression. The creative problem for Springsteen, who takes as his subject everyday dreams, "is that the line between democratic populism (the argument that all people's experiences and emotions are equally important, equally worthy to be dramatized and made into art) and market populism (the argument that the consumer is always right, that the market defines cultural value) is very thin."[6] Especially poignant are Springsteen's homoerotically suggestive depictions the common consumer does not expect and may in fact prefer to ignore, for the commercial imperative or "wedding of rock music and aesthetic visual forms drawn partly from advertising" of music video production would seem to prohibit unconventional portrayals which are not subverted through irony.[7]

I will content myself with a brief study of the last third of the *Bruce Springsteen Video Anthology/1978–88,* beginning with the electrified "Born to Run" composite of clips of different performances on numerous stages that were assembled in 1987 and ending with the rather subdued acoustic rendition capping his Tunnel of Love concerts recorded a year later in the Los Angeles Sports Arena.[8] Between those two vastly different productions of the song Springsteen hoped would be regarded as the greatest rock & roll piece ever made are video performances of "Brilliant Disguise," "Tunnel of Love," "One Step Up," "Tougher Than the Rest," and "Spare Parts," three of which were filmed at Springsteen's beloved Jersey shore, all of which are from the *Tunnel of Love* album.[9] To peruse the videos in this sequence, I shall begin by reading the performances of "Born to Run."

Performed with the entire E Street Band, "Born to Run's" electric version features Springsteen among his crowds. In concert footage spanning the last decade, Clarence Clemons is the most prominent, with numerous shots featuring him in various suits and usually intimate poses with the star of the show; depicted almost as frequently, Miami Steve mugs with Bruce and with Van Zandt's replacement Nils Lofgren; when the camera lens turns to ex-wife Julianne, an instant shows her dancing with her husband, then a few long seconds project Springsteen's sister, Pam, laughing and singing on stage with backup singer Patti Scialfa; significantly, one of the longest shots is far from the stage at a Meadowlands concert where wave upon wave of fans bounce before a tiny figure of Bruce, who performs in front of a giant video screen filled with the scene of the crowd. In marked contrast, the acoustic version of "Born to Run" features Springsteen alone in the spotlight, in a black tank top revealing his muscular build, surrounded by darkness and by an audience that might be considered a kind of edge of town. Prose commentary introduces both performances: for the first, Springsteen exhorts, "Remember, in the end, nobody wins unless everybody wins"; before he croons his anthem to conclude the anthology, he reminds listeners "that individual freedom—when it is not connected to some sort of community or friends or the world outside—ends up being pretty meaningless" and that what he is looking for, even in his performances, are "connections."

Camping out on Hester's dark edge of town throughout this portion of the video anthology framed by variant "Born to Runs," Springsteen repeatedly explores perhaps the most dangerous territory of all—the Tunnel of Love. About gathering songs together to produce *Tunnel of Love*, Springsteen has proclaimed: "I wanted to make a record about what I felt, about really letting another person in your life and trying to be part of someone else's life. That's a frightening thing, something that's always filled with shadows and doubts and also wonderful things and beautiful things."[10] For him, writing and singing about "something you get from engagement with people, from a connection with a *person*," clearly entails much more than musing on the particulars of an individual romance.

One of the first images of intimate connection offered in the "Born to Run" composite is a stage-wide Springsteen slide, on his knees, to plant a big kiss on none other than the Big Man. Fifteen years before, the Boss told listeners that behind "Wild Billy's Circus" tent, the "hired hand tighten[ed] his legs on the sword swallower's blade." That he would dare to highlight the homoerotic overtones of this long-term friendship in the photomontage production of his anthem and choose a homosexual encounter as one of the salient details of carnival life in a song produced for commercial consumption underscores the fact that one of rock's wealthiest stars is not merely a slave to the marketplace. Even though ours is a country by and large enthralled with football—a game in which men jump all over one another and pat each other's behinds—and with a literary history in which Jim beckons Huck down to the raft, Queequeg and Ishmael enjoy a night beneath the counterpane, and Whitman adores the adhesiveness of manly love, America is not a culture that welcomes displays of erotic love between men, nor one in which men customarily greet one another with a kiss. Americans do not expect popular culture figures—especially those whose fans celebrate their faith that he's "just a regular person; he [Bruce] doesn't come out with earrings and makeup;" he reflects "people's lives back to them in some fashion"—to depict undeniably homoerotic images. Though loyal to his fans, Springsteen clearly "hasn't let that loyalty constrain the development of his art or his audience."[11]

By 1988, the sword swallower in the "Tunnel of Love" music video carnival is female, not male, but is haunted by a Queequeg-like figure who keeps peeping around the corner to watch her slowly envelop, then carefully withdraw, the long, double-edged blade. Similarly, Springsteen's constructions of romantic and connective encounters often seem double-edged, contextualizing publicly honored heterosexual couplings with ambiguous or homosexual unions publicly repudiated. And, in keeping with the zeitgeist of the late twentieth century, Springsteen names his beloveds in a most ambiguous fashion: Does the male speaker of "Backstreets" share an "old abandoned beach house" with a male or female Terry? Does the speaker of "4th of July, Asbury Park (Sandy)" tell a male or female Sandy that "the Aurora is rising behind us"? Doesn't the male speaker address another male when he affectionately remembers, "We liked the same music, we liked the / same bands, we liked the same clothes," and says, "I / miss you baby, good luck, goodbye, Bobby Jean"?[12]

To whom are Springsteen's poetically professed passions directed, anyway? What gender are all those beloveds whom he christens so indeterminately? Even Marsh, who likes to emphasize his subject's heterosexual escapades, acknowledges that the "homoerotic undercurrent" of Springsteen's recorded and live performances is "undeniable."[13] Extramusical facets of the Springsteen persona also hint at homoeroticism. To whom is his recent bodybuilding most appealing? Indeed, on the 1989 Amnesty International Human Rights tour, the husky-voiced hunk looked fit for a leather bar. Yet such speculation meets resistance in the media-verified facts of what appears to be aggressive heterosexuality. Sharing more than the stage with the "Boss," moving into more than "Clarence's old position," and becoming more than Bruce's "onstage foil," Patti Scialfa has supplanted Julianne as wife and the E Street Band as significant other, a shift *People* magazine has so jubilantly documented with its publication a couple of years ago of a picture of the rocker on a Rome balcony, cavorting in his underwear with the Jersey girl, and its more recent publication of a portrait of the happy family—mom Patti, son Evan James, and dad Bruce.[14]

The gaps between Springsteen's polymorphous onstage "wildness" and his offstage fodder-for-the-tabloids heterosexual "innocence" shuffle and blur culturally constructed differences of sexuality and gender. Springsteen precludes definitive determination of sexual preference, mooting a fundamental constraint whereby our culture knows us and names us. Such mooting matters not just because inquiring minds want to know, but because undermining this constraint calls into question conventional representations of love and traditional musical constructions of desire, as well as the way popular culture transforms private pronouncement and ostensibly intimate revelation into cultural commentary. Does living his life as a heterosexual invalidate his staged homoeroticisms? Where/who is Bruce and how does anyone know him? Why would he allow his kiss with Clarence and vignettes of homosexual couples in the "Tougher Than the Rest" video to be emphatically framed when there are so many other possibilities for televisual portrayals and when omission of these would probably not even be noticed? In raising such questions, Springsteen exposes many assumptions and illusions underlying sex- and gender-determined divisions of our culture, and leads audiences into "dangerous"—at least to conventional categorizations and schemes for understanding sexuality—territory. Implicitly, Springsteen both concurs with and modifies Eve Kosofsky Sedgwick's assertion that an "essentialism of sexual object choice is far less easy to maintain, far more visibly incoherent, more visibly stressed and challenged at every point in the culture, than any essentialism of gender," for his stage antics and speakers' performances call essentializing notions of the masculine and feminine as well as of sexuality into question.[15]

When, discussing the blockbuster success of *Born in the U.S.A.*, Marsh notes that conventional wisdom of the star-making machinery holds that a pop star's "sexuality should be simultaneously provocative and reassuring," he specifically identifies the powerful, indisputably homoerotic male bonding in Springsteen's performances as an element sure to unsettle or at least intrigue those attempting to claim him as heterosexually All-American.[16] The "fiery rage and sense of utter betrayal" at the core of Springsteen's "Born in the U.S.A." performances challenge those who try to claim the song for Reaganaut jingoism; likewise, his blatant homoeroticisms challenge insistences that "Bruce" is simply "the most heterosexual person I ever met" or that "he's not a queer, thank God," revealing both the naïveté of such statements and their tendency to displace accession of the power of the majority and a separative political stance onto judgments about sexuality.[17] Such views politicize sexual behavior by territorializing authorized from unauthorized sexualities; and by critiquing national politics and the politics of sexuality through mass cultural media, Springsteen questions the politics of cultural hierarchies that valorize the "highbrow." Andreas Huyssen reminds us that the "lure of mass culture . . . has traditionally been described as the threat of losing oneself in dreams and delusions," of realizing Marx's nightmare and "merely consuming rather than producing."[18] By interrogating the ways in which we publish ourselves—sexually and textually—to the world, Springsteen turns the tables on traditional notions (which have only recently begun to lose their force) that have persistently gendered "mass culture as feminine and inferior." Springsteen invariably holds out the microphone for the audience to sing "Show a little faith, there's magic in the night." Introducing the song "War," he usually exhorts his listeners: "Don't blindly follow your leaders . . . because blind faith in your leaders or in anything will get you killed." Are his calls for audience participation in performance, and for action beyond the concert, merely disguised forms of commodification encouraging more consumption? Is this yet another feminizing popular culture threat "against which high art has to shore up its terrain"? Or is something else going on here? Like the homoerotic, the feminine has been devalued in our culture. This performer, who superficially looks and sounds like the hometown lusty boy enticing Mary off her front porch and into his front seat, assumes both these devalued positions, perhaps never so clearly as in his concert staging of "Thunder Road," which contextualizes my remarks on the video anthology's "Tunnel of Love" sequence in crucial ways.

In "Thunder Road's" erotic expressions, there is no ambiguity. The speaker is clearly male, wooing a Mary who is plainly female. Yet like the juxtapositions he arranges for the six televisual renditions of the songs I am discussing here, the staging of "Thunder Road" throws the lyrics' ostensible pronouncements into question. Anyone who has seen a Springsteen and E Street Band concert in which he warbles "The screen door slams / Mary's dress waves / Like a vision she dances across the porch / As the radio plays" is familiar with his "soul kiss with Clarence."[19] As he does in the electric "Born to Run" video, Springsteen slides across stage at the end of "Thunder Road" and kisses Clarence Clemons firmly on the lips. When Marsh pictures this performance ritual in *Glory Days*, he reproduces four photographs: the first shows Bruce with his face in his hands appearing to weep, and Clarence with his arm around him offering solace; in the second, Clarence's arm wraps around a smiling, presumably comforted Bruce, who clutches the Big Man's coat; in the third, Bruce, on his knees between saxophone-playing Clarence's legs, holding his guitar in a phallic position, looks longingly (and rather seductively) up at the Big Man; and in the fourth, Clarence locks Bruce in a loving embrace for a lingering kiss. This fourth pose is especially significant, and not simply because of the kiss. Still between Clarence's legs, Bruce finds himself in what we might call a feminine position. First, Clarence leans down and towers over his friend. But, just as important, Clarence's right arm grips Bruce's shoulder while he holds his left arm aloft, as if he has just proclaimed, like a Baptist or fundamentalist preacher presiding over a rite of immersion, "And I baptize you in the name of. . . ." Thus Clarence assumes the ministerial, stand-in for God, masculine position, while Bruce assumes the believer, church member, feminine place. Is it into the feminine, as well as the homoerotic, that Clarence baptizes him? Contrary to traditional masculine fears of being swallowed up by and lost in the feminine, Springsteen begins to find himself as his eyes adjust to that dark womb of a place, so long banished to the outskirts of culture (or town).

As he does in his stage relation to Clemons, in which the kiss becomes an integral part of the performance of "Thunder Road," Springsteen makes something of a ritual of imagining the plight of the female in at least one song on each of his albums and this, too, is important for contextualizing the "Tunnel of Love" music videos. Of course such male scripting of female stories is not new; male artists have long portrayed female characters. Yet, to borrow his phrase, there is "something" quite distinctive in Springsteen's portrayal of "the night" of female experience. As most will suspect, if not remember, Springsteen concerns himself with the working-class woman—often unwed, deserted mothers or those "ladies of the night" who have made sexual performance their capital to purchase means for survival. In "Candy's Room," "strangers from the city" come, bringing toys to purchase her favors; the song's speaker does not pay her, but claims to love her, really, yet "no man can keep Candy safe" from that "sadness all her own." Unlike traditional plots, this narrative unequivocally acknowledges that romance will never prove to be her salvation. In another song, the man who chants "I Wanna Marry You" declares that "true love can't be no fairy tale" and that to "say I'll make your dreams come true would be wrong." The sad woman in "Point Blank" does not "wait on Romeos," but "on that welfare check." There are no fairy-tale endings here, no distraught women rescued from their plights by dashing handsome men. In fact, except for one "Tunnel of Love" story, there are no happy endings for abandoned women in Springsteen's narratives, and the sole satisfying resolution he depicts is not one that popular culture fans have come to expect. In "Spare Parts," the song televised next to last on the anthology, Janey, a young unwed mother abandoned by a Bobby full of vain promises, "[w]ent to a drawer in her bureau and got out her old engagement ring," then "[w]ent straight down to the pawn shop man and walked out with some good cold cash." As Springsteen tells us when he introduces the song, Janey has learned to "value . . . her own independent existence."

Lest you think I contradict myself, having remarked at this article's beginning that Springsteen pleads for connections, not for the romance of each to his own independent existence, some vital differences between pronouns and key terms warrant scrutiny. The great American romance has been that of individuality, the isolated figure, like Ahab, smashing "through the pasteboard mask" to make his mark on the world. That is the romance of independent existence, and, as Annette Kolodny, Nina Baym, and numerous others have astutely observed, a masculinist dream. Springsteen's Janey learns the value of her independent existence, and value is a matter very different from romance. Romance is a fiction that need not account for the necessities of life; valuing oneself and human connections requires, among many other things, taking responsibility for material sustenances necessary for life.[20]

"Spare Parts" tells us that, forced to support a child by herself, without the help of the father, Janey hears a story about a mother's infanticide: "a woman over in Calverton / Put her baby in the river let the river roll on." She considers similar action, imagining, therefore, a dark but nevertheless romantic end to her story: "Janey held her son down at the riverside / Waist deep in the water how bright the sun shone." But unlike the woman who sought to drown her despair, Janey "lifted" her son "in her arms and carried him home." So Springsteen's woman rises above the romance surrounding the anguish of a woman victimized by male irresponsibility and broken promises, and thus rises above a plot that ends with a rescuing knight

in his shining limousine or the woman in utter ruin. Janey sells the
symbols of romantic promises so she can deal competently with the
material facts of life. Departing from the standard for popular culture
storytelling and sounding much more like a woman writer and re-
visionist mythmaker, Springsteen writes beyond the ending of patriarchal resolution.[21] Janey's "independent existence" is not isolated,
but one in which she recognizes the responsibilities of her connection
to her son. What Janey has learned is that, though she needs human
relationships, she does not need to be connected to a husband to be
valuable. Instead of drowning her child, she baptizes him and herself
into a new life in which she has a worth all her own. The revision
of the biblical myth of the mother with her holy child need not be
elaborated, though I should acknowledge in passing that Springsteen
also revises himself here. In the power dynamics and the iconography
of this baptism, a mother, instead of a black man, occupies the minister's place, and a baby stands in for the Believer/Boss of "Thunder
Road." Interrelatednesses impel and underscore Springsteen's artistic
vision.

The video produced for "Spare Parts" begins with shots of the
English countryside—lush green trees blowing with an approaching
rain shower, cottages along small roads, and crowds going to a "pop
concert"—scored by Roy Bittan's piano interlude. When Springsteen
and the rest of the E Street Band break into the opening chords of
"Spare Parts," the camera cuts from shots of waving leafy limbs to
shots of thousands upon thousands of fans swaying and waving before a stage in Sheffield, then to Bruce singing the opening stanza
by himself, then to him repeating it passionately, sometimes unto
hoarseness, as Patti begins to sing along. In the performance memo-
rialized on the video, Patti's role is as one half of a duet rather than
as the backup singer playing a substantially lesser part on the version
recorded for the album. Like Janey, Patti asserts herself to lead Springsteen himself in the chorus, and thus through performance proclaims
that she is not (like a spare part) dispensable, but is in fact an integral
part of the band.

In the video immediately preceding, other of society's "Spare
Parts" are also recuperated by featuring conventional and unconventional video "snapshots" to accompany performance of the love song

"Tougher Than the Rest." These vignettes—in which couples smile at one another, at the camera, rub one another, kiss one another or goofily grin standing side-by-side—allude to the four-for-a-quarter (or dollar or whatever the price now) picture-taking booths found on boardwalks, in carnivals, in arcades, and in bus stations. One of Richard Poirier's remarks about the Beatles pertains to such performances generated by Springsteen: "Maybe the most important service of the Beatles and similar groups is the restoration to good standing of the simplicities that have frightened us into irony and the search for irony; they locate the beauty and pathos of commonplace feelings even while they work havoc with fashionable or tiresome expressions of these feelings."[22] The lyrics to "Tougher Than the Rest" are ordinary enough to frighten one into irony: "Well it's Saturday night / You're all dressed up in blue / I been watching you awhile / Maybe you been watching me too." But the chorus offers something of an unexpected twist: "Well if you're rough and ready for love / Honey I'm tougher than the rest." Those lines in themselves are not really so extraordinary, particularly in these days when sadomasochism fills the airwaves. Still, the choice of subjects and arrangements in the video scripted for this song disrupt the viewer's expectations.

The opening shots show us the Tunnel of Love, then cut to the stage where a rather corpulent, cigar-smoking carnival man is selling tickets to ride. As members of the E Street Band purchase these, the camera carefully frames and viewers can clearly see only two take their "passport": first Clarence, then Patti. Throughout much of the song, Springsteen looks straight at Patti and she looks right back as he sings to her, an apparent televisual testimonial that Springsteen has grown out of his passionate male bonding and into Freud-sanctioned heterosexual maturity. Yet even as interpreting *Tunnel of Love* "as a report from the marital front is far too facile," so reading the music video "Tougher Than the Rest" as a report on the successful wooing of Patti severely limits understanding of Springsteen's artistic project.[23] The vignettes of adult romances interspersed throughout the scenes of Bruce crooning to Patti (or at play, lying on his back and kicking his feet in the air with other band members, or jumping on speakers, or leaning down into the audience to receive a quick kiss) move back and forth between snapshots of homo- and heteroerotic couplings.

Each of these twenty or so snippets shows a couple, and most are of course heterosexual. But, without irony, Springsteen's video also features one gay and two lesbian couples. As with his kissing Clarence, these pictures are not the lascivious or decadent play of the Rolling Stones or David Bowie.

In contrast to Bowie- or Jaggeresque flamboyance, the homosexual couples in "Tougher Than the Rest" are presented to the viewing audience routinely, as part of a photomontage of all-American lovers. Showing them in a more or less matter-of-fact way, Springsteen's video love song exhorts his audience to expect such romantic unions. However understated, by the very fact of their existence these presentations challenge some of the most deep-seated American attitudes that surely contributed to Springsteen's drawing the conclusion: "One of the problems in the United States is that 'united in our prejudices we stand,' you know? What unites people, very often, is their fear."[24] As his homoerotic play and dress destabilize preconceptions of the emphatic heterosexual, so the homoerotic snapshot portrayals disrupt traditional notions of legitimate and/or "natural" relationships and implicitly critique these biases. The audience's perspective is like that of a camera in one of the booths or that of a video-cam in the hand of someone conducting person-on-the-street interviews: couples being filmed look right out at viewers who look right back at them. Since erasures of homosexual unions from representations of America's quotidian experience have been so pervasive, the gay and lesbian couples could easily have been omitted and no one would have noticed. But by refusing conventional silences and calling attention to the homoerotic facts of life many would just as soon forget or disregard, Springsteen protests the agenda of the narrow-minded who mark homoerotic affections as aberrant and who seek to police desire accordingly. By implication, he also challenges those who, like Jesse Helms, would police artistic representations of desire.

His challenges are more sophisticated than mere objections to those who would oppress others. Rigid schematizations of sexuality, pugilistic definitions that depend on excluding the Others to stake their territories, are questioned as well. Sexual textualities in publicly funded art are bound up by notions of artists' intentions and conceptions of images "proper" enough for community sponsorship, and

Springsteen's depictions demand scrutiny of the definitions and presumed consensus many citizens take for granted. Though in the turn toward the twenty-first century audiences are more willing to accept sexual desires not necessarily substantiating the myth of an unswerving heterosexual highroad, when reading beyond heterosexuality the prevailing urge has been to distinguish that which is Not Me from that which is Like Me. Consequently, lawmakers formulate proprietary codes that defund those who are designated as alien, very different, and threatening to the norm. Such dichotomies are as overly simple as they are easier and more soothing to read.

As there is for steady demarcation between male and female, there is still a nostalgia, heterosexual and homosexual, that maintains that homoeroticism is entirely different from heteroeroticism and that wants "natural, fixed" differences in sexual desire as well as between the sexes. Though often a strategy for gay and lesbian will to power, such insistence can also be used to brutalize and oppress homosexuals. It has yet to be seen how, like the promotion of fixed sexual differences, the promotion of fixed differences in sexual desire— "whether they are described as natural or culturally constructed— does anything but maintain an all too familiar system of oppositions and stereotypes."[25] The 1989 legislation stipulating what kinds of artistic enterprises may and may not be funded by the National Endowment for the Arts, approved by a United States Senate voice vote on 26 July and passed in slightly modified form in September, justifies itself according to such an ideology of difference. In the first specification of this amendment, which was not altered, blatant stereotyping equates sadomasochism, homoeroticism, and the exploitation of children:

> None of the funds authorized to be appropriated pursuant to this Act may be used to promote, disseminate, or produce— (1) obscene or indecent materials, including but not limited to depictions of sadomasochism, homoeroticism, the exploitation of children, or individuals engaged in sex acts.[26]

Obviously, the thrust of this proposal is to protect the heterosexually pure from any contaminating deviant body. Key to the assumptions delineated is the belief that homoeroticism and sadomasochism can be readily identified, labeled dangerously different, then prohibited.[27] Most dangerous is the faith in consensus and in stable definitions that labels the homosexual as Not Like the law-abiding rest of "us." In fact, heterosexist notions of "normality" persist, even within deconstruction.[28]

The very idea that the homoerotic can be identified and separated from some monolithic heterosexual norm and then proscribed from federal funding is a political stance that allows little understanding of the complexities of human sexuality. This belief in an ability to separate pure from profane bodies expresses yearnings for stable definitions of sexual desires and parallels yearnings for stable definitive demarcations between male and female. Consonant with those who proclaim Springsteen "the most heterosexual person" are those who, like George Will, triumphantly declare that "there is not a smidgeon of androgyny in Springsteen" and who nostalgically seek to claim him as a manly icon for "a mythical America" and the continuing patriarchal project of manifest destiny.[29] Will and others frightened by homosexuality and by those who blur masculine/feminine distinctions invest "the deviant" with a kind of demonic power, and consequently treat it as something to be exorcised. At issue is the power over (and of) interpretation. As in so many critical struggles, "the battleground is representation itself," for "identity and reality are created within representation," and interpretations appear easier to control in realms of definitude.[30] As Sedgwick points out, since "virtually all people are publicly and unalterably assigned to one or the other gender, and from birth," gender orientation appears to be much more stable than sexual orientation, which has a "far greater potential for rearrangement, ambiguity, and representational doubleness."[31]

The performances of Springsteen, the virile rock & roller who superficially seems so far removed from these matters of philosophy and sexual theory, challenge audience complacency and force readers to ask not just "what are the guidelines for reading these matters of sex and texts?" but "can there be guidelines for reading sex and texts?" Instead of insisting on determining discrete bodies—sexual beings who are definitively heterosexual, lesbian, bisexual, or asexual—and imposing rules of order, Springsteen relays his "sense of the underlying fraud of all order, the undeniable fact that the universe contain[s] as much randomness as structure."[32] In "Brilliant Disguise," the second video on the Tunnel of Love sequence, Springsteen perches atop a stool in a rather plain kitchen, an unadorned figure in black and white looking right into the camera at the audience looking right back at him. But the words of the song belie this apparently straightforward presentation by the performer so many think, as Simon Frith has pointed out, conforms to order as "The Real Thing." At a recent benefit for the Christic Institute and in response to a fan screaming, " 'We love you, Bruce,' Springsteen responded, without a shred of irony, 'But you don't really know me.' "[33]

On the surface of things, Bruce Springsteen seems so male, so heterosexual, so frank, so knowable. But close attention to his artistic productions reveals not only how inscrutable he may be, but also how tenuous knowledge is of that most basic element of human nature—sexuality. Homoeroticism permeates his performances, assumption of the feminine is one of his repeated artistic maneuvers, and, though he writes and sings about Adam, he finally seems much more like Eve in his approach to knowledge. Instead of obeying instructions and submitting to divine edict, Eve opts for critical inquiry. In Judeo-Christian mythology, Eve's questions—why not eat of the fruit of knowledge? why accept a state of ignorance?—lead to her and Adam's expulsion from Eden and to the first travel or exploration of new horizons. When she refuses imposed order, Eve learns that one question leads to another and that knowledge about good and evil and about the nature of things is not fixed.

Springsteen's performances highlight the fact that the limits of various paradigms for sexuality are as obvious as are their applicabilities. Extending Adrienne Rich's continuum beyond lesbian to include male sexualities begins to describe the diversities of lived sexualities— heterosexual, lesbian, bisexual, homosexual. Yet the continuum metaphor establishes a scale of passions that finally retains polarities as it measures who is more or less erotic, who is more or less hetero- or homosexual. How can such a metaphor be elaborated to account for the myriad and disparate social contexts and constructions of sexual being? The same might be asked of universalizing metaphors that posit an innate bisexuality in each and all. Freud's hypotheses that "*everyone* has made a homosexual object choice," if only unconsciously, helps us see the "fundamental and crucial proposition, call it deconstructive, poststructuralist, postmodern, whatever," that "what a culture designates as alien, utterly other and different, is never so." In our Freudian-inflected world, how can formulations of a normative heterosexuality that represses perverse desire resist reinscribing the violent hierarchies Derrida descries? With so many willing to posit a universal goal of heterosexuality, such a paradigm becomes a convenient tool for those who want to legitimate persecution of the bodies who, having succumbed to their "weak," darker side, threaten civilization itself.[34]

However defined and theorized, homosexualities have persisted in every culture and heterosexualities have never been subverted out of being. As Anthony DeCurtis observes, what Springsteen demands of himself and asks of his audience are continuing "explorations of how self-deceit, romantic illusions, and fantasies of control corrupt the bedroom and the boardroom, personal as well as political affairs, and poison human experience": "Inclusiveness is at the heart of his vision."[35] And Springsteen pleads that it be at the heart of ours, urging a refusal of replications of exclusionary dichotomies and theories of knowledge that lay violent claims to imaginary territories. Such exhortations echo Hans Robert Jauss's description of understanding in the "open horizon of onmoving experience" as the "search for or investigation of a possible meaning." In this approach, paradigms for understanding sexuality (or anything else for that matter) are always in the process of revision, and, when allowed to degenerate into instruments for imposing order and presuming control, work against their professed goals. If we heed Jonathan Dollimore's advice to expose the displacement of the political onto the sexual by continually "taking sexuality apart and revealing the histories within it," we will probably, as Springsteen did when evaluating a dance mix of his "Dancing in the Dark"—which radically restructures each composition, "dismantling some sections of a song to its skeleton, doubling other parts, stretching and extending and bending" and reassembling "the record to a danceable commentary on itself"—discover that, like music, sexuality "isn't as fragile" as many have thought.[36] Historically and even to the present day, however, human understanding, especially of an aspect like sexuality that so many desperately want to control, has been regarded with a premodernist "closed horizon of expectations," as if it were "the recognition and interpretation of a professed or revealed truth."[37] Taking sexuality apart to explore and reconstitute it for a deeper, more inclusive understanding may just prove to be an approach "tougher than the rest."

Notes

Through their enthusiastic conversation, several people contributed significantly to this essay: Jim Bloom, David Van Leer, Marshall Grossman, Orrin Wang, David Wyatt, Bill Keach and Sheila Emerson, Beth and Bill Loizeaux, Bill Malloy and Deborah Burns, Linda Kauffman, Marilee Lindemann, and, for his encouragement and assistance locating certain articles, Anthony DeCurtis.

1 The first quotation is from a conversation with Ronald Reagan that Jefferson Morley fantasizes in "Bruce Springsteen Born in the U.S.A.: The Phenomenon," *Rolling Stone*, 5 October 1985, 75. What follows are three of Springsteen's remarks: the first is quoted by Dave Marsh, *Glory Days: Bruce Springsteen in the 1980s* (New York, 1987), 152; the second, by Mikal Gilmore, "Bruce Springsteen" interview, *Rolling Stone*, 5 November 1987, 23–24; and the third, by Kurt Loder, "The Rolling Stone Interview: Bruce Springsteen," *Rolling Stone*, 6 December 1984, 21.

2 The albums to which I refer are Bruce Springsteen, *Greetings from Asbury Park, N.J.* (Columbia Records, 1973), *The Wild, the Innocent & the E Street Shuffle* (Columbia Records, 1973), *Born to Run* (Columbia Records, 1975), and *Darkness on the Edge of Town* (Columbia Records, 1978); the individual songs cited are "Darlington County," *Born in the U.S.A.* (Columbia Records, 1984), "Highway Patrolman," *Nebraska* (Columbia Records, 1982), "Brilliant Disguise," *Tunnel of Love* (Columbia Records, 1987), and "Darkness on the Edge of Town," title track, *Darkness*.

3 Marsh, *Glory Days*, 229.

4 Though I could have cited many more, I choose two of the most well-known feminists theorizing about gendered identity formation. See Nancy Chodorow, *The Reproduction of Mothering: Psychoanalysis and the Sociology of Gender* (Berkeley, 1978); and Carol Gilligan, *In a Different Voice: Psychological Theory and Women's Development* (Cambridge, Mass., 1982).

5 E. Ann Kaplan, *Rocking Around the Clock: Music Television, Postmodernism, and Consumer Culture* (New York, 1987), 1. A useful collection of theoretical perspectives on video culture is *Video Culture: A Critical Investigation*, ed. John G. Hanhardt (New York, 1986).

6 Simon Frith, "The Real Thing—Bruce Springsteen," in *Music for Pleasure: Essays in the Sociology of Pop* (New York, 1988), 101. See also Simon Frith's "Toward an

Aesthetic of Popular Music," in *Music and Society: The Politics of Composition, Performance, and Reception,* ed. Richard Leppert and Susan McClary (Cambridge, 1987), 133–49.

7 Kaplan, *Rocking Around the Clock,* 11. On politics, commercialism, and art in popular music, particularly rock & roll, see Greil Marcus, *Mystery Train: Images of America in Rock 'n' Roll Music* (New York, 1975), and *Lipstick Traces: A Secret History of the 20th Century* (New York, 1989).

8 *Bruce Springsteen Video Anthology/1978–88* (CBS Music Video Enterprises, 1989). The televisual performances generated in response to his songs are of course collaborative, incorporating the energies of the producer, director, camera crew, and various performers as well as those of Springsteen.

9 To read about Springsteen's high hopes for "Born to Run," see Gilmore's "Springsteen" interview, 24. "Brilliant Disguise" was filmed at Sandy Hook; "Tunnel of Love" at Asbury Park; and "One Step Up" in Wall Township.

10 This and the quotation in the following sentence are from an interview by Steve Pond, "Bruce Springsteen's 'Tunnel Vision,'" *Rolling Stone,* 5 May 1988, 39–42.

11 Merle Ginsberg, "Bruce Springsteen Made in the U.S.A.: The Fans," *Rolling Stone,* 10 October 1985, 31; Bruce Springsteen, quoted by Kurt Loder in "Bruce!" *Rolling Stone,* 28 February 1985, 23; and Christopher Connelly, "Still the Boss," *Rolling Stone,* 26 September 1985, 125.

12 Springsteen, "Backstreets," *Born to Run;* "4th of July, Asbury Park (Sandy)," *The Wild, the Innocent, and the E Street Shuffle;* "Bobby Jean," *Born in the U.S.A.*

13 Marsh, *Glory Days,* 216.

14 Pond, "'Tunnel Vision,'" 40.

15 Eve Kosofsky Sedgwick, "Across Gender, Across Sexuality: Willa Cather and Others," *South Atlantic Quarterly* 88 (1989): 56. For various analyses of sexualities and their representations, readers should consult this entire issue, *Displacing Homophobia,* ed. Ronald R. Butlers, John M. Clum, and Michael Moon.

16 Marsh, *Glory Days,* 216. Here I have in mind both the "star-maker machinery" mentioned in Joni Mitchell's "Free Man in Paris," and Geoffrey Stokes, *Star-Making Machinery: The Odyssey of an Album* (Indianapolis, 1976).

17 On Springsteen's "Born in the U.S.A.," see David Fricke, "Bruce looks down the long road," review of *Bruce Springsteen & the E Street Band Live 1975–1985, Rolling Stone,* 15 January 1987, 50–52. On speculative characterizations of Springsteen's sexuality, see Curt Fluhr quoted by Joseph Dalton, "Bruce Springsteen Made in the U.S.A.: My Hometown," *Rolling Stone,* 10 October 1985, 78. For extended analysis of "the displacement of the political into the sexual," see Jonathan Dollimore, "The Cultural Politics of Perversion: Augustine, Shakespeare, Freud, Foucault," *Genders* 8 (July 1990): 1–16. Such displacements remind one of Springsteen's balladeer/murderer in "Nebraska" who displaces responsibility for his actions onto the young woman he kidnaps for his killing spree ride by repeatedly referring to "the things that we done." His final request is "Sheriff when the man pulls that switch sir and / snaps my poor head back / you make sure my pretty baby is sittin' right / there on my lap."

18 Andreas Huyssen, "Mass Culture as Woman," in *Studies in Entertainment: Critical Approaches to Mass Culture,* ed. Tania Modleski (Bloomington, 1986), 199–200. For an interesting analysis of artistic hierarchies in America, see Lawrence W. Levine, *Highbrow/Lowbrow: The Emergence of Cultural Hierarchies in America* (Cambridge, Mass., 1988).

19 Marsh, *Glory Days,* 216.

20 Echoes of Adrienne Rich's *Necessities of Life* (New York, 1966) are intentional.

21 Rachel Blau DuPlessis, *Writing Beyond the Ending: Narrative Strategies of Twentieth-Century Women Writers* (Bloomington, 1985). I also would like to thank DuPlessis for her substantial contribution to my thinking in the discussion of theorizing sexuality at the end of this article.

22 Richard Poirier, "Learning from the Beatles," in *The Performing Self: Compositions and Decompositions in the Languages of Contemporary Life* (New York, 1971), 124.

23 Steve Pond, "Bruce's Hard Look at Love," review of *Tunnel of Love, Rolling Stone,* 3 December 1987, 77–79.

24 Loder, "Bruce Springsteen," 70.

25 For an illuminating discussion about sexual difference, see Janice Doane and Devon Hodges, *Nostalgia and Sexual Difference: The Resistance to Contemporary Feminism* (New York, 1987), 3–14ff. Doane and Hodges's attentions are focused on differences between male and female, but many of their insights enrich analysis when transposed to discuss the uses of ideologies of difference to evaluate heterosexual and homosexual desires. Also, for a discussion of problematic uses of the terms "power," "desire," and "difference" in feminist theorizing, see Judith Kegan Gardiner, "Power, Desire, and Difference: Comment on Essays from the *Signs* Special Issue on Feminist Theory," *Signs* 8 (Summer 1983): 733–37.

26 See Senator Jesse Helms's amendment to the *Fiscal Year 1990 Interior and Related Agencies Appropriations Bill, H.R. 2788.* In an astounding denial of its own intolerant agenda, specifications 2 and 3 proceed, by association, to parallel homoeroticism with various bigotries (denigration of adherents of a particular religion or nonreligion and denigration of a group or class of citizens on the basis of race, creed, sex, handicap, age, or national origin). For a similar argument exposing the ideological oversimplifications of this amendment, see Catharine R. Stimpson, "President's Column," *MLA Newsletter* 22 (Summer 1990): 3; and Judith Butler, "The Force of Fantasy: Feminism, Mapplethorpe, and Discursive Excess," *differences* 2 (1990). Butler concludes: "In my view, it is in the very proliferation and deregulation of such representations [of categories of women and homosexuality]— in the production of a chaotic multiplicity of representations—that the authority and prevalence of the reductive and violent imagery produced by Jesse Helms and other pornographic industries will lose their monopoly on the ontological indicator, the power to define and restrict the terms of political identity" (121).

27 I have neither the time nor space to cite all the literary examples of homoeroticism (some of Shakespeare's sonnets [e.g., Sonnet 33], Huck and Jim, the *Pequod*'s crew) and sadomasochism (the death of Marlowe's Edward II and the tyranny of Captain Ahab, as well as, if we also refer to psychological brutality, Gilbert

Osmond) that would be excluded by this amendment.

28 Heather Findlay, "Is There a Lesbian in this Text? Derrida, Wittig, and the Politics of the Three Women," in *Coming to Terms: Feminism, Theory, Politics,* ed. Elizabeth Weed (New York, 1989), 59–69.

29 Marsh, *Glory Days,* 257; and Loder, "Bruce Springsteen," 21.

30 Doane and Hodges, *Nostalgia and Sexual Difference,* 3, 12.

31 Sedgwick, "Across Gender, Across Sexuality," 56. Sedgwick's point may be true for most people, but cases like that of Maria Jose Martinez Patino call even such an apparently unassailable generalization into question; the hurdler was disqualified from competing with women because she "failed" her sex chromosome test. See "When Is a Woman Not a Woman?" *Women's Sport and Fitness* 13 (March 1991): 24–29.

32 Marsh, *Glory Days,* 149.

33 Anthony DeCurtis, "Springsteen Returns," *Rolling Stone,* 10 January 1991, 15.

34 Dollimore, "Cultural Politics," 10, 12. For elaboration of a "lesbian continuum," see Adrienne Rich, "Compulsory Heterosexuality and Lesbian Existence," in *Women: Sex and Sexuality,* ed. Catharine R. Stimpson and Ethel Spector Person (Chicago, 1980), 62–91. Three other theorists have contributed significantly to my thinking about theorizing sexuality: see Michel Foucault, *The History of Sexuality,* trans. Robert Hurley (New York, 1978); for a discussion of the "proliferation of lesbian sexualities/ethnicities," see Katie King, "Producing Sex, Theory and Culture: Gay/ Straight Remappings in Contemporary Feminism," in *Conflicts in Feminism,* ed. Marianne Hirsch and Evelyn Fox Keller (New York, 1990); and, for a perspicacious discussion of "minoritizing" and "universalizing" definitions of homosexuality, see Eve Kosofsky Sedgwick, *Epistemology of the Closet* (Berkeley, 1990), esp. "Introduction: Axiomatic" and "Epistemology of the Closet."

35 DeCurtis, "Springsteen Returns," 16–17.

36 Dollimore, "Cultural Politics," 15; and Marsh, *Glory Days,* 231.

37 See Hans Robert Jauss, *Question and Answer: Forms of Dialogic Understanding,* ed. and trans. Michael Hays (Minneapolis, 1989), 197–231, for extended analysis of horizons of expectations and reception of ideas.

Alan Light

About a Salary or Reality?—Rap's Recurrent Conflict

In 1990, rap dominated headlines and the pop charts as never before. Large segments of the American public were introduced to rap—or at least forced to confront its existence for the first time—through a pack of unlikely and sometimes unseemly performers. The year started with the January release of Public Enemy's single "Welcome to the Terrordome," which prompted widespread accusations (in the wake of remarks made by Professor Griff, the group's "Minister of Information," that Jews are responsible for "the majority of wickedness that goes on across the globe") that rap's most politically outspoken and widely respected group was anti-Semitic. The obscenity arrest of 2 Live Crew in June filled news, talk shows, and editorial pages for weeks. The concurrent rise of graphic, violent "Gangster Rap" from such artists as Ice Cube and the Geto Boys stoked these fires, even if their brutal streetscapes often made for complex, visceral, and challenging records.

It's easy to vilify any or all of these artists.

Newsweek lumped several of them together and ran a cover story (19 March 1990) entitled "Rap Rage," which proved to be a savage attack on the form (including, by some curious extension, the heavy-metal band Guns n' Roses) as "ugly macho boasting and joking about anyone who hangs out on a different block," and as having taken "sex out of teenage culture, substituting brutal fantasies of penetration and destruction." Certainly, Luther Campbell and 2 Live Crew aren't exactly the First Amendment martyrs of the ACLU's dreams; their music consists of junior high-school locker-room fantasies set to monotonous, mighty uninspired beats. The "horror rap" of the Geto Boys is deliberately shocking, and songs such as "Mind of a Lunatic," in which the narrator slashes a woman's throat and has sex with her corpse, raise issues that are a long way from the Crew's doo-doo jokes. Public Enemy, for all of its musical innovation and political insight, has an uncanny knack for talking its way deeper into trouble, and leader Chuck D.'s incomprehensible waffling during the Griff incident, first dismissing Griff, then breaking up the group, then reforming and announcing a "boycott of the music industry," was maddening and painful to watch.

But there was also a different side to the rap story that was at least as prominent in 1990. M. C. Hammer's harmless dance-pop *Please Hammer Don't Hurt 'Em* became the year's best-selling album and rap's biggest hit ever. It was finally displaced from the top of the charts by white superhunk Vanilla Ice's *To the Extreme*, which sold five million copies in twelve weeks, making it the fastest-moving record in any style in five years.

Hammer has been defended by the likes of Chuck D. for being rap's first real performer, a dancer/showman/business tycoon of the first order, but his simplistic regurgitation of hooks from familiar hits quickly wears thin. Vanilla Ice not only lacks Hammer's passable delivery, he also manufactured a none-too-convincing false autobiography to validate his appropriation of black culture and subsequent unprecedented commercial success. Both are given to a self-aggrandizement so far beyond their talents that the biggest problem is simply how annoying they are.

There's nothing criminal about bad music or even simple-mindedness. And it's nothing new for the most one-dimensional, reductive purveyors of a style to be the ones who cash in commercially. But the most unfortunate result of the year of Hammer, Ice, and the Crew is that it may have determined a perception of rap for the majority of America. Any definitions of rap formed by the millions of Americans introduced to it in the last year would probably (and, sad to say, reasonably) center on a simplified analysis of the genre's basest cultural and sociological components and the most uninspired uses of its musical innovation.

If, in 1990, people new to rap gave it any thought at all, they would have concentrated on the crudeness of 2 Live Crew—who may have a constitutional right to be nasty, but there is no way around the ugliness of their lyrics. Newcomers might (understandably, given much of the mainstream press coverage) have dismissed Public Enemy, self-styled "prophets of rage," as mere traffickers in hate. Whatever one thinks of the controversial sampling process, in which pieces of existing records are isolated and digitally stored and then reconstructed as a kind of montage to form a new musical track, the derivative, obvious samples of Hammer and Ice represented the triumph of the technology at its worst. And rap diehards and novices all had to contend with the cheers of "go, white boy, go" as Vanilla Ice became the biggest star yet to emerge from this black-created style.

This has made for a lot of sociocultural analysis and interpretation, which is perfectly appropriate; rap is unarguably the most culturally significant style in pop, the genre that speaks most directly to and for its audience, full of complications, contradictions, and confusion. But what gets lost in this discussion, tragically, is that rap is also the single most creative, revolutionary approach to music and to music making that this generation has constructed.

The distance between M. C. Hammer and the Geto Boys seems to be the final flowering of a contradiction built into rap from its very beginning. Though the polarity may seem inexplicable—is it progress now that we hear not just "how can both be called music?" but "how can both be called rap?"—it is actually a fairly inevitable progression that has been building for years. We can be sure that rap artists are more aware than anyone of the current condition; a press release touting the new group Downtown Science quotes rapper Bosco Money's definitive statement of purpose for 1990: "Our crusade is to fuse street credibility with a song that's accessible to the mainstream."

Rap, however, has seen problematic moments before, times when people were sure it was dead or played out or irrelevant. It has, with relatively alarming frequency for such a young art form, repeatedly found itself at seemingly impassable stylistic crossroads. Off and on for years, it has been torn between the apparently irreconcilable agendas inherent in such a radical pop creation. Throughout the decade of its recorded existence, though, rap has always emerged stronger due to its openness to musical and technological innovation and diversification.

We should not forget that 1990 was also the year that the bicoastal post-Parliament-Funkadelic loonies in Digital Underground had a Top 10 hit with "The Humpty Dance," and Oakland's gratuitously nasty Too Short released his second gold-selling album. L. L. Cool J was booed at a Harlem rally for not being political enough, but then recorded an "old-school" style album that reestablished him as a vital street force. It was a year when Public Enemy, so recently a strictly underground phenomenon, shipped over a million copies of the *Fear of a Black Planet* album; a year when the Gangster scene redefined "graphic" and Hammer and Ice redefined "crossover." It was a year when there could be no more arguing that rap sounded like any one thing, or even any two things. Despite the increasing perception among insiders that rap is a sellout or, to outsiders, that it's just a cheap, vulgar style, it is this expansion and flexibility that is the real story of rap's decade on record.

Five years before Vanilla Ice, rap had made its initial breakthrough into mainstream culture, but it looked like it had gone as far as it was going to go. Rap records had managed to cross over to the pop charts as novelty hits on occasion, beginning in 1980 with the startling Top 40 success of the Sugarhill Gang's "Rapper's Delight." By 1985, hiphop culture, rap, graffiti, and especially breakdancing were receiving widespread popular attention; after a brief breakdancing sequence drew notice in the movie *Flashdance*, other movies like *Breakin'* and *Beat Street* quickly followed, and breakdancing became a staple in young American culture, turning up everywhere from TV commercials to bar mitzvah parties. The soundtrack to all this head spinning and 7-Up drinking was an electrosynthesized hip-hop, with lots of outer space imagery, sounds and styles borrowed from the year's other rage, video games, and featuring a burbling, steady electronic pulse (Jonzun Crew's "Pack Jam" is the most obvious example, but the style's real masterworks were Afrika Bambaataa and Soulsonic Force's "Planet Rock" or "Looking for the Perfect Beat"). Maybe it was the rapidity of its appropriation by Hollywood and Madison Avenue, maybe it was just too obviously contrived to last, but the break-dancing sound and look quickly fell into self-parody—much of it was dated by the time it even got released.

There was, at the same time, another strain of rap that wasn't quite as widely disseminated as the break-beat sound but would prove to have a more lasting impact. Grandmaster Flash and the Furious Five's 1982 hit "The Message" offered a depiction of ghetto life so compelling and a hook so undeniable ("Don't push me / 'Cause I'm close to the edge") that it became a pop hit in spite of the fact that it was the hardest-hitting rap that had ever been recorded. (Harry Allen, Public Enemy's "media assassin," recently offered an alternate view when he wrote that the song was the "type of record white people would appreciate because of its picturesque rendition of the ghetto.") In its wake, "socially conscious" rap became the rage. Plenty of junk, including Flash's top rapper Melle Mel's follow-ups "New York, New York" (which was listenable if awfully familiar) and "Survival" (which was just overblown overkill), was released in attempts to cash in on this relevance chic, but the most important and influential rappers to date were also a product of "The Message." Run-D.M.C.'s first album came out in 1984.

With its stripped-to-the-bone sound, crunching beats, and such accessible but street-smart narratives as "Hard Times" and "It's Like That," in addition to more conventional rap boasting, the album *Run-D.M.C.* was the real breakthrough of the underground. One irony was that the three members of the group came from black middle-class homes in Hollis, Queens, and their "B-Boy" gangster wear was just as much a costume as the cowboy hats and space suits of Grandmaster Flash or Afrika Bambaataa. "With Run-D.M.C. and the suburban rap school," says producer and co-founder of Def Jam Records Rick Rubin, "we looked at that [ghetto] life like a cowboy movie. To us, it was like Clint Eastwood. We could talk about those things because they weren't that close to home." This "inside" look at the street, though, was enough to impress an unprecedented, widespread white audience when combined with Run and D.M.C.'s rapid-fire, dynamic delivery. To the street kids, the group's sound was loud and abrasive—and therefore exciting and identifiable. "It wasn't a hard record to sell to the kids on the street," says Def Jam's president (and Run's brother) Russell Simmons. "But it was a hard record to sell to a producer or the rest of the industry. There was no standard to compare it to."

Run-D.M.C. was the first great rap album. Even as David Toop was writing in *The Rap Attack* (now out of print, Toop's book is one of very few decent extended writings on hip-hop) that "rap is music for 12-inch singles," *Run-D.M.C.*'s release demonstrated that the form could be sustained for longer than six or seven minutes. The next year, though, as breakdance fever continued to sweep the nation, the group released *King of Rock*. It sold over a million copies, but the group sounded tired. The title song and its video were funny, crunching classics, but the in-your-face rhymes and jagged scratching style seemed stale. The tracks which experimented with a rap-reggae mix were flat and unconvincing. And though seventeen-year-old hotshot L. L. Cool J was the first and best rapper to pick up on the Run-D.M.C. style in his spectacular debut *Radio*, he was obviously second-generation, not an innovator. It was 1985, rap had been split down the middle into two camps, and it was becoming harder to care about either one.

What has sustained rap for its (ten-year? fifteen? decades-old? the argument continues . . .) history is its ability to rise to the challenge of its limitations. Just at the points at which the form has seemed doomed or at a dead end, something or someone has appeared to give it a new direction. If 1985 was hip-hop's most desperate hour (the rap magazine *The Source* recently referred to this era as "The Hip-Hop Drought"), in 1986 it rose triumphant from the ashes. Run-D.M.C. was at the forefront of this renaissance, but it was the group's producer, Rick Rubin, who inspired it. He thought that a cover, a remake of a familiar song, would be a way to make the group's new

album a "more progressive" record. "I went through my record collection," Rubin recalls, "and came up with [Aerosmith's] 'Walk This
Way,' which really excited me because the way the vocals worked it
was already pretty much a rap song. It would be cool to have a high-
profile rap group doing a traditional rock & roll song and really not
having to change that much."

Rubin brought Aerosmith's lead singer Steven Tyler and guitarist
Joe Perry into the studio with Run-D.M.C. and the resultant "Walk
This Way" collaboration made rap palatable to white, suburban youth
across the country. It reached Number 4 on the pop singles charts
and catapulted the *Raising Hell* album to multimillion selling heights.
The recent massive successes of Michael Jackson and Prince had been
exceptional crossover developments, opening up MTV to black artists
and reintroducing these artists to pop radio. "Walk This Way" drove
those opportunities home, and it did so without compromising what
made rap so special, so vibrant; the beats and aggressive, declama-
tory vocals made it an undeniable rap record, heavy-metal guitars
or no.

Rap was established as a viable pop form, at least as long as its
connections to the traditional rock & roll spirit were made explicit.
Nowhere was that connection more obvious than with the next major
development in hip-hop. Hot on the heels of *Raising Hell* came the
Beastie Boys' *Licensed to Ill*, at the time the biggest-selling debut
album in history. The Beasties were three white Jewish New Yorkers
who had played together in a punk-hardcore band before discovering
rap and hooking up with Rick Rubin. For them, rap wasn't a way to
establish racial pride or document hard times: it was a last vestige of
rock & roll rebellion, a vaguely threatening, deliberately antagonistic
use for their bratty, whiny voices.

Licensed to Ill sometimes rang hollow when the Beastie Boys
rhymed about a criminal, decadent life beyond the fantasies of their
listeners, but when it worked—as in their breakthrough hit "Fight
for Your Right [to Party]"—you could hear young America laughing
and screaming along. Their rhymes were simple and unsophisticated
compared to those of Run or L. L. Cool J, but that made it easier for
their audience of rap novices to follow. Besides, technical prowess
wasn't what their yelling and carousing was about.

The strongest legacy of the album, however, was purely technical. *Licensed to Ill* introduced a newly expanded rap public to the concept of sampling. Until this time, rappers were backed up by DJs who would spin records, cross-cutting between favorite beats on multiple turntables, scratching and cutting up breaks from other songs as a musical track by manually manipulating the records under the needle (the definitive scratch record was Grandmaster Flash's cataclysmic "Grandmaster Flash on the Wheels of Steel"). The advent of the digital sampler meant that a machine could isolate more precise snippets of a recording and loop or stitch them into a denser, more active backdrop. One drumbeat or a particularly funky James Brown exclamation could form the backbone of an entire track, or could just drift in for a split second and flesh out a track.

The Beasties were the perfect group to exploit this technology, because the musical accompaniment they sought was the sound they and Rubin had grown up with, heavy on Led Zeppelin riffs and TV show themes, and packed with in-jokes and fleeting goofy references. Along with a handful of dance singles, most notably "Pump Up the Volume" by a British production duo called M/A/R/R/S, the Beasties made this bottomless, careening flow of juxtaposed sound familiar to the world. After "Walk This Way" made suburban America a little more open to the idea of rap, the Beasties, with the novelty of their personalities, attitude, and sound (and, of course, their color), won huge battalions of teenagers over to the form. But just as significantly, they rewrote the rules regarding who could make this music and what, if anything, it was supposed to sound like.

———

Surprisingly, in the wake of the Beastie Boys, there was not a massive, immediate explosion of white rappers. In fact, within the rap community the Beasties were cause for backlash more than celebration, and the next critical development was a move toward music "blacker" than anything ever recorded. Public Enemy emerged out of the hip-hop scene at Long Island's Adelphi University, encouraged by, once again, Rick Rubin. Their first album, 1987's *Yo, Bum Rush the Show*, didn't have the militant polemics that would characterize their later, more celebrated work, but it did have a sound and attitude as new to the listening public as the Beasties or Run or Flash had been. "When we came into the game, musicians said we're not making music, we're making noise," said producer Hank Shocklee, "so I said, 'Noise? You wanna hear noise?' I wanted to go out to be music's worst nightmare." With such open defiance, Public Enemy sculpted jarring, screeching musical tracks and wrote of the hostility they felt from and toward the white community. Public Enemy was offering an extension of rap's familiar outlaw pose, but they grounded it in the realities of contemporary urban life, with a sharp eye for detail and a brilliant sonic counterpoint that raised rap to a new level of sophistication.

If rap had crossed over, however tentatively, Public Enemy was not going to allow anyone to forget that this music came from the streets and that no rappers should feel any responsibility to take it away from there. Having found a pop audience and the kind of mass acceptance any pop form strives for from its inception, rap was now faced with the challenge of retaining its rebel stance and street-reality power. Public Enemy went on the road, opened for label-mates the Beastie Boys, and featured an onstage security force dressed in camouflage and bearing replicas of Uzis. They intimidated the young Beasties crowd and didn't really catch on with rap devotees until "Rebel without a Pause" exploded in urban black communities months later.

Rappers could now sell a million records without ever being picked up by pop radio or crossing over, and the artists were becoming aware of the kind of power that such independence meant. "Rap is black America's CNN," said Chuck D., and he would go on to claim that Public Enemy's goal was to inspire five thousand potential young leaders in the black community. This mindset ran through the work of Boogie Down Productions, who came out as hard-core gangster types (championing the honor of the Bronx in hip-hop's ongoing borough supremacy battles), but soon brought rapper KRS-One's intelligence and social concern up front in raps like "Stop the Violence." The Public Enemy mindset was there in the menacing, slow-flowing style of Eric B. & Rakim, who made the sampling of James Brown rhythm tracks and breaks the single most dominant sound in hip-hop. It was there even in the less revolutionary work of EPMD (the name stands for Erick and Parrish Making Dollars), hardly oppositional in their priorities, but uncompromisingly funky above all else.

It was an attitude that reached its fruition in 1988 when Public Enemy released *It Takes a Nation of Millions to Hold Us Back*, rap's most radical extended statement and still the finest album in the genre's history. Chuck D. castigated radio stations both black and white, fantasized about leading prison breaks, eulogized the Black Panthers, and thunderously expanded rap's range to anything and everything that crossed his mind. Shocklee and Company's tracks were merciless, annoying, and sinuous, using samples not for melodic hooks or one-dimensional rhythm tracks but as constantly shifting components in an impenetrably thick, dense collage. *It Takes a Nation* exploded onto city streets, college campuses, and booming car systems; it was simply inescapable for the entire summer. Jim Macnie wrote in the *Village Voice* that "it seemed that no one ever put in the cassette, no one ever turned it over, it was just on."

After that album, politics and outspokenness were de rigueur, simple boasting way out of style. Public Enemy's sound couldn't be copied—it still hasn't been rivaled—but that screech, once so foreign and aggressive, was soon filling dance floors in hits like Rob Base and D.J. E-Z Rock's propulsive smash "It Takes Two." Public Enemy had thrown down the gauntlet, as much musical and technological as lyrical and political, and they could just wait and see when and how the hip-hop community would respond.

Public Enemy's artistic and commercial triumph crystallized two lessons that had been developing in hip-hop for some time. Number one: anything was now fair game for rap's subject matter. Number two: a rap album could sell a lot of copies without rock guitars. Rap had, after struggling with its built-in contradictions for several years, established its long-term presence as a pop style without being required to compromise anything. Terms like "underground" and "street" and "crossover" were becoming less clear as records that would never be allowed on pop radio were turning up regularly on the pop sales charts. It didn't take long for these successes sans radio and the expansion of rap's subject matter to sink in and to set in motion the forces that put rap in the unsettled, divided condition it faces today.

The most visible immediate result was geographic. Virtually all of the rappers mentioned thus far have been residents of New York City or its environs. In 1988, galvanized by Public Enemy's triumphs, the rest of the country began to compete. Most significantly, five young men from the Los Angeles district of Compton joined together and recorded their first single, "Dope Man," which may or may not have been financed by their founder Eazy-E's drug sales profits. This group called themselves Niggas With Attitude (N.W.A), and demonstrated that the West Coast was in the rap game for real. Their only real precursor in Los Angeles was Ice-T, the self-proclaimed inventor of "crime rhyme" whose sharp, literate depictions of gang life were inspired by ghetto novelist Iceberg Slim. N.W.A took Ice-T's direct, balanced, and morally ambiguous war reporting to the next level with brutal, cinematically clear tales of fury and violence. The titles said it all: "Gangsta Gangsta" or even, in a gesture truly unprecedented for a record on the pop charts "[Fuck] tha Police."

Rap's single biggest pop hit in 1988 didn't come from New York or Los Angeles, however, but out of Philadelphia. DJ Jazzy Jeff and the Fresh Prince released a pleasant trifle chronicling teen suburban crises called "Parents Just Don't Understand," which hovered near the top of the pop charts all summer (Fresh Prince went on to become the first rapper to star in a prime-time sitcom). *Yo! MTV Raps* debuted on the music-video network and not only gave hip-hop a national outlet, but quickly became the channel's highest-rated show. Miami's 2 Live Crew released *Move Somethin'*, which went platinum long before they became hip-hop's most famous free-speech crusaders, and cities such as Houston and Seattle were establishing active rap scenes.

A dichotomy was firmly in place—rappers knew that they could cross over to the pop charts with minimal effort, which made many feel an obligation to be more graphic, attempt to prove their commitment to rap's street heritage. As with the division first evident in 1985, rap had split into two camps with little common ground, and the polarization again led to a period of stagnation. N.W.A's *Straight Outta Compton* simply defined a new subgenre—hard-core, gangster rap—so precisely that those who followed in their path sounded like warmed-over imitators. On the other side, like the breakdance electro-rap before it, poppy MTV-friendly hip-hop quickly grew stale. L.A.'s Tone-Lōc, possessor of the smoothest, most laid-back drawl in rap history, released "Wild Thing," the second best-selling single in history (right behind "We Are the World"), but it didn't feel like a revolution anymore.

━━━━

Into the abyss in early 1989 jumped De La Soul, heralding the "DAISY Age" (stands for "da inner sound, y'all," and hippie comparisons only made them mad) and sampling Steely Dan, Johnny Cash, and French language instruction records on their debut album *3 Feet High and Rising*. After two full years of James Brown samples, with the occasional Parliament-Funkadelic break thrown in, it took De La Soul to remind everyone that sampling didn't have to mean just a simpler way to mix and cut records. It was a more radical structural development than that—sampling meant that rap could sound like anything. Michael Azerrad wrote in *Rolling Stone* that many saw the group as "the savior of a rap scene in danger of descending into self-parody." It's an unnecessarily sweeping statement—there were still first-rate hip-hop albums being released—but De La Soul did quickly and assuredly reenergize the form. It was the group's peculiar vision, their quirky intelligence and, just as significantly, their awareness of the true possibilities of sampling technology that made possible such a leap forward.

In De La Soul's wake came a new look (colorful prints, baggy jeans, Africa medallions) and music from De La Soul's cohorts in the Native Tongues movement, including the Jungle Brothers and A Tribe Called Quest. The sound was varied, funny, and gentle, and the "Afrocentric" emphasis of the rhymes was warm, ecologically and socially concerned, and not too preachy. Soon there was also a whole new audience; De La Soul acquired a large collegiate following, drawn to their looser grooves, accessible hooks, and appealing goofiness. This was rap that was nonthreatening, politically correct, and didn't have the tainted feel of a crossover ploy.

In addition, De La Soul helped introduce Queen Latifah and Monie Love to the public, and thus proved instrumental in the emergence of a new generation of women rappers in 1989. Women had been part of rap from the beginning; the three women in Sequence comprised one of the first rap groups to sign a recording contract, and Salt-n-Pepa had several major hits, including "Push It," one of 1988's biggest dance hits. Latifah, however, was something new. In the face of ever-increasing graphic misogyny, she (and MC Lyte, Monie, and then in 1990 Yo-Yo and numerous others) offered a strong female alternative. For all of the attention given to 2 Live Crew or N.W.A's "A Bitch Iz a Bitch," rap was allowing a voice for women that was far more outspoken, far more progressive than anything found in other styles of pop music.

Ultimately, this new strain of headier hip-hop offered some kind of uncompromised middle ground between rap's pop and gangster sides, but it didn't slow down their ever-widening divergence. This "new school" became its own movement, while the two camps were far too entrenched to adapt the lessons of the DAISY age to their music. Los Angeles continued to dominate the East Coast in producing new sounds and styles. Young M. C., a University of Southern California economics major who had helped write Tone-Lōc's hits, recorded his own raps that featured even more danceable grooves and middle-class lyric concerns, and became a star on his own. The members of N.W.A, meanwhile, took to the road with the threat of arrest hanging over their heads if they chose to perform "[Fuck] tha Police," and by the end of 1989 had received an ominous "warning letter" from the FBI. After a decade on record, the biggest challenge hip-hop faced was not survival, but avoiding overexposure and irreparable co-optation.

Hip-hop is first and foremost a pop form, seeking to make people dance and laugh and think, to make them listen and feel, and to sell records by doing so. From its early days, even before it became a recorded commodity, it was successful at these things—Russell Simmons recalls promoting rap parties with DJ Hollywood and drawing thousands of devoted New Yorkers years before rap made it to vinyl. "It's not about a salary / It's all about reality," rap N.W.A; even if they didn't claim that life "ain't nothing but bitches and money" on the same album, the fallacy would be clear. On a recent PBS rap special, San Francisco rapper Paris said that "[e]verybody gets into rap just to get the dollars or to get the fame."

At the same time, rap by definition has a political content; even when not explicitly issues-oriented, rap is about giving voice to a black community otherwise underrepresented, if not silent, in the mass media. It has always been and remains (despite the curse of pop potential) directly connected to the streets from which it came. It is still a basic assumption among the hip-hop community that rap speaks to real people in a real language about real things. As *Newsweek* and the 2 Live Crew arrest prove, rap still has the ability to provoke and infuriate. If there is an up side to this hostile response, it is that it verifies rap's credibility for the insider audience. If it's ultimately about a salary, it's still about reality as well. Asked why hip-hop continues to thrive, Run-D.M.C.'s DJ Jam Master Jay replied, "because for all those other musics you had to change or put on something to get into them. You don't have to do that for hip-hop."

At a certain level, these differences are irreconcilable. Since Run-D.M.C. and the Beastie Boys established rap's crossover potential, and Public Enemy demonstrated that pop sales didn't have to result from concessions to more conventional pop structures, the two strains have been forced to move further apart and to work, in many ways, at cross-purposes. It is a scenario familiar in the progression of rock & roll from renegade teen threat to TV commercial music. Perhaps more relevant, the situation is reminiscent of punk's inability to survive the trip from England, where it was a basic component of a radical life, to America, where it was the sound track to a fashionable life-style.

If this conflict is fundamental to all pop that is the product of youth culture, it is heightened immeasurably by rap's legitimately radical origins and intentions. But success with a wide, white audience need not be fatal to the genre. The rage directed by much of the rap community at Hammer and Vanilla Ice is ultimately unwarranted—if they make bad records, they're hardly the first, and if that's what hits, it's not going to take the more sophisticated listeners away.

Rap has thus far proven that it can retain a strong sense of where it comes from and how central those origins are to its purpose. If this has sometimes meant shock value for its own sake—which often seems the norm for recent Gangster records, such as N.W.A's *100 Miles and Runnin'*—and if that is as much a dead end as Hammer's boring pop, the legacy of De La Soul is that there are other ways to work out rap's possibilities. Some of the best new groups, such as Main Source and Gang Starr, may have disappeared by the time this article appears, but they have been integrating melody, live instruments, and samples from less familiar sources into their tracks, learning from De La Soul and Digital Underground and company that hip-hop has other roads still left untrodden.

The paradigmatic hip-hop figure of 1990 would have to be Ice Cube, formerly N.W.A's main lyricist. He recorded *AmeriKKKa's Most Wanted* with Public Enemy's production team, the first real collaboration between the two coasts, and it ruled the streets for most of the year. The album's layered, crunching, impossibly dense sound set a new standard for rap production, the progression we've been waiting for since *It Takes a Nation of Millions to Hold Us Back*. Ice Cube's technical verbal prowess is astonishing; his razor-sharp imagery is cut up into complicated internal rhymes, then bounced over and across the beat, fluid but never predictable, like a topflight bebop soloist.

The content, though, is somewhat more troublesome. When rhyming about the harsh realities of ghetto life, Ice Cube is profane, powerful, and insightful. When writing about women—make that bitches, since he uses that word a full sixty times on the album—things get more disturbing. He has defended "You Can't Fade Me," a first-person account of contemplating murderous revenge on a woman who falsely accuses him of fathering her expected child, by saying that he's just telling a story and illustrating that people really do think that way. It's a fair enough defense, but it's hard to believe that many listeners won't hear it as Ice Cube's own attitude. If part of rap's appeal is the "reality" of the rappers, their lack of constructed stage personae and distance from the audience, Ice Cube simply doesn't establish the constructedness sufficiently to make the song's "objective" narrative effective.

But here's the surprise. At a press conference late in 1990, Ice Cube said that "a lot of people took mixed messages from my album, so I'm just going to have to try to make my writing clearer in the future."

It's something rappers have always had a hard time doing—when a performance style is so rooted in boasting and competition, admitting that you might be wrong or even just imperfect is a risky matter. If Public Enemy had been willing to take such an attitude, of course, they could have handled the Griff affair much more gracefully. But if Ice Cube is sincere about improving his expression without compromising it (and his moving, somber antiviolence track "Dead Homiez" bodes well), he may have shown us the future. Like De La Soul's radical rewriting of sampling and hip-hop personae, gangster rap that moves beyond gore and shock is evidence that rap is not trapped in a dead-end dichotomy.

Writing about rap always has a certain dispatches-from-the-front-lines quality; sounds and styles change so fast that by the time any generalizations or predictions appear, they have often already been proven false. At any moment, a new rapper or a new attitude or a new technology may appear and the troubled times hip-hop faced in 1990 will be nothing but ancient history. This may be its first real struggle with middle age, but rap has never failed to reinvent itself whenever the need's been there.

Dan Rubey

Voguing at the Carnival: Desire and Pleasure on MTV

Music videos on television available in the seductive plenitude of MTV's 24-hour format have raised characteristic anxieties in parents and educators since the cable network's beginnings in 1981. Parents have feared that violent and sexual video images would stimulate dangerous behaviors in the teenage target audience, and that MTV's round-the-clock accessibility would place those images beyond parental control. But those fears have been addressed in audience response studies demonstrating that the level of violence in music videos is inversely related to appeal, and that while increased sexual imagery increases appeal, explicit sex decreases it.[1]

E. Ann Kaplan's *Rocking Around the Clock* (1987) voices more sophisticated anxieties drawn from a Frankfurt School analysis of mass media, Jean Baudrillard's theory of the televisual apparatus, Fredric Jameson's critique of postmodernism, and a Lacanian/feminist analysis of images of women in film. Kaplan argues that the cultural codes structuring MTV programming are symptomatic of

Reagan's America in its materialism, sexism, and racism, and that MTV reinforces those "codes" or "reading formations" in young viewers.[2]

The manipulations of advertising and the implantation of empty desire are the primary substance of MTV, Kaplan argues, because music videos are themselves ads for music products interspersed with ads for other products:

> . . . [I]n its overall, 24-hour flow, MTV functions like one continuous ad. . . . MTV, more than any other television, may be said to be *about* consumption. It evokes a kind of hypnotic trance in which the spectator is suspended in a state of unsatisfied desire but forever under the illusion of *imminent* satisfaction through some kind of purchase. This desire is displaced onto the record that will embody the star's magnetism and fascination.[3]

MTV's unending flow duplicates real life in its constant availability, giving the viewer less cause to resist ideological construction by the images. The TV spectator (as opposed to the film viewer) "is drawn into the TV world through the mechanism of consumption (i.e., constant unsatisfied desire, the constant hope of a forthcoming but never realized plenitude)." MTV's four-minute texts "maintain us in an excited state of expectation. . . . We are trapped by the constant hope that the next video will finally satisfy and, lured by the seductive promise of immediate plenitude, we keep endlessly consuming short texts."[4]

This endless flow of short unrelated texts is, for Kaplan, a perfect expression of postmodernism. The TV screen "replaces the cinema screen as the controlling cultural mode, setting up a new spectator-screen relationship." MTV in particular reproduces "a kind of decenteredness, often called 'postmodernist,' that increasingly reflects young people's condition in the advanced stage of highly developed, technological capitalism evident in America." It prepares spectators for and embodies "a postmodern consciousness." In that consciousness (following Baudrillard), fiction and reality coalesce into "simulacra," where the "celebration of the look—the surfaces, textures, the self-as-commodity—threatens to reduce everything to the image/representation/simulacrum." Distinctions between "subject" and "image" are blurred.[5]

Following Jameson's critique of postmodernism in his essay "Postmodernism and Consumer Society," Kaplan notes that postmodernist discourse collapses other differences and boundaries as well: the difference between high art and commercial art, the difference between past and present, the difference between signifier and signified.[6] For Jameson, the disappearance of a sense of history that characterizes the perpetual present of postmodernism is similar to the schizophrenic breakdown of language in which signifiers (words as material objects—sounds, written script) become detached from signifieds (their meanings), and function simply as images. In postmodernist discourse signifiers and signifieds can no longer be coherently organized into a comprehensive chain of meaning. It is no longer possible to speak from a particular point of view, to make distinctions, to articulate a cultural position critical of society. While modernism could criticize and oppose bourgeois society, it is not clear that postmodernism can do more than reproduce (and reinforce) consumer capitalism.

Kaplan's position is more hopeful than Jameson's. On the one hand, MTV's "management" cannot control everything: "[T]he short four-minute texts embedded within a continuous 24-hour flow leave gaps for some alternate positions," such as the U.S.A. for Africa and Bob Geldof's Live Aid events, or "videos with working-class settings and social commentary."[7] Even postmodernism's lack of respect for historical positioning and the distinctions between high art and popular culture may be liberating:

> Rock videos may be seen as revitalizing the dead images by juxtaposing and re-working them in new combinations that avoid the old polarities. This may be the only strategy available to young artists struggling to find their place in society and to create new images to represent the changed situation they find themselves in.[8]

This split between Kaplan's two contradictory positions toward TV is mirrored in current debates about TV's role in developing consciousness and information-processing skills. In the January 1991 *American Educator*, Jane Healy attacked "Sesame Street" (which uses many of the same visual techniques as music video) for its failure in helping children learn to read, making some of the same points that

Jameson made in his critique of the schizophrenic language of post-modernism and postmodern art.[9] According to Healy, "the habits of mind necessary for reading are exactly those that *Sesame Street* does *not* teach: language, active reflection, persistence, and internal control." Children may learn letters or even words from the show's fast-paced, dancing graphics, but they do not gain "metalinguistic awareness," the understanding that (among other things) "letters make up words and that written words must be linked together into meaningful sentences."[10] In Jameson's terms, the signifiers are detached from the signifieds and logical meanings cannot be produced. "One of the most serious charges leveled against television viewing," Healy says, "is that it robs children of the ability to make pictures in their own minds." Poor readers have trouble "projecting anything on their screens of imagination." Instead, TV projects its images onto *them*.[11]

But others feel that TV develops different cognitive skills. Robert Pittman, senior executive at Time/Warner Inc. and the man who made MTV operational in 1981, argued last year in an op-ed page article in the *New York Times* (24 January 1990) that generations "who grew up with TV communicate differently than previous generations." According to Pittman, "pre-TV adults are the 'one thing at a time' generation. They read a magazine article straight through from beginning to end; then they make a phone call or watch TV." TV babies, by contrast, process "information from different sources almost simultaneously. They really can do their homework, watch TV, talk on the phone and listen to the radio all at the same time. . . . And at the end of the evening, it all makes sense." TV babies perceive visual messages better: "They can 'read' a picture or understand body language at a glance."

Pittman describes himself as learning primarily from visual media. During the Vietnam War, TV generation Pittman watched the pictures on the TV newscasts while his radio generation parents listened to the commentary. "The video message conflicted with the narrative one. And so, when it came to an opinion about the war, I was in conflict with my parents." Toby Goldstein wrote in the April 1982 issue of *Creem* that Pittman "is a man who says he learns about the news from skimming headlines and is proud that his attention span is so brief as to render him incapable of reading a publication like *The New Yorker*."

In Pittman's view, "creators of media and advertising are learning to speak the language of this post-TV generation," but it is "far
more critical to us as a society that public service campaigns catch
on." Thus Nancy Reagan's anti-drug messages were ignored because
they were framed in the old style of communication. Pittman suggests that the new communication techniques be incorporated into
traditional classroom approaches. "Likewise, we need to get through
on discrimination, crime, AIDS and the environment. Talking about
solutions in a new language may be the ticket." Pittman was in a
position to implement his ideas on MTV. Anti-drug Nike commercials or spots like the "If You're Gonna Do This" video that promoted
condoms have benefited from Pittman's ideas, as have music videos
on social issues like Neneh Cherry's stunning AIDS video "I've Got
You under My Skin."[12]

Both of these positions see TV as a powerful cultural force that
shapes the consciousness of viewers. But is TV actually that powerful, monolithic, and conspiratorial? The effects of consumer capitalism are complex and not always ideologically consistent. TV is
primarily a commercial enterprise, but even "high" art has been commercial since the Renaissance.

Are viewers really hypnotized tabulae rasae, passively determined
subjects constructed by TV's postmodern discourse? If that were true,
all viewers should receive the video texts in a similar way. But a
recent study of reactions to Madonna's "Papa Don't Preach" found
several variables dependent on the viewer's race, sex, and feelings
toward the performer. White viewers saw the video as about teenage pregnancy, blacks saw it as about father-daughter relationships
and identified "baby" as the boyfriend.[13] These findings suggest that
music videos, because of their nature as a visual medium, inevitably
foreground issues of race and gender, which were invisible on radio.

When I began watching music videos systematically for this essay,
I wanted to watch around the clock for a day or so, to get "hypnotized," to be "lured by the seductive promise of immediate plenitude" into "endlessly consuming short texts." Unfortunately, I found
I couldn't watch for more than two-and-one-half hours before bore-
dom and information overload tossed me out of the loop. Watching
MTV turned out to be surprisingly similar to listening to rock radio
in the Long Island suburbs in the late 1950s, when rock & roll was

just breaking into white radio. Just like music videos, rock songs on the radio were ads, played to sell records and other products.

I listened frequently but in different circumstances—alone, with friends, at the beach, at parties, in the car—and with variable attention. We used the radio as texture, listening with one ear until something we particularly liked came on, and then turning up the volume. While there was general agreement about hits, everyone had somewhat different tastes, and there was a certain amount of self-definition and turf building attached to individual preferences. There were also a number of ways to position oneself as a consumer. Most of us bought singles: some bought only songs we'd heard several times; others bought everything in a category. Some were hip enough to buy records that became hits before they got much airplay. Some people bought albums. A legendary few actually went into "the City" for concerts at places like the Apollo.

After a while I watched MTV in the same way, paying different degrees of attention to different videos, liking some more and wanting to see them again, being bored by most others. All this may seem tediously obvious; I'm just mentioning it to counter the notion that viewers are "hypnotized" by the flow of texts. If anything, there is a constant process of sorting and evaluation at the preconscious level. UB 40's video "The Way You Do the Things You Do" (1990) suggests that modern teenagers use videos as background music in much the same way we used radio.

As I watched, I had to develop watching strategies. I was frustrated by glimpsing things that never appeared again. Rather than an uninterrupted flow of videos, MTV is structured like radio, with shows hosted by different Vee Jays with different play lists repeated in different time slots within the week. So beyond random viewing of MTV and alternative shows like *Video Soul*, *Reggae Videos*, or *Rap City* on other channels, I watched *Yo! MTV Raps* and the *Top 20 Video Countdown* because I could find them regularly.

I thought that the *Countdown* would show the most popular videos, but it wasn't that simple. Top 20 lists are compiled from national album sales, video airplay, MTV requests, and MTV research, building circularity and subjectivity into the process. Network research is based on phone interviews and can be only as good as the questions, interviewers, and sampling techniques.[14] Album sales don't mark the popularity of individual videos. Requests reflect fan-dom rather than video quality or even popularity. Video airplay simply reflects what MTV producers think viewers want to see, or what they want them to see to push sales. Still, the Top 20 lists give some idea of what viewers want to watch; apparently what most viewers wanted to watch at the turn of 1990 was heavy metal video.

But while the process of watching music videos resembles listening to radio, decoding the videos themselves is a more complex experience. Videos combine three overlapping elements: performance, with various modes adapted from stage shows and music performance films; narrative or "concept" drawn from traditional Hollywood cinema, documentaries, or TV shows but always highly abbreviated and stylized; and visual presentation drawn from advertising graphics, Hollywood musicals, and both traditional and experimental film.

The direct historical roots of music videos include Busby Berkeley films, jukeboxes with movie visuals, and Richard Lester's Beatles films.[15] The first videos were based primarily on performance; now narrative or "concept" videos predominate, but the two categories overlap. There tends to be a rough match between the performance/ narrative mix and visual style (camera work and editing), and the musical genre and stage image of the group or singer. Most video genres have an instantly recognizable look that invites or repels. Heavy metal videos use fairly simple camera and editing techniques, while "alternative" music videos use experimental techniques from German expressionist or French surrealist films.[16]

Second for second, visual images contain far more "information" than radio or the written word. Video images present information simultaneously in a number of different semiotic codes. Viewers decode (consciously and subconsciously) semiotic markers that include the music and its level of emotional arousal, song lyrics, the accompanying narrative (which may illustrate the lyrics or have little direct relationship), choreography and performance style, musical style and genre, costume and fashion, physical characteristics of the actor/performers (including body language and facial expressions), mise-en-scène (settings, musical equipment and props, color, screen graphics, sound), camera work (camera angles, shot ratios, camera movement), and editing techniques (fast cuts, superimpositions, dissolves, etc.).

What do viewers do with all this "information"? Charles Acland says the audiovisual bombardment of the fragmented, repetitious, rapid, disorienting videos "begs for hermeneutic organization, for a resolution of the disorder through interpretation." Spectators construct and elaborate their own narratives and fantasies around the suggestive shots, lyrics, and stylized fast-forward narratives of the videos, as Marsha Kinder has pointed out.[17] There is always the danger, as Kinder and Kaplan argue, that interpretation will be determined by the cultural logic of consumer capitalism and reinforce racism, sexism, and passivity.

On the other hand, as Acland suggests, precisely because of the overdetermined cacophony of information, there is always a wide range of "possible meanings available to a diverse and heterogeneous public." And the process of interpretation is not limited to the visual text. "The complete, or rather infinitely incomplete, popular music text," Acland says, "is comprised of any source of information or practice that the individual fan or group of fans can relate to the song, such as lyrics, style (dress, hair, dance), concerts, politics, other fans, etc." "In other words," Acland adds, "the individual is able to negotiate the limits of the texts by considering and interpreting certain elements and refusing others, either deliberately or due to unfamiliarity."[18]

Andrew Goodwin's critique of Kaplan's book points out that the images of pop star faces trigger meanings that are established beyond MTV, and that music videos can be read as documentaries about stars, either as people or pop personae. Individual videos always intersect with *macro-narratives* existing above and beyond any particular video or its individual narrative—other videos, live performances by the band, promotional campaigns, media articles, etc.[19]

Unpacking the various codes of music videos is complex because of their densely allusive construction. Character backgrounds and motivations that would require lengthy development in conventional Hollywood films are condensed into seconds in music videos, and recovery of the larger texts they allude to with this fast-forward narrative shorthand is problematic. But since videos move so quickly, they have to refer to iconic themes and images to avoid degeneration into random incoherence.

≡≡≡

Judging from the high number of heavy metal videos on the *Top 20 Video Countdown* and the call-in request show *Dial MTV*, heavy metal is the most popular music for MTV viewers. Heavy metal appeals primarily to the young white males of MTV's twelve-to-thirty-five-year-old target audience. But some bands also attract young women, and they have a complex image problem in making their music appeal to young men and yet not alienate female buyers. Warrant's lead singer said in a recent MTV interview that the band was concerned because the sound of its first record wasn't as "heavy" as the band's sound in concert, and that while they didn't want to "turn off" young women, they needed to make their second record's sound "heavier" to appeal to young men.

There's a great deal of macho posturing in MTV interviews, and the violent, sadistic imagery of many heavy metal videos—the leather, whips, chains, bare chests, and biker gear—is perhaps a defense against sexual ambiguity. The de rigueur long hair (often achieved with hair extensions) functions as a sign of androgyny. For some groups, like Nelson, the long straight blond hair seems particularly feminine. For others, like Motley Crüe, it functions as a phallic sign. In Motley Crüe's video "Without You," the lead singer evokes Sampson and his hair by pushing apart the pillars of the Philistine temple. Allusions to Delilah portray women as seductive and castrating. The most disturbingly sexist and sadomasochistic images of women have appeared in heavy metal videos. But the anger these images represent is also expressed toward male authority figures. As Kaplan puts it, the "men seem to be in an impossible Oedipal situation, caught between the seductive mother and the castrating father." [20]

Heavy metal videos seem endlessly to represent the male rite of passage from the Lacanian Imaginary, the lost world of plenitude and unity with the mother, to the Lacanian Symbolic, the world of language in which castration is institutionalized and gender is assigned—the world of the Law and the Name of the Father. That process of construction of the male subject has been seen by feminist theorists as the social process by which men inherit and replicate the structures of male power, structures that oppress women. Within the structure of the Lacanian schema and from the point of view of the male spectator, women in heavy metal videos tend to represent either the lost plenitude of the early childhood Imaginary, or the seductive, treacherous, threatening women of the Symbolic who function as signs of castration. But images of women are not essential in heavy metal videos, because the band itself fills the space left by that primal loss.

Nelson's "After the Rain," produced in 1990 and at the top of the charts in early 1991, provides a straightforward example of how music videos use psychological developmental conflicts to construct viewers as consumers. The video begins with a shot of an air-stream trailer set in a barren landscape in the middle of a thunderstorm; the trailer is a sign for the isolated claustrophobia of nuclear family life, and the weather mirrors the emotional storm inside. An unseen man yells, "It's time he grew up. . . . [Y]our son ain't nothing but a worthless dreamer . . . will never amount to anything." The mother, an absent presence, apparently tries to intercede, but is silenced.

The shot switches to a teenage boy wearing a headband and listening to the argument. He's crying, frustrated, and helpless. He lies down on the bed and puts on headphones; the camera pans over a Walkman and the cassette tape for this album (the product the video is selling). As he turns on the Walkman, a pulse of blue electricity runs along the wires into his ears. He turns toward a Nelson poster on the wall (another product); the Nelson twins reach out of the poster and pull him in; he tumbles through a vortex and finds himself in a womb-like cave, sitting between the Nelsons and across from an old Indian shaman.

The Indian shows the boy two floating globes concealed in his hand, one red, the other blue (the earth), and hands an eagle feather to the Nelsons, who disappear. The Indian leads the boy to a stairway, magically changes into traditional costume and face paint, holds an eagle feather out to the boy, and vanishes. The boy finds his way out of the cave (an initiatory rebirth motif) and discovers the band performing in a natural amphitheater, complete with light and smoke

effects. He joins the enthusiastic crowd, taking on their group identity and participating in the ecstatic ritual performance; the camera
cuts between the Nelsons on stage and the crowd.

The presence of the Indian as a guide calls up American heartland fantasies of spiritual unity with the land and a sense of shared
tribal identity, road warriors on motorcycles. The Indian is a spiritual guide who gives the boy access to a mystical vision—the band's
performance. The lyrics of "After the Rain" have nothing to do with
the video narrative, but certain lines provide a minimal linkage. The
words address someone suffering over a broken love affair. The singer
offers help ("Take my hand and I'll pull you through") and reassurance ("After the rain, you'll find true love again"). Words and music
strike an elegiac tone characteristic of heavy metal songs, leaving
details up to the listener.

The video, on the other hand, suggests a psychological narrative in
which the lost love is the absent mother, with the band functioning as
a transitional androgynous helper. The doubling of the Nelson twins
suggests the mythical hermaphrodite, both phallic and nurturing. As
the song ends, the crowd disappears, leaving the boy watching the
Nelsons. The scene shifts back to the trailer where the boy awakens.
The camera pulls back slowly to take in the boy's guitar (present in
the earlier shot of the room but not foregrounded), and the Nelson
poster. The boy picks up an eagle feather from the bedside table, a
sign of the dream vision's persistence in the real world. The image
freezes as the group's name, the name of the song, the album, and the
record producer reappear in the lower left-hand corner of the screen.

It would seem, then, that the function of the video is not simply to
supply illustrative images that someone listening to the lyrics might
have supplied. It is to create a different level of analysis and associations that create a psychological dynamic not available in the lyrics
alone, and to attach that dynamic to music products—the Walkman, the cassette, the poster, concerts, and the guitar. The presence
of the guitar suggests the boy can become a musician himself, like
the Nelsons. However unrealistic this may be, the video does provide
an image of the nurturing parenting unavailable within the prevailing sexual dynamic of powerful, abusive father and silent, castrated
mother.

This critique of family structure and abusive fathers occasionally becomes stylized political analysis. Poison's "Something to Believe In" begins with a shot of a man and boy standing behind a coffin in a stylized church setting, the man comforting the boy for what is apparently the death of his mother. The lyrics of the song are about loss and the pain of growing up and assuming responsibility: "Sometimes I wish to God I didn't know now the things I didn't know then."

The video moves back and forth between the singer and TV images of tarnished male leaders—Jim Bakker, Presidents Kennedy and Johnson in the context of the Vietnam War—while the lyrics describe a crippled Vietnam vet in a wheelchair inside some institution, crippled by "a time I don't remember and a war he can't forget." Lyrics and images switch to homelessness and class difference ("poor eating from hand to mouth, rich drinking from a golden cup"). An image of a poor woman and her children in the back of a truck recalls James Agee's Depression photographs. The video depicts a world of bankrupt male authority and asks for "something to believe in." But while the images make the critique emotionally powerful, the video never moves beyond elegiac lament for lost innocence. The final image is a silhouette of the singer with phallic guitar on a TV screen, the only icon available "to believe in."

As these videos suggest, "good" women function as silent absences or powerless victims in heavy metal videos. When they are shown as sexual and powerful, they call up the Oedipal narrative and become seductive betrayers. The Scorpions' "Tease Me, Please Me" loads class conflict onto Oedipal drama. A rich man (shades, suit and tie, greying temples) drives away from a palatial Beverly Hills house in a Mercedes as a truckload of young men drives up, and one young man in a tank top gets out with a tool box. As the young man works digging a post hole, he is watched from the balcony by the older man's wife, dressed in a negligee. They look at each other, but the point of her looking at him first seems to be to establish her as the initiator and relieve him of guilt, rather than to establish a female gaze.

She runs her hand up his bare chest, they make love in a series of soft-focus montages as the band sings "Tease me, please me, no one ever needs to know." The husband returns as the young man is leaving, and asks "Get any work done around here today, kid?" establishing himself as a condescending patriarchal oppressor. The youth smirks and says "Oh yeah!" In the final shot, the wife tells her husband that the "punk kid" (her husband's term) "worked very hard today, but he didn't quite finish. I'd like to have him back tomorrow."

In this Oedipal revolt, the youth/son and the wife/mother share insider language codes and turn them against the husband/father. The older man is successful and wealthy, but he is isolated and alone, laughed at and deceived behind his back, while the youth has his friends in the truck and the woman. But the picture of the woman is not much more positive than that of the man; she has no life of her own beyond lounging around the pool and amusing herself with yard-boys. It's a dismal picture of the suburban wasteland, where fathers go off to the real world of the city, leaving wives and children to harem intrigues in the sterile suburbs.

The anger at women as seducers and betrayers lurking below the surface of "Tease Me, Please Me" becomes overt in Damn Yankees' "High Enough." The video mixes a color performance sequence of the band singing separation anxiety lyrics ("don't say goodbye, say you're going to stay forever") with a framing black-and-white narrative of a robbery and police shootout. In the narrative, a young man robs a gas station and a liquor store, then jumps into a convertible driven by a beautiful gum-chewing blonde in a short dress. The blonde counts the money as he kisses her, suggesting she is the motive for the robberies, the lure that traps men into the world of money and law.

The police arrive as they make love in the convertible; he jumps over a fence, but she's caught. The scene shifts to a house where the man is trapped; as the band performs on the porch, the police shoot into the house, apparently killing the young man in the fusillade. The scene switches to the woman in a prison cell. A priest arrives to give her last rites; she is handcuffed and led out of the cell, apparently to be executed. In the final shot, the priest turns his head to reveal a ponytail and his identity as one of the band members; he smiles into the camera. The ambiguous ending leaves it up to the viewer to decide whether the band member is there to rescue the girl or gloat over her execution.

Heavy metal videos create a tribal identity for young white men caught psychologically in the throes of the Oedipal situation, and caught economically in the prolonged dependency of adolescents in modern American society, cut off from meaningful work or apprenticeship, without clear role models. These young men seem valuable only as consumers; they resist entry into a tarnished adult world but seem incapable of constructing any alternative beyond the androgynous fantasies of the bands. The inability (or unwillingness) of these videos to provide any positive images of adults functioning in the real world keep their political and social criticism trapped at the level of Oedipal revolt.

Much of this may reflect normal teenage angst, but there's also a sense that this is a difficult time for the construction of white male identity. If white male adulthood has become the category of oppressor, where are the possibilities for male relationships and solidarity other than solidarity as oppressor? The appropriation of magical tribal identities from a mythic past devoid of any historical or cultural context seems a desperate and doomed solution, even in fantasy.

=======

If heavy metal is the music of tribal identity for young whites, rap music serves a similar function for young blacks. The two musical, performance, and dress styles collide in Run-D.M.C.'s video "Walk This Way" (1986), one of the first rap videos to get heavy play on MTV. "Walk This Way" was a popular song recorded by the heavy metal band Aerosmith in the 1970s, and the collaboration of Aerosmith and Run-D.M.C. on this video was a successful attempt to introduce rap music to white audiences.

At the beginning of the video, Run-D.M.C. is performing for a black audience; the camera pulls back to show a wall, and the heavy metal group Aerosmith on the other side, pounding on the wall to complain about the music. Aerosmith's Steve Tyler breaks through the wall and sings the lyrics while Run-D.M.C. watches with arms folded in disgust. Then Run-D.M.C. breaks through into Aerosmith's space and sings to their white audience while Aerosmith watches in disgust. The musical competition is matched by a competition of style: Run-D.M.C. is dressed in minimal rapper style with black suits and hats; Aerosmith wears long colorful robes in heavy metal style. By the end of the video, Run-D.M.C. and Tyler are singing and dancing together arm-in-arm, a sign of the crossover of black rap music to white audiences, and of the roots of rock & roll in black music.

This crossover phenomenon was recognized on MTV with a special called *Rap Sunday* that aired on 6 August 1988, and was institution-alized soon after by the regular rap video show, *Yo! MTV Raps.*[21] In 1990, M. C. Hammer's rap/dance video "U Can't Touch This" was the most requested video on MTV's *Dial Up* and the best music video of the year on MTV's music video awards show. Hammer (Stanley Kirk Burrell) made it to the top of the charts by combining rap lyrics with flashy, energetic dance routines and fast, stylish editing technique. The video avoids both narrative and images of the group performing before an audience. Images of the dancers are edited in a style that draws on experimental film and images from previous videos. But the look also draws from art design and fashion graphics, interspers-ing images of a city school yard (in which Hammer functions as a teacher—"Ring the bell, school's back in") with neutral, graphically abstracted stage backgrounds featuring the dancers.

What "U" can't touch are the beautiful, energetic bodies of the black women dancers with their butts thrust out at the camera in fast cuts, and Hammer himself, whose success is displayed as a goad for the home boys and girls ("let 'em know that you're too much"), but also for anyone else willing to take Hammer as a model. Hammer's message (like many rap artists') is "I've made it big" ("I'm living large"), and in that context the staircase and tilted camera angle in many of the shots are visual signs of upward mobility.

Lacking any narrative thread, the dance "plot" of the video is the sexual dynamic established by cuts from lines of male dancers in baggy shirts and pants to lines of female dancers in lycra and spandex shorts and halter tops. The female dancers are sexy and attractive, but the energy and skill of their dancing combined with the athleti-cism and fleshy muscularity of their bodies presents them as women enjoying and displaying their own bodies, not passive objects of a victimizing male gaze. The video ends with Hammer dancing with a blonde above him on the staircase. She is the only white in the video; she doesn't appear in dance lines with the black women, and she seems to function as a densely loaded sign of upward mobility, female objectification, and interracial sex.

Hammer's success has drawn predictable condescension from black rivals and white critics who assume he is not sufficiently political or has sold out to achieve success. But that analysis may be inappropriate within contemporary social and economic realities. Kaplan pointed out in 1987 that MTV systematically excluded black music; the fact that this exclusion seems to have ended offers an interesting example of how consumer capitalism works. It would be naive to deny that media often function as instruments of sexist or racist ideologies held by people in power. But those positions can succeed within the consumer capitalist model only as long as they accurately reflect views held by members of the target audience. As those views shift, people in positions of authority face pressures to adapt or lose money—the ultimate bottom line. When the product starts losing money, the individuals in power become vulnerable.

Robert Pittman's career at MTV seems a good example. Pittman has gotten much of the credit for MTV's success, but he was primarily a producer and CEO; the conceptual architect of MTV was John Lack. Pittman seems to have been primarily responsible for marketing strategies, and one of those strategies was the exclusion of black music videos. According to interviews in *Rolling Stone*, Pittman's own taste in rock ran to modern pop groups like Talking Heads and the Pretenders, and away from heavy metal and black music.[22] Pittman claims that MTV's play list was based on a format that reflected what suburban American (white) youths wanted to see.

What they wanted, research showed, was "rock & roll," a category that, Pittman believed, excluded black groups. Black music belonged in the rhythm & blues category excluded by the format. This grotesque distortion of the history of rock & roll has been perpetuated by heavy metal figures who claim that only heavy metal or "hard" rock is "real" rock & roll, and that black music is "dance" music. David Bowie turned the tables on Vee-Jay Mark Goodman during an interview early in 1983 by asking why so few black artists were shown on MTV.[23]

If Steven Levy's analysis in *Rolling Stone* is correct, it was Michael Jackson's album *Thriller* (1983) and pressure from CBS Records to air the "Billie Jean" video that broke MTV's resistance to black groups. So the MTV "format" created in response to the apparently mistaken belief that white suburban audiences weren't interested in seeing black artists was broken by pressure from the music industry itself, both artists and producers, and ultimately by favorable audience response.

The popularity of *Thriller* videos "Billie Jean" and "Beat It" indicated that the market research had been wrong, or at least had been wrongly interpreted. MTV executives may not have been racists themselves, but their mistaken assumption that white Americans didn't want to see black artists denied those artists exposure in the same way that black music was banned from mainstream radio in the 1950s. The irony is that even though the consumer capitalist system is perfectly willing to sell anything that can be sold, it can't always avoid tripping over its ideology. We may be reaching a time when racism and sexism are no longer economically viable.

Given that context, it's important to be careful about writing off Hammer's achievements as blatant commercialism. Certainly Hammer is a master merchandiser, and his videos wouldn't have the same crossover popularity if they expressed anger at whites, or if they advocated violence. MTV management vetoed a video for *Yo! MTV Raps* by Los Angeles rappers N.W.A (Niggas With Attitude) because of the lyrics, "When I pulled out my sawed-off / Bodies got hauled off." [24]

Lines like "Now I just think that you can do whatever you want," or "But nothing happened until that day that I prayed," from Hammer's video "Pray (Jam the Hammer Mix)" may seem naive and even cynical in the face of the realities facing urban black children. But Hammer isn't ignoring racism; black viewers know who "We" and "these people" are in lines like "We got to pray just to make it today" and "I kept on knockin' but these people wouldn't let me in." Even if the virtues of self-confidence, hard work, and perseverance that Hammer preaches seem disturbingly middle class, at this point in history they look like more realistic models than revolution or reparation.

Hammer sells community to his youthful fans, but he's also used his success to build Bust It Productions, the record label and music factory he started in 1987 that employs nearly a hundred people and sponsors ten groups (according to *People* magazine).[25] All of this is paradoxical and difficult in terms of any conventional leftist political analysis. On the one hand, Hammer's videos play to the same kind of consumer desire for style and flash pushed by the commercials that accompany them on MTV, the vicious consumerism that leads black kids to shoot each other on the street for Nikes and shearling coats. On the other hand, Hammer's own display of success markers like designer suits and limousines makes him a believable role model, just as his energetically eccentric dancing style marks him as an individual talent.

It's a tricky game: reaching and teaching black youths is something both the rappers and the product sellers are trying to do. The message of the rappers, cloaked in matching costumes and rigidly identical, symmetrical dance choreography, is to be yourself, do your own thing, don't copy others. The message of the advertisers, cloaked in the language of freedom and individuality, is that you are identified by what you consume, not who you are.

MTV commercials try to win over kids by appealing to their natural antipathy to parents and teachers, those easily parodied authority figures who, among other things, tell kids that products and consumer goods aren't everything in life. Hammer seems to be trying to rehabilitate some of those male role models—teacher in "U Can't Touch This," preacher in "Pray"—in order to fill the void of sympathetic adult male role models in heavy metal videos, and in the lives of many inner-city black youths as well. It may be that in this historical period, such rehabilitation can be accomplished only by black or Hispanic men.

For related reasons, the church setting of "Pray" may function differently for black audiences than for white. For white teenagers, church and family tend to represent the seat of hypocritical male authority, as in the opening shots of Poison's "Something to Believe In" or Nelson's "After the Rain." But for blacks, family and church are potentially positive images (although not without their complexities), just as they have been for immigrant groups who came to this country more willingly. Historically, the church has been "a rallying point for resistance, a shelter from the storm of racial prejudice and repression, a safe harbor where black people could walk out re-

charged and girded for the battles they must wage in a hostile world,"
according to a recent *New York Times Magazine* piece on the Rev-
erend Calvin Butts of the Abyssinian Baptist Church in Harlem.[26]

"Pray" moves between shots inside the church (with Hammer as
preacher) and the mean ghetto streets where a young girl is gunned
down in a battle between black and Hispanic drug dealers: the video
juxtaposes what black people can do for themselves, and what they
are doing to each other. Certainly the killing is rooted in larger issues
like racism and colonial imperialism. But the point is, as one black
minister put it recently, there aren't any *white* pushers selling drugs
to black children in the projects. The violence against black youths
may be the product of a racist society and consumerist values, but
other black youths are pulling the triggers.

In contrast to heavy metal, Hammer's videos offer involvement in
music and dance, not just passive spectatorship. Young black males,
and black and white females, are more likely than white males to say
that they watch music videos to learn the latest dances and fashions.
Rap/dance videos are close to Mikhail Bakhtin's vision of carnival in
Rabelais and His World. Carnival is participatory, open to everyone;
it endorses freedom and equality, reversal of social hierarchy; it is
oriented to the future, not the past. The invitation in C&C Music
Factory's "Gonna Make You Sweat (Everybody Dance Now)," the
hottest video at the beginning of 1991, is to "Take a chance, come
on and dance," to "Let the music take control, let the rhythm move
you." Bakhtin's carnival is (in part) a return to the mother, to the
womb, to the realm of the Lacanian Imaginary.

But Hammer's desire to serve as a role model—and blacks are more
likely than whites to say they watch because they want to be like the
people in the videos[27]—probably inhibits any full-scale endorsement
of carnival in his videos. Because Hammer is interested in rehabilitat-
ing authority and role models rather than dissolving or overturning
them, he avoids embracing the grotesque, the raucous laughter and
abusive language of rap, the emphasis on lower bodily strata which is
part of the carnival spirit. Hammer's dancers are attractive and sexy,
but their dancing seems more energetic than erotic.

On the other hand, Digital Underground's "The Humpty Dance"
seems like a programmatic adaptation of Bakhtinian carnival's ele-

vation of the grotesque body over the classic, the ridiculous over the serious. The rapper in "Humpty Dance" wears a silly white fur hat with a tag hanging from it, a loud plaid jacket (ridiculing rap fashion), a big phallic false nose, and black Marx Brothers glasses. The lyrics begin, "I'm about to ruin the image and the style that you're used to, I look funny, but Yo! I'm making money." He's both funny ("I'm the new fool in town. . . . Sometimes I get ridiculous") *and* sexual ("My name is Humpty, Yo! ladies, Oh how I'd like to pump thee").

The acceptance of nonclassic body types and insistence on their sexuality is typical of rap, and of carnival: "Yeah, I called you fat, look at me, I'm skinny, but that never stopped me from getting busy." There is a carnivalesque linkage of food and innuendo—"I like my oatmeal lumpy." The lyrics play with profanity, with words bleeped out by the band—"Oh yes ladies, I'm really being sincere, because [bleep] my humpty nose will tickle your [bleep]." "Humpty Dance" calls up many of the darker sexual grotesqueries of rap groups like 2 Live Crew, but treats them with sophisticated humor and a sense of fun, playing with verbal transgressions rather than simply voicing them.

Digital Underground highlights its distance from M. C. Hammer and its exploration of areas of experience that Hammer avoids. Describing the Humpty Dance, the rapper says he was "shaking and twitching like I was smokin'. . . . [P]eople say you look like M. C. Hammer on crack, Humpty, that's alright because my body's in motion, it's supposed to look like a fit or a commotion." The allusion to crack is a flirtatious appropriation of the dangerous energies associated with the drug and a claim to underground knowledge, not an invitation to smoke crack (or a warning against it).

In contrast to the athletic, professional dancers and precise choreography in Hammer's videos, the Humpty Dance is loose and easy —"anyone can play this game." Throughout the video everyone is dancing, the rapper and members of the audience. The stage is low and close to the audience, not set up on a higher plane, as are heavy metal stages. At the end of the video, the invitation to "do the humpty hump" is addressed to everyone, to "black people . . . white people, Puerto Ricans, Samoans." Carnival is open to everyone willing to abandon pretension and rank, and join in.

Within the context of consumer capitalism, the music of M. C. Hammer and Digital Underground suggests black enterprise (or self-help philosophy) and utopianism, both of which have been viewed with suspicion by Marxist cultural critics. Jane Gaines argues that "Black capitalism's one big success [Motown Industries] thrives on the impossibility of Black enterprise: soul entertainment as compensation and release sells because capitalism cannot deliver well-being to all."[28] But no social or economic system can deliver well-being to all. Certainly capitalism has exacerbated and institutionalized racial tensions, and the vision offered on MTV of a society integrated through music is also a consumer utopia where everyone dances in designer clothes and buys products together.

But that vision has some attractive elements, not the least of which is an opportunity to see a wide range of black and white performers on something approaching their own terms. It may be that racism is perpetuated more by the personal prejudices of powerful individuals than by any inevitable mechanisms of capitalism. Because popular culture depends on the consumption of massive numbers of relatively inexpensive products like records, all consumers are created equal and the more consumers who have the money to buy, the better. As Gaines points out, "popular culture can accommodate the possibility of both containment and resistance," and capitalism erratically supplies "subversive 'needs' as well as 'false' desires."[29] Gaines quotes Simon Frith on the "need" supplied by rock fantasy:

> Black music had a radical, rebellious edge; it carried a sense of possibility denied in the labor market; it suggested a comradeship, a sensuality, a grace and joy and energy lacking in work.

But Frith goes on to point out the value of rock music as a "source of vigor and exhilaration and of good feelings" as well:

> One of the reasons why rock has been the most vital form of popular culture in the last twenty years is that it has expressed so clearly the struggle involved: rock has been used simultaneously as a form of self-indulgence and individual escape *and* as a source of solidarity and active dissatisfaction.[30]

Music, as Frith points out, is about "fun," about pleasure. The sexual images in music video call up a generalized desire that producers hope viewers will attempt to satisfy by spending money. But the music is also a source of pleasure in itself, a visceral, body-oriented pleasure. Perhaps white males are the least likely to use music videos to learn to dance because they fear they have the most to lose by entering the anti-hierarchical world of carnival.

The question of visual pleasure is more complicated. The objectification of women for the voyeuristic pleasure of male viewers characteristic of film has been replicated in music videos. But at the same time, creation of a female gaze by women artists is one of the most important trends in music video, suggesting that TV may offer women a space for a new investigation of female spectatorship.

Laura Mulvey's 1981 essay "Visual Pleasure and Narrative Cinema" established a ten-year orthodoxy which argued that the gaze constructed by traditional Hollywood cinema was inevitably male, and that images of women were restricted to fetish (von Sternberg) or voyeuristic (Hitchcock) object. Mulvey called for a "new language of desire," an avant-garde feminist film practice that would abandon narrative and visual pleasure (scopophilia). But Mulvey later questioned the inevitability of the male gaze, clearing the way for consideration of a gaze that is female.[31]

The fifth chapter of Kaplan's *Rocking Around the Clock* begins an analysis of possibilities for a female gaze in music videos. Kaplan discusses "socially conscious" videos that make feminist statements (Pat Benatar's "Love Is a Battlefield," 1983), videos directly commenting on the male gaze (Tina Turner's "Private Dancer," 1984), and videos that "attempt to set up a different gaze altogether, or to address some (possible) female gaze" (Aretha Franklin/Annie Lennox's "Sisters Are Doin' It for Themselves," 1986). Kaplan's discussion of Madonna's "Material Girl" (1985) argues that Madonna is not controlled by male desire in this reworking of *Gentlemen Prefer Blondes*. In contradiction to the "self-abnegating urge to lose oneself in the male that is evident in the classical Hollywood film," Kaplan argues that Madonna's appeal for female spectators is based on her "success in articulating and parading the desire to be desired in an unabashed, aggressive, gutsy manner."[32] Since Kaplan's book was written, both

Madonna and Janet Jackson have produced videos that explore the possibilities of a female gaze. Their enormous commercial success has given them a personal power which, although not free from market realities, allows them creative latitude and access to financial resources and mass-market distribution.

Janet Jackson's video "Nasty" (1986) reads like a feminist film theorist's programmatic deconstruction of the male gaze.[33] The video begins with a taxonomy of male sexist affronts within the gender dynamic of male as owner of the gaze and female as object, males as intrusive of female space, males as verbally aggressive and females silently passive. Jackson and two women friends are ogled by young men as they enter a movie theater; the ticket taker runs the beam of his flashlight up Jackson's body. She is annoyed, but says nothing. The men follow the women into the theater and sit next to them. One says to Jackson, "Come on baby, you know you want me," and strokes her thigh.

Jackson yells "Stop!" freezing both the men in the audience and the men on the screen. She jumps onto the stage, calls for a "beat" and begins dancing, and then backflips into the screen, becoming part of the movie image. This avant-garde rupture of the cinematic illusion destroys the traditional relation between spectator and film image, the posture that presents the image to be watched but not entered (or resisted, or reconfigured). Jackson's penetration of the space of the male characters on the screen reverses the penetration of the young women's space by the men in the theater, and it also stops the flow of the on-screen narrative, a flow feminist critics have seen as inevitably Oedipal, inevitably reproducing traditional gender categories.

Jackson imposes her own text onto the film, attacking "nasty boys" and "nasty talk," asserting that "I'm not a prude, I just want some respect." Jackson's demeanor is one of controlled anger; her sharp, staccato dance movements look like karate blows. She is dressed completely in black, with a jacket and tight turtleneck and pants, revealing a full figure emphasized in several angry pelvic grinds.

Her anger is tempered by moments of pleasure from the music ("a nasty groove") and the dancing ("I could get to like this"). Toward the end of the video, the camera shifts back to the audience to show Jackson's girlfriends watching and singing along, an image of female spectatorship as active and participatory. The video ends with all the men (from the movie *and* the theater) trapped inside the screen, and Jackson and her two friends outside, looking at them, a final reversal of the gaze.

But if "Nasty" is primarily an assault on the male gaze within terms structured by Mulvey's analysis, Jackson's allusions to female pleasure and spectatorship raise issues from the second generation of feminist film critics. Carol Vance has argued that feminism "must put forward a politics that resists deprivation and supports plea-sure. It must understand pleasure as life-affirming, empowering, de-sirous of human connection and the future, not fear it as destruc-tive, enfeebling, or corrupt." And Teresa de Lauretis contends that Mulvey's agenda for a feminist cinema stripped of narrative, closure, and visual pleasure resulted in a cinema that was unwatchable by anyone not steeped in theory. In particular, as Gaines points out, the Mulvey approach has not been attractive to black women film-makers, who tend to be interested in remaining in touch with popular audiences.[34]

In this context, Jackson's videos in *The Rhythm Nation Compila-tion* (A&M Video, 1990) represent a fascinating exploration of the possibilities of constructing a "new language of desire" and a new female spectator. The compilation begins with a prologue of com-ments by the different directors of the seven videos, stressing Jack-son's role as creative force. It ends with an epilogue in which Jackson presents two girls who, she says, returned to high school and gradu-ated because of the song "The Knowledge" on *Rhythm Nation*. How-ever literally one takes this, it's clear that Jackson wants to present herself as a professional, as the creative intelligence behind a product that has as one of its aims the betterment of black people and the creation of role models for black women.

The title video "Rhythm Nation" begins with a credo—"We're a nation with no geographic boundaries . . . pushing toward a world rid of color lines." Inside a stylized factory, a young black man in tears watches as Jackson and members of the Rhythm Nation dance. The lyrics call for communal efforts to improve social conditions: "Lend a hand to help your brother do his best. . . . Let's work together to improve our way of life." The choreography expresses that agenda in terms of self-control and militaristic discipline. Jackson and the dancers are dressed identically in black paramilitary uniforms; they move precisely in unison, with robotic, stiffly angular arm movements. The black-and-white color scheme, together with the grim factory setting and the martial arts choreography, underscores the mood of grim determination. Jackson herself seems asexual in her uniform and almost anonymous—foregrounded, but still one of the troops.

But the next video, "Escapade," suggests carnival as an alternative to militarism. The video opens on a Latin American or Caribbean village square, with shots of women and men wearing masks and carnival costumes. An old convertible adorned with flags and full of people in carnival masks drives into the square, watched by sinister-looking soldiers with rifles. Flanked by two friends, a white girl with dark hair and a black girl, Jackson strides and dances down the dusty street, surrounded by dancing villagers in colorful costumes. By the end of the video, one of the soldiers has joined the dancers.

The lyrics recount a chance encounter and an invitation for weekend escape from the working week: "Let's save our troubles for another day, let me take you on an escapade." They're linked to the video by a young Hispanic man who watches Jackson from the edge of the street, following her progress but never approaching her. The video ends with a disturbing image of the young man standing still, facing the camera, as a painted skull mask with glowing eyes swings in front of his face.

The issues raised by this video are complicated, but two in particular stand out. One is the question of Jackson's presence as a black woman in this setting. Jackson's light skin and her facial features (like those of her brother Michael) locate her in the marginal area between black and white, the culturally loaded space of the mulatto, and her position in the street between a black woman and a white one mark her racial liminality.[35] Her presence in this environment calls up the roots of black music in African and Caribbean cultures, roots that are problematic for black North Americans: a source of identity and strength, or just as much of a cultural other as they are for whites. Jackson's video appropriates the energy and joy of the carnival, but she seems to position herself as a tourist, someone who can move back and forth between cultures. In "Escapade," Jackson's cultural liminality is eroticized by the gaze of the male villager, who himself remains trapped and marginal.

The carnival masks that exaggerate or disguise identity and gender recall questions posed in Mary Ann Doane's essay, "Film and the Masquerade: Theorizing the Female Spectator." Drawing on Joan Riviere and Michèle Montrelay, Doane suggests that for women, masquerade "constitutes an acknowledgment that it is femininity itself which is constructed as a mask—as the decorative layer which conceals a non-identity." In flaunting femininity, the masquerade holds it at a distance: "Womanliness is a mask which can be worn or removed." Quoting Montrelay, Doane says that "the woman uses her own body as a disguise." "By destabilizing the image," she concludes, "the masquerade confounds this masculine structure of the look."[36]

Jackson positions herself as a liminal figure with respect to gender as well as race. She characteristically dresses in a long jacket, pants, and boots—stylized male dress. For Doane, sexual mobility is a "distinguishing feature of femininity in its cultural construction." Wearing male clothes ("Clothes make the man") allows a woman the possibility of "attaching the gaze to desire," of distancing herself from her own image in order to reappropriate it as an image of desire. The masquerade allows the woman who has appropriated the "male" gaze to compensate by exaggerating "the gestures of feminine flirtation." In the video "Alright," Jackson, dressed in a 1940s zoot suit that exaggerates and flaunts masculinity, watches herself emerge from a limousine dressed in a white evening gown that flaunts femininity. Jackson encourages spectators to see socially constructed gender identities as masquerades, to be taken up and put down, modified, reversed, or eliminated.

Doane's sense of a woman using "her own body as a disguise" may help to explain the radical departure in Jackson's presentation of her own body in "Love Will Never Do (without You)," the final video in the *Rhythm Nation Compilation*. Hélène Cixous has remarked that "more so than men who are coaxed toward social success, toward sublimation, women are body."[37] In "Love Will Never Do," Jackson exhibits her own body in a way she has never done before. That body was, in a sense, a "new" body, a "different" body from the one in the *Control* videos, a markedly thinner body shaped and defined by weight training, a face resculpted by weight loss and makeup (and perhaps by plastic surgery) to emphasize her cheekbones. This new body is itself a masquerade, a sign of feminine desirability constructed by a Nautilus machine, a body Jackson can now display and enjoy looking at. Jackson displays her new body in silhouettes, running her hands over her own body and up the chest of one of the men. She bends forward to accentuate her breasts. Shot in both black-and-white and subdued color and set in the starkly minimal desert, "Love Will Never Do" looks like fashion photography from *Vogue* or *Glamour*. There is no narrative beyond the celebration of a successful love affair, only voyeuristic pleasure.

In the "Love Will Never Do" video, Jackson not only gazes at herself but appropriates the gaze by looking at male bodies, turning them into objects of desire for female spectators, and for male spectators as well. The video celebrates hedonism and voyeurism; there are languorous displays of Jackson's body in ripped jeans and brief top, and of several muscular male bodies, black and white, with bare arms and chests. In one striking image a muscular, bald, black man in a bikini rolls down the desert salt flat in a white wheel frame, his arms and legs extended, looking something like Leonardo da Vinci's drawing of the human body describing a perfect circle.

Some feminists have argued that only men are voyeurs. But second-generation feminist film critics have attempted to recapture visual pleasure for women. Gaines argues that both lesbian and straight women watch with pleasure the bodies of the female dancers in the film *Flashdance*. Lucie Arbuthnot and Gail Seneca describe their "voyeuristic pleasure" in watching Marilyn Monroe and Jane Russell in *Gentlemen Prefer Blondes*.[38] But the voyeuristic enjoyment by women of images of male bodies displayed as sexual objects has not been theorized by feminist film critics, perhaps partly because such images have not been created by female directors up to now, and partly because the theory does not allow for it. According to psychoanalytic theory as adapted by feminist critics, the objectification of women as fetish serves the needs of the male psyche in dealing with castration anxiety.[39]

But voyeurism (as opposed to fetishism) seems grounded in power structures. As long as the cinematic power structure was made up of heterosexual males and erotic display of the body was seen as a power issue, men in Hollywood films looked at women and women seldom looked back. Male spectators enjoyed voyeuristic images of women, female spectators were denied such images of men. But now that women and gays are moving into positions of power, we are seeing more male skin and a new pressure on male stars to get into the gym and work on their bodies.[40]

Despite early claims that women were not interested in looking at images of men, several women friends have said they enjoy watching the men in "Love Will Never Do." A "gay gaze" may complicate these questions, but it seems likely that images can be appropriated by anyone regardless of their own sexual orientation or that of performers and directors, just as lesbian women appropriated images from *Personal Best*.[41] Spectators can enjoy images of people of their own sex and use them for narcissistic purposes. The point is that Jackson's tentative display of her body in "Love Will Never Do" is not inevitably a capitulation to male voyeurism forced by economic pressures.

A preternatural ability to reappropriate and capitalize on media images of women has made Madonna the most prominent female sexual icon of music videos and, at the same time, the prime example of role shifting, transformation, and metamorphosis—the queen of masquerade for whom the mask is the only identity. Madonna raised the question of the male gaze and photography in one of her earliest videos, "Borderline" (1984), and addressed pornography directly in "Open Your Heart" (1986).

In the Fellini-esque "Open Your Heart," Madonna dances in a Times Square-style peep show for sad-looking men isolated in cubicles. Her tightly laced leather top and long legs suggest a fetish object like Marlena Dietrich, the magical sign of protection against castration anxiety. As the men watch, she sings "Open your heart to me," suggesting they can have love, a relationship with a woman instead of this sad alienation, if only they will turn the key to their closed hearts.

In the theater lobby a young boy stares at posters of Madonna; he tries to get in but is refused by the elderly male ticket taker. He's on his way to being constructed as a lonely voyeur like the men inside.

Madonna appears in the lobby dressed in clothes exactly like his; she laughs and dances with him, and they leave the theater together, suggesting new possibilities for the construction of male sexuality under the guidance of nurturing women instead of alienated, fearful men.

But if "Open Your Heart" attacks voyeurism, "Vogue" (1990) explores the pleasures of the masquerade and the impulse to display oneself, to be looked at. "Vogue" played on MTV at the same time as Jackson's "Love Will Never Do," and both videos shared a similar black-and-white fashion magazine aesthetic. But whereas Jackson's video was set outdoors and had a playful, joyous feeling, "Vogue" was shot indoors in glamorously mysterious settings recalling Cocteau's films and the glamour photography of Helmut Newton.

In New York gay subculture, "voguing" is pretending to be a fashion model on a runway, dancing and striking exotic poses—a masquerade, an escape from everyday identity. The dancer/models in "Vogue" are light-skinned blacks, Hispanics, or dark Europeans, making Madonna's white skin, dress, and diamonds stand out in the high-contrast black-and-white color scheme. She functions as a mistress of ceremonies, balancing the foregrounded male dancers as they turn and strike poses in their designer clothes, shirts open and billowing around them like robes.

The lyrics say "It makes no difference if you're black or white, if you're a boy or a girl. . . . [Y]ou're a superstar, yes, that's what you are." Bodies become works of art, like the statues at the beginning of the video; personal identity is a construct to be put on or taken off, like Madonna's signature Marilyn Monroe poses. Madonna chants an incantatory catalog of Hollywood stars—"Greta Garbo and Monroe, Dietrich and DiMaggio, Marlon Brando, Jimmy Dean, on the cover of a magazine." The glamorous Hollywood past is available for appropriation—"Beauty is where you find it." In one recurring image hands pass in front of faces, framing them, applying makeup, but never actually touching, creating a language of surface and image rather than sensuality.

Madonna crossed that border in the "Justify My Love" video (1990), causing a mini-scandal that served as a pretext for marketing the video as a single, and as the center of the promotional campaign, when MTV banned it.[12] It is difficult to know exactly what turned MTV off—the serpentine Freddy Kruger/Joel Grey androgyne who writhes through the video, the S&M leather and mesh costumes modeled in postures of dominance and submission, the nipples of the dominatrix wearing only pants, suspenders, and a Nazi cap, or what the magazines have called the "lesbian kiss," the image of Madonna kissing a woman while her lover watches. It seems clear the video was intended to transgress, to cross as many boundaries as possible—look/touch, straight/gay, male/female, dominance/submission, black/white, real life/TV, America/Europe.

Set in a Paris hotel peopled by figures of a "European demimonde" just back from Berlin in the 1930s, Madonna's exploration of sexual fantasy has some of the feel of the "Open Your Heart" video, also directed by Jean Baptiste Mondino. This time "open your heart" means share your fantasies. Madonna's lover in the video was her current lover in real life, Tony Ward. She wants to kiss him in Paris, "make love in a train cross-country": "Talk to me, tell me your dreams, tell me your fears. Are you scared? Tell me your stories." The S&M visuals flirt with danger, but Madonna is in control. She enters this hotel of dreams alone, as a tourist; she's exhausted, lugging a suitcase. At the end she leaves alone, refreshed and energetic, her bare-chested lover reclining on the sofa, watching her leave. "Justify My Love" speaks for freedom of sexual fantasy; an anti-censorship phrase from the lyrics is inscribed on the screen: "Poor is the man whose pleasures depend on the permission of another."

Madonna has been triumphantly touted by Camille Paglia in the *New York Times* as "the true feminist":

> She exposes the puritanism and suffocating ideology of American feminism, which is stuck in an adolescent whining mode. Madonna has taught young women to be fully female and sexual while still exercising total control over their lives. She shows girls how to be attractive, sensual, energetic, ambitious, aggressive and funny—all at the same time.[43]

Madonna's images may reproduce images of women that feminists have found degrading and offensive, but as Chuck Kleinhans and Julia Lesage remind us, fantasy "is precisely what people desire but do not necessarily want to act on. It is an imaginative substitution and not necessarily a model for overt behavior." And, as Madonna said on *Nightline* about her "Express Yourself" video (1989), "I have chained *myself*. . . . There wasn't a man that put that chain on me."[44]

Still, it seems reasonable to question whether Madonna's aggressive appropriation of the traditional male gaze is the kind of women's counterpleasure that second-generation feminists have been looking for. Madonna the producer, the businesswoman, markets Madonna the performer, the sexual icon. Videos like "Justify My Love" seem designed to turn the male gaze on its head, to hoist it on its own petard, so to speak. Madonna's appropriation of Marilyn Monroe's image strips away the vulnerability and replaces it with control, but it still retains the basic dominance-submission structure of sexual relationships. Her vision seems primarily ironic, camp, rather than the creation of a "new female gaze," or a "new language of desire." My point here is not to impose some notion of politically correct fantasy. Fantasy is fantasy, everyone's entitled. But in the end, Jackson's "Love Will Never Do," with its gentle touch and smiling faces, may turn out to be more genuinely transgressive than the cabaret images of "Justify My Love."

In any case, it seems important that Madonna's reversed male gaze seems most comfortable with dark-skinned objects, male and female. That object choice reserves for her the culturally dominant position of white skin. Madonna is the white, blonde goddess entering other cultures (gay, Hispanic, black, European) and leaving them at will, the male gaze reconstituted as the colonizing white American gaze. There's a sense of voguing at the carnival about Madonna, of striking the pose but never engaging.

In "Justify My Love" one woman pencils a moustache on another; Madonna's face appears between but behind theirs, out of their line of vision. She giggles at the camera, creating a distance from the "lesbian" women and establishing her connection with the viewer who, presumably, is finding all of this a bit outré. Madonna's bleached blonde identity is significant at a time when most videos cast blondes as representatives of white power, as bimbos, the racial Other, the sadistic object. Madonna appropriates all that and cashes it in, insisting on both her solidarity with minorities and marginal groups, and on her ability to move between worlds, to leave the hotel when she's tired of dressing up. Across the persona and masks of individual videos, Madonna presents herself as a female icon of white power functioning without or against white men. In this context, the assertion "It makes no difference if you're black or white, if you're a boy or a girl" seems cynical rather than naive.

═══════

Madonna's success makes her the ultimate postmodern video star. That she was "shockingly inarticulate" on *Nightline*, according to Caryn James, simply indicates that Pittman is right, that television represents a new way of thinking in terms of images rather than words. That Madonna has been enormously successful without mastering the conversational skills that make for a good interview says something about the relationship of school curricula to success in the outside world.

Music videos are never going to teach anyone to read, but they may help to develop a visual literacy that seems increasingly important. They don't seem likely to actually deprive anyone of imaginative powers; decoding these densely packed visual texts requires attention and imagination. They are too variable and contradictory to brainwash anyone. Because of their short length and sheer numbers, they provide more opportunities for experimentation and creativity than films or regular TV shows.

Perhaps the most interesting thing about current music videos is that by foregrounding issues of gender and race that were invisible on radio, they provide infinitely more possibilities for thinking about and experiencing the variability of these social constructions than has ever been available before. The paradoxes of consumer capitalism that first banned and then promoted black music videos suggest that fears of a corporate ideological monolith replicating itself by controlling the fantasy life of young viewers are probably misplaced. If anything, written words tend to dichotomize gender and race while visual images, especially images in color, soften those binary categories. Men and women display themselves in any number of gender variations in music videos; skin color isn't simply black or white, but a spectrum of shades. Music videos are about desire, but they're about pleasure as well.

Notes

1 Christine Hall Hansen and Ranald D. Hansen, "The Influence of Sex and Violence on the Appeal of Rock Music Videos," *Communication Research* 17 (April 1990): 212–34.

2 E. Ann Kaplan, *Rocking Around the Clock: Music Television, Postmodernism, and Consumer Culture* (New York, 1987).

3 Ibid., 12.

4 Ibid., 28, 4.

5 Ibid., 44.

6 Kaplan quotes from Fredric Jameson's essay in *The Anti-Aesthetic: Essays on Postmodern Culture*, ed. Hal Foster (Port Townsend, 1983), 111–25. Jameson's essay ends by raising an unanswered question about resistance in postmodernism:

> There is some agreement that the older modernism functioned against its society in ways which are variously described as critical, negative, contestatory, subversive, oppositional and the like. Can anything of the sort be affirmed about postmodernism and its social moment? We have seen that there is a way in which postmodernism replicates or reproduces—reinforces—the logic of consumer capitalism; the more significant question is whether there is also a way in which it resists that logic. But that is a question we must leave open.

7 Kaplan, *Rocking Around the Clock*, 31.

8 Ibid., 47.

9 Jane M. Healy, "Chaos on Sesame Street: Does This Carnival of Images Help Students Read?" *American Educator* 14 (Winter 1990): 22–39.

10 Ibid., 24–25.

11 Ibid., 27. See, for example, Marsha Kinder, "Music Video and the Spectator: Television, Ideology and Dream," *Film Quarterly* 38 (Fall 1984): 2–15.

12 For articles that support Pittman's position on the positive role of music videos in developing flexible, nonlinear patterns of thinking and understanding, see Dave Laing, "Music Video: Industrial Product, Cultural Form," *Screen* 26 (1985): 78–83; H. Stith Bennett and Jeff Ferrell, "Music Videos and Epistemic Socialization," *Youth & Society* 18 (June 1987): 344–62; and Steve Jones, "Cohesive But Not Coherent: Music Videos, Narrative and Culture," *Popular Music and Society* 12 (1988): 15–29.

13 Jane D. Brown and Laurie Schulze, "The Effects of Race, Gender, and Fandom on Audience Interpretations of Madonna's Music Videos," *Journal of Communication* 40 (Spring 1990): 88–102. Charles Acland pointed out the basic ambiguity and indeterminateness of the video on this question in "Look What They're Doing on TV: Towards an Appreciation of the Complexity of Music Video," *Wide Angle* 10 (1988): 4–14.

14 For a discussion of MTV's market research, see Steven Levy's "Ad Nauseam: How MTV Sells Out Rock & Roll," *Rolling Stone*, 8 December 1983, 33–34.

15   For historical accounts of music video and MTV, see David Ehrenstein, "Pre-MTV," *Film Comment* (August 1983): 41–42; Arnold S. Wolfe, "Rock on Cable: On MTV: Music Television, the First Video Music Channel," *Popular Music and Society* 9 (1983): 41–50; Joan D. Lynch, "Music Videos: From Performance to Dada-Surrealism," *Journal of Popular Culture* 18 (Summer 1984): 53–57; and John K. Hartman, "I Want My AD-TV," *Popular Music and Society* 11 (1987): 17–23.

16   David Lee Roth, then Van Halen's lead singer and video star, commented on the experimental film look for a *Rolling Stone* article:

> Fancy editing, cutaway, flash dissolves, slow motion, double-trick fadeaways going into solarization . . . shit, man, give me some slack. . . . It's still some jerk dancing, lip-syncing the words to a song about "baby, baby, baby." This thing of standing next to the Venetian blinds with the light coming through, making bars on your face . . . how many times have you seen that in the last two hours on MTV? (Levy, "Ad Nauseam," 76)

17   Acland, "Look What They're Doing," 5. See also Kinder, "Music Video and the Spectator," 12. Kinder points out that music videos function very much like dreams, and that they put images into viewers' heads which supplement "the dreamer's ordinary experience with thousands of prefabricated moving visual images that are directly absorbed into the cultural dreampool and influencing both the form and content of dream texts." According to Kinder (and Kaplan), TV helps to position "the spectator in the public marketplace where one becomes an active consumer purchasing products one has been trained by television to desire, thereby contributing to the capitalist economy" (11). Because of its characteristics of "unlimited access, structural discontinuity, decentering, structural reliance on memory retrieval, live transmission and the omnipresence of the spectator," Kinder says television "trains the spectator to focus on one's personal powers of choice and reception while ignoring the remote sources of transmission—the true Remote Control—whose ideological determinants and manipulative strategies remain mystified" (14–15).

18   Acland, "Look What They're Doing," 6–8. And see Lawrence Grossberg, "I'd Rather Feel Bad Than Not Feel Anything at All: Rock and Roll, Pleasure and Power," *Enclitic* 8 (1984): 94–111.

19   Andrew Goodwin, "Music Video in the (Post) Modern World," *Screen* 28 (1987): 36–55.

20   Kaplan, *Rocking Around the Clock*, 109.

21   For an account of the creation of *Yo! MTV Raps*, see Jamie Malanowski, "Top Hip-Hop," *Rolling Stone*, 13 July 1989, 77–78.

22   R. Serge Denisoff, "Review Essay: Historicism and MTV: E. Ann Kaplan's *Rocking Around the Clock*," *Popular Music and Society* 12 (1988): 63. See also interviews with Pittman printed in *Rolling Stone*: Jefferson Graham, "Heavy metal on the outs at MTV," *Rolling Stone*, 11 April 1985, 15; and Steven Levy, "Ad Nauseam," 37. Pittman was edged out as MTV CEO in 1986 after the network's decline in

Neilsen ratings. See Anthony DeCurtis, "Pittman leaving MTV," *Rolling Stone*, 25 September 1986, 17.

23　Levy, "Ad Nauseam," 37.

24　Malanowski, "Top Hip-Hop," 78.

25　See Lisa Russell, "M. C. Hammer couldn't make the big leagues in baseball, so he began rapping out hits in a different league," *People*, 6 August 1990, 59–60; Jeffrey Ressner, "Hammer time: America's most popular rapper is also a demanding taskmaster," *Rolling Stone*, 6 September 1990, 40ff.; Craig Rosen, "Direct-Hammer: 'Some of these kids have never gotten letters before,'" *Billboard Magazine*, 9 June 1990, 96.

26　Joel Dreyfuss, "Harlem's Ardent Voice," *New York Times Magazine*, 20 January 1991, 22.

27　Brown and Schulze, "Madonna's Music Videos," 90.

28　Jane Gaines, "White Privilege and Looking Relations: Race and Gender in Feminist Film Theory," in *Issues in Feminist Film Criticism*, ed. Patricia Erens (Bloomington, 1990), 206.

29　Ibid., 206–7.

30　Simon Frith, *Sound Effects: Youth, Leisure, and the Politics of Rock'n'Roll* (New York, 1981), 264–65.

31　Laura Mulvey, "Visual Pleasure and Narrative Cinema," *Screen* 16 (Autumn 1975): 6–18. The essay has been reprinted many times in anthologies on film and the visual arts. See also Mulvey's "Afterthoughts on 'Visual Pleasure and Narrative Cinema' Inspired by *Duel in the Sun*," *Framework* 6 (1981); and E. Ann Kaplan, "Is the Gaze Male?" in *Powers of Desire: The Politics of Sexuality*, ed. Ann Snitow, Christine Stansell, and Sharon Thompson (New York, 1983). The material of this essay appeared in another form in Kaplan's *Women in Film: Both Sides of the Camera* (London, 1983).

32　Kaplan, *Rocking Around the Clock*, 126.

33　Six videos of songs from *Control* were packaged to sell independently, and "Nasty" was the first video in the two-volume set *Control: The Videos* (1986, A&M Video).

34　Carol S. Vance, "Pleasure and Danger: Towards a Politics of Sexuality," in *Pleasure and Danger: Exploring Female Sexuality*, ed. Carol S. Vance (Boston, 1984), 23–24; and Teresa de Lauretis, "Oedipus Interruptus," *Wide Angle* 7 (1985): 34–40. Several essays of special interest in this regard appeared in Erens, ed., *Issues in Feminist Film Criticism*. See, for example, Jane Gaines, "Women and Representation: Can We Enjoy Alternative Pleasure?" 82.

35　In a discussion of Diana Ross's *Mahogany*, Jane Gaines says:

> From Afro-American history, we should recall the white male's appropriation of the Black woman's body which weakened the Black male and undermined the community. We need to develop a theory of Black female representation which takes account of "passing" as an eroticizing alternation and a peculiar play on difference, and the corresponding double consciousness it requires of

those who can seem either Black or White. ("White Privilege and Looking Relations," 208)

36 Mary Ann Doane, "Film and the Masquerade," in Erens, ed., *Issues in Feminist Film Criticism*, 48–49.
37 Hélène Cixous, "The Laugh of the Medusa," quoted by Doane, "Film and the Masquerade," 46.
38 Jane Gaines, "Women and Representation," 86; see also Lucie Arbuthnot and Gail Seneca, "Pre-Text and Text in *Gentlemen Prefer Blondes*," in Erens, ed., *Issues in Feminist Film Criticism*, 115.
39 See, for example, Mulvey's "Visual Pleasure and Narrative Cinema" or Doane's "Film and the Masquerade."
40 See Peter Watrous, "Pop Turns the Tables—With Beefcake," *New York Times*, 10 February 1991, Arts and Leisure section.
41 Elizabeth Ellsworth argues that lesbian feminist reviewers launched a "radical rewriting" of the film and appropriated it as a lesbian film (see "Illicit Pleasures: Feminist Spectators and *Personal Best*," in Erens, ed., *Issues in Feminist Film Criticism*, 192–95).
42 Marshall Cohen, MTV's executive vice president of corporate affairs and communications, said Madonna never had any intention of getting the video on MTV (quoted by Benjamin Svetkey, "Some Like It Hot . . . Some Not," *Entertainment Weekly*, 14 December 1990, 19). Whatever the truth of that claim, being banned has made the video successful. As Madonna said on ABC's *Nightline* when Forrest Sawyer pointed out that she would make even more money because of the controversy, "Yeah? so lucky me."
43 Camille Paglia, "Madonna—Finally, a Real Feminist," *New York Times*, 14 December 1990.
44 Chuck Kleinhans and Julia Lesage, "The Politics of Sexual Repression," *Jump Cut* (March 1986): 24–26 (quoted by Jane Gaines in "Women and Representation," 87); see also Caryn James, "Beneath All That Black Lace Beats the Heart of a Bimbo," *New York Times*, 16 December 1990, Arts and Leisure section.

Jeff Calder

Living by Night in the Land of Opportunity: Observations on Life in a Rock & Roll Band

. . . what we need are good pictures . . . hand-made with love and passion and care by individual picture-makers, not by banks, or committees, or accountants, or lawyers, or office boys, or boards of directors who are really in the real estate business.
—Frank Sinatra

Gigantic screwjacks will be required in order to raise the culture of the masses.
—Leon Trotsky

The sense of the size of the margin . . . by which the total of American life . . . is still so surrounded as to represent . . . but a scant central flotilla huddled as for very fear of the fathomless depth of water, the too formidable future, on the so much vaster lake of the materially possible.
—Henry James

You've had your shot, and now you're dead in the water.
—Show-biz axiom

Thirteen years ago I began my journey along the margin of America's Pop Republic. The margin isn't such a bad place, unless, of course, one needs to eat. Unlike many on the margin, though, I've always thought that rock music could still be a creative mass medium. As a consequence, and after a great deal of frenzy and frustration, I was drawn to the center of James's vaster lake. Then one day while hard charging into the fog bank of the future, I suddenly met myself going in the opposite direction. That can't be me, I said. What happened to . . . him? It was a chance meeting, no doubt, but I knew then that a part of myself would always be roving around the margin, now with new tales about strange places with names like "Hollywood," where the squares blot out the sun. In the sudden shade on the vaster lake things happen more quickly than show-biz stoats with pinkies can bare their teeth and tell everyone the option's up.

The movie industry operates under a famous dictum formalized best by the screenwriter William Goldman: "The single most important fact, perhaps, of the entire movie industry [is] NOBODY KNOWS ANYTHING." Its withered twin, the music industry, is the same. They all act as if they know what they're doing. No one does. Which is why under no circumstance should anyone take seriously anything anybody at a record company ever says. This is particularly true regarding the merits of things musical. With rare exception record company people are so terrified of losing their jobs that they can't begin to listen to the first note of a song.

It may always have been this way, but somehow good stuff used to slip past. I grew up in the great era of rock and soul music. My favorite artists took risks; they had a way with words and a sense of vision. These qualities have been eliminated from commercial radio in America today. Back then, my favorite artists ruled the seedy AM stations and transistor receivers. Later, like many other teenagers in the late 1960s, I saw popular music at a point of departure. It would grow as we would grow, strictly onward and upward. By the end of that decade, pop music had become almost a religion for a big part of my generation. Now, twenty years later, the sanctuary has been defiled by market research. Visionary artists are still out there, but the stream of rampant invention has lost access to the "mainstream": the powerful radio systems of America. If the most exciting pop music can't reach people, what's the point?

In 1953 Gore Vidal commented that "as the novel moves toward a purer, more private expression it will cease altogether to be a popular medium, becoming, like poetry, a cloistered avocation." Along with film, the novel was a popular medium of Vidal's youth. Fifteen years after his earlier observation Vidal would conclude:

> Our lovely vulgar and most human art is at an end, if not the end. Yet that is no reason not to want to practice it, or even to read it. In any case, rather like the priests who have forgotten the meaning of the prayers they chant, we shall go on for quite a long time talking of books and writing books, pretending all the while not to notice that the church is empty and the parishioners have gone elsewhere to attend other gods, perhaps in silence or with new words.

Those who grew up with artistic aspirations in the field of pop music now face a similar situation. We've become musical monks making music for other musical monks. How could it have come to this?

It was to be rock history's main irony. Much of American music in the 1960s was a promotion of freedom and openness. Its tremendous success generated huge profits. The profits brought in the experts: lawyers, accountants, marketeers. Their job was to maximize profits, and the way to do that in a volatile business is to create a more controllable situation. Threat had to be eliminated, and threat is defined as anything that might cause a listener to change the station. Station switching is reflected in surveys as a decline in listenership, or market share. A lower market share means a lower advertising rate. The corporation—in this case the radio system—then makes less money, so any song perceived as being a threat—politically, culturally, or emotionally—must not be given airplay.

In the 1970s, through a combination of consulting firms, advertising agencies, and radio stations, a "manufacture of consent" occurred. The audience came to expect and accept popular music of little vitality or depth. By the time the Sex Pistols arrived in Atlanta in 1977, the process was complete. The Sex Pistols had the biggest media blitzkrieg since the Beatles thirteen years before. But they sold very few records. Why? No airplay. Why? Because the radio systems found them threatening. For once the program directors were right. Johnny Rotten and the Sex Pistols *were* threatening to a business that had become irrelevant even to itself. The Sex Pistols fell apart, and around the same time it looked like the music business might fall apart, too.

At the close of World War II André Breton was asked his thoughts on the future of poetry. Breton replied: "Poetry would betray its ageless mission if even the most harrowing historical events could induce it to diverge from its own royal road and turn against itself at a crucial juncture on this road. Poetry must ceaselessly advance." If one makes the pop analogue, some old questions arise: Can pop music actually be a vehicle on the royal road, or is music making imbued with Breton's idealism only futile? How can one ceaselessly advance in a popular medium when access to a viable audience is denied? In rock & roll today the royal road can be a lonely one. When you're living by night in the land of opportunity, it's nice to have a flashlight, but what happens when the people at the battery concession have a vested interest in *dark*? America's radio stations may once have been laboratories of experiment, but at the squalid dawn of the Reagan/Bush era they were ruled by formula. Where was one to turn if one brought Breton's idealism to pop music? To Las Vegas and John Davidson, of course.

In 1982 John Davidson published "The Singing Entertainer." It was created as a guide for someone who wanted to be a professional performer. Like Breton, Davidson and "The Singing Entertainer" are hefty counsel. Had such a manual been around in 1978 I would have been spared a great deal of public humiliation. "The Singing Entertainer" contains many helpful hints, like how to hold a microphone properly and body positioning ("Mike hand should be relaxed," and limp wrists are too "blasé"). On the other hand, I was spared the following rosy picture: "As we approach the '80's, the country is literally laughing, dancing, jogging and dressing up again. We have entered The Glitter Era." My experience approaching the 1980s doesn't quite correspond to John Davidson's, though I do recall a number of people dancing and jogging on my head.

Davidson's other historical analysis would have struck home, however: "If you want to be a singing entertainer you probably couldn't pick a better time than right now. The role of the singing entertainer in show business never has been more significant." Sometimes, when opportunity knocks, the best move might be to slip out the back way. But then I would have been denied the pleasure of my band's first critical notice: "Just plain awful." Or, a dozen years later, the following: "Kind of a sad story, really."

In the meantime, I had little preparation for being in a rock band. In high school I sold clothing in the afternoon and briefly managed a combo called the Prone Position. As "manager" I could occasionally land onstage and perform a song called "Torture Chamber" under the moniker the Black Cock. Later, in the mid-1970s, I put together a band in Florida named the Fruit Jockeys. That lasted two gigs because no one could stand the huge papier-mâché globe-heads painted orange that I asked everyone to wear. By 1978, though, I had become more serious about songwriting, which for me was an outgrowth of literary pursuits. Forming a real band became inevitable. Traveling through Atlanta on several occasions, I had met a prodigal teenage guitarist, Bob Elsey. We home-recorded some songs together and decided to call ourselves the Swimming Pool Q's. During this early New Wave period, band names were frequently essay-length. As far as the name goes, marketing strategy was no consideration. The name the Swimming Pool Q's seemed appropriate for a band that was partially Floridian. We would spend years being asked to justify the name, but at the time it was a little less life-threatening than the Fruit Jockeys, especially in the South.

Something called southern boogie was still big at that time. The Swimming Pool Q's were one of the first groups in the region to stand in opposition to it. The wiggy twist was that in 1980 I would have epithets hurled at me for having short hair by clodhoppers with long hair, who ten years before were hurling the same epithets at me for having long hair when they had short hair. Only this time it became important to savor the baiting. At gas stations, for instance, the usual site of hayseed hassles, it's always fun to leap out of the car covered in lace and demand the location of the closest rare book shop. Back then, the hip log-telegraph was pounding out signals in London and New York City. Some provincial ears were standing up, and with those ears arose the spirit of aesthetic opposition. Bands were formed by people who all seemed to come from the worlds of art and retail. Few had "musical backgrounds" or any knowledge of how to play their instruments. One learned along the way. Spirit was all. The word "career" wasn't in the vocabulary, and the prospect of making an album was about as realistic as time travel. I couldn't tune a guitar (not necessarily a disadvantage in this circle). My singing was croaking. My concept of "songwriting" was to jam showboat words and gags into an impossible musical structure with no sense of melody. There was no band, either, so we had to get one of those. Our initial lineup was assembled from friends and disgruntled musicians (note: musicians are always disgruntled). Unlike most New Wave bands during this period (any band with the barest pretense to originality was considered New Wave) we always had great players. This would come to create problems. In the narrow world of the margin, self-conscious incompetence was becoming sanctified. The spirit-was-all crowd held in disdain any display of technical mastery as a concession to faulty values.

The first thing to do with a band is to find something to do. At this point one initiates a chain of events to unfold in disorderly fashion over a five-year period, The Sphere of Work (booking and travel) which gets one to The Gig (the act of entertainment which is both Work and Art) that ultimately transforms The Sphere of Art (songwriting and musical ability), allowing for the creation of the first mechanical product (The Album). This process used to be called dues paying, a concept frowned upon during New Wave as careerist. Nevertheless:

THE REHEARSAL

Usually a horrid nightmare. The less said about this the better. All it takes is one Bad Head to ruin a rehearsal, and at least one musician always has a Bad Head. Bad Head is usually the result of an unhip daytime job or a forever-failing love interest. Bands rehearse more often in the early days. After performing the material for awhile, they get together only to learn new songs. The first practice location is a parent's basement. This never lasts too long. The only alternative is to find a regular rehearsal space. This costs money. To get money, one must secure an engagement. This requires:

BOOKING

To cajole or con. . . . Whatever it takes to achieve The Gig. This usually necessitates a telephone. Always remember, the telephone is your friend. Sometimes a friend must be punished. The punishment can take many forms (a hammer, the hand receiver, the back tires of an automobile) and usually occurs after a particularly nasty colloquy with a club owner: "You're only as good as your last gig, and now I'm going to cut the wire!" Generally speaking, club owners don't care much about music. They care about money. Money is generated by smashing as many human beings as possible into The Club. Both the club owner and you know that there's the possibility of a bad night. That's the club owner's cue to say, "Okay, I'll give you the guarantee, but if you don't make it back at the door you can just lose my phone number. You don't know me. You can forget I ever existed!"

Living by night is not the province of the dainty.

Booking, continued: a big part of booking is lying. Always lie. About what? Anything, from the weather and the number of cover songs you know to whether or not you wear thin ties. In booking there are no moral or ethical consequences to lying. At the end of the engagement the club owner is going to pretend he doesn't remember anything you talked about regarding money, and you won't be able to find him anyway. Someday you'll get a big booking agency to handle the band and take the load off your shoulders. That's when your problems really begin.

Our first engagement was on June 1, 1978. It was an art collective's fashion show called the Underwear Invitational. We weren't paid but received enough notoriety to con our way into a local club on a Monday night. Having almost no stage experience, it was to be an evening of terror and total confusion. It took months to feel comfortable on a plywood stage covered in dime-store carpet.

There was no New Wave or Alternative circuit in 1978. The best you could hope for was the open-minded club with an eclectic format of jazz/blues/folk with a little rock on the side. Early-in-the-week (Monday through Wednesday) gigs were no-risk situations. The Swimming Pool Q's played countless "New Wave Nights" on the no-risk evenings. The last New Wave Night we played was in the mid-1980s in Florida. The club owner said, "If you don't have a good night you'll finish New Wave forever in Orlando." To our mutual relief, we didn't, and we did.

After gigging around Atlanta for several months, we played our first out-of-town date on November 18 as the opening act for the B-52's at the University of Georgia in Athens. A month later we had our first big show as the warm-up act for Devo in Atlanta. The club management forced us to play *two* forty-five-minute sets in front of twelve hundred people. It was trial-by-blowtorch in a kangaroo court. The rabble hurled pointed remarks and other pointed things, but we survived.

With the Devo slot as ammunition and a few telephone numbers laid upon us by one of the B-52's, we duped some nightclubs in Manhattan into booking us during a week-long blizzard. We weren't what they expected but poured on enough fake charm to get the hook at only one disco of the New Wave persuasion. We got the same question I'd heard asked of the Allman Brothers in 1969: "Are you guys really from the South?" Our rental van got us home ten days later with fifty-eight dollars. More important, we were a mean little rock band now, able to lie and say that we'd taken Manhattan as we set out to conquer our own region.

THE ROYAL ROAD
The process of driving around in circles and becoming an alcoholic. It increases a band's resolve or destroys it. As a result of relative affluence, young middle-class white people develop bizarre tics which can create tremendous tension in the confines of a small vehicle jammed to the roof with gear and threatening to throw every imaginable rod at any given moment. There's never enough money for food. You never know where you're going to spend the night. You drive eight hours, and you're still late for the gig, and some club owner with one bucktooth is screaming at you to throw the amplifiers up on the stage and play. People in black leather make fun of your tie tack. The club manager is jacked on the white lady and doesn't recall anything about the guarantee. A tiny detail that you forgot to take care of

suddenly blows up in your face like the Hindenburg. I remember only the good things, like driving through Popeye's Fried Chicken and ordering a can of spinach.

Before The Royal Road, during the embryonic phase of the band, hometown supporters came to the gig and provided a cushion, allowing everyone in the group to overcome the panic of the first shows. Once the city limits appeared in the rear view mirror, however, the cushion disappeared. Traveling in the South required resourcefulness. Sure, there were towns like Tampa where the local radio promoted us as "a punk group from CBGB's in New York City!" We packed in a partisan crowd so starved for something new that it didn't matter we weren't Punk or New Wave, only different. The problem was in getting to the Tampas: that is, the gigs routed along the way to make the whole thing pay. Most of the joints were still mired in boogie. These places weren't exactly prosceniums flanked by Doric columns. The audiences were skeptical and not very interested in art songs with titles like "Walk Like a Chicken." They were more like potential pipe bombs which we had to disarm quickly to survive. It was frightening, but it was also fun and new.

Back to The Bible: In "The Singing Entertainer," John Davidson writes, "You must take the audience on a well-planned journey, a journey on which the ride must be as enjoyable and fulfilling as arriving at the destination." To be honest, most performances in which I've been involved have been more like mazes with the occasional sinkhole opening up in the pathway. Which brings us to entertainment. Like most jobs, entertainment is a learn-on-the-job situation. It's the only way to learn what works and what doesn't work. You learn to improvise in order to get off the hot seat (equipment failures, broken guitar strings, Bad Head). You learn to handle the heckling jackass by inviting him onstage, sticking a microphone in his face, and introducing him as "Chuck."

At first you stand in one place because you're scared. Then you leap up and down because you're still scared and don't want to be anymore. Then you leap up and down because it signifies commitment to the massive energy and spontaneity of the music. Then you stalk the stage in order to demonstrate command. Then you go back to doing what you did in the first place—standing still—because it signifies even greater command. Then you do all of the above whenever you feel like it because you've finally learned not to care. The Tao of Performance: not caring is entertaining.

Above all, entertaining is a willingness to make a fool of oneself in public and enjoy it. It's not often while playing in front of a bunch of hopped-up kids that I ask, "What's the meaning of entertainment in America?" Ruminations interfere with the process which, when working smoothly, is like getting lost and found simultaneously.

Some exploding zeppelins include The Opening Act Situation and The Showcase. The Opening Act Situation normally takes place on a bigger stage than one is used to performing upon. The length of the set is usually quite limited. Stage goons are there to insure that no one touches any of the headlining act's idiotic props. These constraints make improvisational flights-of-fancy almost impossible. The audience doesn't care about you. They're there to see the headlining act. The only sensible course is to take as little time between songs as possible. That way the yahoos and town scruff don't have enough time to scream the name of the headlining act ad nauseam while you labor in The Pit of Hell. And moving swiftly from song to song confuses the undecided part of the audience into thinking you might actually be good.

The Showcase, or "The Blowcase," is the occasion when the record company hacks fly in from The Coast to check out your act and maybe give you a recording contract. This means that everybody in the band goes out to buy new clothes and shows up at the gig looking like Napoleon during his scene with the pope. The elaborate new outfits make it impossible to strap the instruments on, much less perform. And it's a complete disaster. Later, the men from The Coast say you're a lot different from what they thought you would be just from listening to the tape, but please stay in touch.

More John Davidson: "A singing entertainer is a mirror for his audience. You must reflect both the time in which you are singing and the people who are listening." Here Davidson is not that far off the mark. Successful performers of any genre—hip or unhip—tend to reassure their audience through song and dress, and they allay the audience's insecurities: it's okay to have a certain haircut or sexual persuasion because the performer has one, too. This seems to be an important function of popular music. Unfortunately, many of us have never figured out quite what we're supposed to reassure the audience about, which has led to a monthly bank statement considerably thinner than John Davidson's.

Writing songs begins as a private pursuit, and as with many private pursuits, the site of composition is the bedroom. There's a tape deck, an instrument (guitar or keyboard), and no awareness of "the general listener," whoever that might be. One writes to please oneself. Lyrics were my initial orientation: the music was there to serve the words. Most of my first songs were overly long narratives. Every time I came up with a new plot twist or good line I'd write another musical part. Now, a song can be many things, but it's not a novel or short story, even if it uses literary devices. By stages I learned that if a song is tedious, verses and details have to be cut at the expense of narrative.

An example of tedium in song: "Shoot a Quick Nine," circa 1979, the story of a Durham family man who gambles away his house on the golf course.

> The kids are hung on the latest kick
> Mommy's fallen for a toothpick prof
> Heart pumping like a two dollar trick
> Can't turn his tummy off
> From a third story office on a Durham street
> He looks through venetian blinds:
> Shoot a quick nine

About ten minutes later he loses the house and the LTD, and we usually lost the audience. As their eyes glazed and jaws went slack, I eventually got the idea that this sort of thing might read better than it sang.

The first two things to transform songwriting are the band and the live performance. The writer subtly adjusts to the strengths, weaknesses, and peculiarities of the band. On a subconscious level he begins to imagine different musical possibilities for new songs. While songs were definite and rigid during the bedroom phase, they become more plastic when introduced to others who have abilities the songwriter doesn't. Once the band is cooking, ideas can be developed collectively by jamming at the dreaded rehearsal (this is not advised during Bad Head). The jam can be taped and taken back to the bedroom, where it can be fashioned into a song. This kind of collaboration can lead to some good work. On the other hand, when five people have five different ideas about how a song should be structured, the possibilities for confusion are extraordinary. This, too, can lead to Bad Head.

As touched upon during the "Shoot a Quick Nine" episode, performing live can change one's songwriting as well. The grinding routine of one-nighters affects the pleasure one derives from singing and playing. As opposed to the big-layout tunes over which the audience might rub their chins to stay awake, songs with more emotional and melodic content become more rewarding for the singer. The oddball things stay, but they function as pace changers and releases. Whether or not this is pandering to the audience is beside the point. The words and phrases become simpler as one begins to fuse them more deliberately to the music. One begins to lose the quirks that gave the songs their unique character in the beginning. Now the challenge becomes giving the new approach an equally personal distinction.

The Royal Road has its own special impact on songwriting in that it provides a portal to the world of rude experience. Travel can be a jarring ordeal that can influence the shape of songs, their emotional qualities. The alienation and fragmentation of the road can only have a deleterious effect on one's personal life. This can lead to much whining, which is the source of much song. It's not uncommon for many songwriters to seek out trouble simply for the sake of new material. This is known as The Scientific Pursuit of Pratfall. A not atypical scenario: songwriter develops a drinking problem for about twenty-four hours, pursues a half dozen indiscretions, gets in a fist-fight that breaks his glasses and lands him in the pokey allowing for a thirty-minute peek at The Underside of American Life, after which he crawls back home and pleads forgiveness for something he denies ever having done in the first place (Figure 1).

At this point, if one isn't too preoccupied with selecting a parole officer, the process of recording begins to make serious alterations

Figure 1. Calder's arrest.

upon songwriting. Recording a song on tape and hearing it played back for the first time can be an enlightening, exciting, and often depressing experience. Besides discovering one's incompetency as a musician, the songs that everyone thought were so brilliant—the real crowd pleasers—sound terrible. On the bright side, the certain embarrassments show promise.

Awareness of one's artistic deficiencies increases as the band moves from the home studio to the more serious and expensive twenty-four track professional studio. Simultaneously, the artist begins to improve as he becomes more comfortable in the studio environment. This is where the trouble known as The Hundred-Dollar-Per-Hour Dupe begins. One is made cocksure by the overwhelming bigness of the studio sound. A vision of thousands screaming in a riot of approval dances in the head. Forty-eight hours later the cassette tape you made for free at rehearsal sounds better. Technology conned you into thinking you were better than you were.

Slowly one develops the capacity to penetrate the deception of modern studio fantasy. In addition to avoiding any future high dollar quandary (usually the result of being unprepared), a recognition of musical clutter emerges, and the songwriter reminds himself of the revealed stylistic excess the next time he writes a song. At some point, too, if the band has the opportunity to spend huge amounts of time in a sophisticated studio, it can develop a half-baked idea into a full-blown song in ways it never could have when jamming in the rehearsal room or playing live. The songwriter and the band are hearing the thing blasting back over the studio monitors as they're creating the music and as any casual listener will be hearing it in the future.

Then there's the factor of radio airplay and its impact on the songwriter. If you're lucky, the recording is boomed over the vaster lake to the vaster audience you no doubt deserve. Suddenly the work is subject to the most intense mass scrutiny and self-analysis. An even greater responsibility suggests itself, but to whom and for what? The songwriter is no longer alone in his bedroom with the tape deck. He's internalized his experiences over the years and, perhaps, evolved from the more intellectual and eccentric to the more emotional and "sensible." He's begun to learn what's "effective," and what's not, but effective for whom? himself? some imagined listener? a perceived radio audience? After a while can he even distinguish among the three? These bewildering questions loom on the horizon, but before they can be answered, one has to make The Album.

In 1979 we released our first single titled "Rat Bait"/"The A-Bomb Woke Me Up." We recorded it in Florida at a small studio that had been converted from a produce market. In the New Wave strategy dominant at the time we released it on our own label, Chlorinated Records. An Atlanta entrepreneur, Danny "The Anti-Mogul" Beard, who had backed the B-52's' independent hit, "Rock Lobster," helped us plug "Rat Bait" in a growing national underground network of retail stores, small radio stations, and alternative press. It brought us some attention outside the Southeast. An A&R representative from EMI Records, a major label, flew in to record a demo tape with the band. It was a typically pitiful though not catastrophic session. Eventually EMI rejected the group ("not focused"). Other major labels gave us the characteristic deaf ear. Undaunted, with our more extensive recording and performing experience, we were ready to make The Album.

To make a first album requires three things besides a pile of cash: a record label, a producer, and a studio. First, I flew to Vegas with my life savings and generated a small fortune which I lost the next night in Reno. That left family and friends. I "borrowed" about ten grand from an old pal who was heir to a supermarket chain. I was set for a return flight to the Green Felt Jungle when I was stopped by the aforementioned Anti-Mogul. He had started his own label and agreed to put out our record. The Anti-Mogul would serve as executive producer, an even vaguer concept than producer. In this case the executive producer would fetch soft drinks, tell jokes from *Humpty-Dumpty* magazine, and run interference between the band and the producer.

At this point none of us was very sure what a producer actually did. We used a fellow who had done some other projects for The Anti-Mogul. He stopped by and heard the group at practice one night. Like most bands' first producer he was a glorified engineer who impressed everyone with incomprehensible gizmos and tried to keep as many overdub ideas off the record as possible. Also, he kept the show running because it was obvious we didn't have a clue. We used the studio of his choice, an old Christian broadcasting facility. We had an enormous pipe organ at our disposal, which we fired up like a lawnmower whenever possible.

We began recording on the night John Lennon was murdered. It took about two weeks to make the record. We played the songs just as we would in a nightclub—with no alterations. The guitar solos, vocals, and pipe organ were overdubbed. Except for a few instances of meaningless tension (Bad Head), things went smoothly. The resulting product, titled *The Deep End*, sounded nothing like we thought the band sounded, but we were pleased. Leaping forward, here is the standard trajectory of a recording career:

ALBUM ONE: Sounds nothing like the band.

ALBUM TWO: More thought given to arrangements and playing in advance of the recording sessions. Still perform the basic tracks as on Album One for "the live feel" (it should be noted here that every band in the world sounds terrible live, but it's always important to get "the live feel" on tape). Overdub experimentation is allowed. More time and attention paid to the mix.

ALBUM THREE: Band is now ready for daring "in-the-studio" moves. Vast amounts of time and money are seemingly squandered by Zen-like producer, but with often fantastic results. Studio Burn sets in; it's like being in a submarine for sixty days. Result A: Band makes first record "taking the listener into account."
Result B: Just when band becomes capable of making a record that sounds like itself, it makes a record that sounds nothing like the band, curiously returning to Album One though with different consequences.

ALBUM FOUR: Since the other records have failed at the cash register, there's no budget to make another Album Three, so the strategy now is to "go for the live feel" and "get back to the roots" and try to make a more sophisticated version of Album

One which never sounded "live" or even like the band in the first place, and which you only learned to make by going through the process of Albums Two and Three.

Ten years after your first record is released you'll adore it because it has "charm." Meanwhile—back then—some of your first fans will hate it because you've gotten new fans and you're no longer their little pocket-pal to rub. However, radio stations will play the album and new faces will turn up at the gig. You might get more money from the club owner who regarded you as a joke only six months before (this is the same clodhopper who'll ask you ten years later if you've "considered doing something else?").

Some records get sold, but no one knows where the money goes so you can't pay back your friend. Your record gets to distant cities to which you begin traveling. The reporters' questions become a little more serious than "Where did the band get its name?" or "Are you New Wave?" Your personal lives become a netherworld of sex and drugs without the sex and drugs; clubs in towns that you can't find on the map rip you off; your records aren't in the stores and the ad wasn't in the paper; personnel changes occur because somebody told the bass player that the band wasn't popular anymore back home. In short, you need more money, better organization, equipment, bookings, and, above all, respect. In long, you need a bigger paddle with which to beat people who you wish would go somewhere and involuntarily explode.

=====

> At any moment in the music business almost nothing can happen.
> —Show-biz axiom

> To a lot of people I am an enigma. The enigma is enveloped in a paradox, and the whole thing is totally surrounded by a paradigm.
> —Kal Rudman

Kal Rudman publishes the *Friday Morning Quarterback*, a music industry tip-sheet. Like all the Kal Rudmans of this world, Kal is talking about Kal. It's a self-portrait in gobbledygook. As a description of a big record company, however, Kal's enigma/paradox/paradigm becomes coherent. A record company is an institution shrouded in a dense fog that obscures all standard operating procedures. In short, almost no one knows what is going on, or what to do to make something go on.

The people who make things like "hits" happen are the master navigators. They always find their way to The Fog Machine. Then they turn off The Fogger and go Top Five. Then they turn The Fogger back on just to make it tough for everybody else. In the presence of these people I'd recommend a powerful grease solvent. On the other hand, they are *the few*. They know how to get the job done while the rest of us just float around. By the time you figure out how to get the job done, the firm wants you to take a long rest. Then they take back the keys to the company car, and your invitation to the annual picnic gets lost in the mail. Yet, when you were unknowing—before the undoing—you managed to get part of the job done: The Record Deal.

Making a record, like making a film, costs a lot of money. Unless you have controlling stock in Raytheon, you'll need The Big Record Deal to make The Big Record. Understanding The Big Record Deal, though, is quite simple. You get money to make a record. If it sells a lot of copies ("moves units") you'll make some money (maybe) and get to keep making records. If it doesn't move units you won't get to make either. If you are with a major record label you will have to sell lots of records. Major labels are not patrons of the arts.

Just to get the record deal, however, you need money to make a "demo tape" and, subsequently, to "shop the deal." This is where a means-to-an-end philosophy becomes necessary. If your band is any good at all it won't have a penny by now. That means somebody's parents have to come up with a credit card. Of course, not many recording studios take American Express, but you'll need plastic to shop the deal, so you might as well start chiseling early.

The demo tape is your first ploy. In theory, a person at the record company's A&R Department (A&R stands for Artist & Repertoire; they're the talent scouts) hears the demo tape and, if he likes it, he signs you to a "deal," a recording contract. Just getting an A&R person to listen to a tape is an achievement. The exception to the demo tape process is The Buzz Factor. An artist may have a "big buzz": hype generated by media or a phenomenal grass-roots ground swell that catches industry czars by surprise. If a band has a big buzz it can sometimes go straight to the deal and obviate the demo tape.

The demo tape takes a lot of work. You need someone outside the band who can give you serious musical advice. He can't just stop by the rehearsal and tell you that everything is fine because everything is never fine. Locating someone capable of giving you the help you need is especially difficult in the provinces, but let's say you get lucky and find someone who really cares about your music. With that person's help you choose the best three or four songs, tear them apart, excise the self-indulgent parts and reassemble them. The tedium of this is always enhanced by a high-frequency whining emanating from the musicians involved. Once the alterations are made, the band plays the songs in front of audiences until the players aren't thinking about the alterations anymore.

Eventually, preparations for recording are complete except in the area of high finance. Here's where The Anti-Mogul steps in. He offers to bankroll the demo session. In return, if you fail to get the record deal, he'll release the songs on his small label. If you get the deal you pay him back the money he's sunk into the project, plus a profit. A handshake occurs, and you cross your fingers behind your back. Then you book studio time and cut your demo. The recording session goes well, perhaps because you're prepared, for a change. It's important to keep the fall-back strategy with The Anti-Mogul in motion, so you shoot a picture for the record jacket cover and "master" the tapes— the final steps before pressing the record. Meanwhile, you're about to run up an even bigger bill with American Express shopping the tape.

Once you get beyond the petty, pointless humiliations, shopping the deal can be fun. First, you can't care whether you're accepted or rejected. Once you attain this carefree state you'll project an air of confidence that will impress record company executives into thinking they might be missing something unless they give you some time. Second, you need to find someplace to go shop the deal. That's easy since there are only two marketplaces, New York City and Hollywood. Third, remember that you can learn everything you need to know about the music business in five minutes because (a) nobody knows anything, and (b) all you need is a telephone. The skills at connivance that you've mastered dealing with nightclub owners must come into play now, because it's time to penetrate The Fog.

At the major record labels the secretaries are the custodians of Fog. They're in place to prevent you from reaching the inner sanctum of the A&R Department. Secretaries are like the sphinx, and the answer to their riddle is to know their names. But how do you get them? Armed with the name of the A&R person you wish to contact, simply call the main switchboard at the record company and ask for the secretary's name. This may require a minor ruse: "Good afternoon, this is Jack Tandy again. I was just speaking with Johnny Starmaker, and I'm supposed to call back some info to the secretary by five o'clock. I'm embarrassed to say I can't quite recall who they said to ask for." The switchboard will be happy to give you a name just to get you off the line.

It's necessary now to give yourself a little pep talk. Say to yourself, "Remember, I'm the artist. Without me there would be no music business." After you've repeated this delusion, call back the record company, ask for the secretary, and say you're returning Johnny Starmaker's call. The secretary falls for the gambit, puts you on hold, and buzzes Johnny, who's in the middle of some mid-morning catastrophe and is in such a state of wild confusion that he can't remember whether he called Jack Tandy or not. So he picks up, and you slip your foot in the door of the inner sanctum.

"Johnny, this is Jack Tandy with [name of band here]. I'm going to be in New York on April 1 for a few days. We've got a great new demo I'd like to send you, and if you like it maybe we could grab a cup of coffee." Johnny thinks he's heard of the group, remembers something about an Indie album and says, yeah, fine, call a week before you come and anything else he can think of to get you off the phone. You say the demo tape will be on his desk tomorrow and ask "Is there a priority code I should put on the envelope?" He gives you the secret code that will get the tape right to his desk and not into the pile of a thousand cassettes on a table across his office.

Now you're in business, and remember: there's no business without you. After you've finished with Johnny Starmaker, call the other New

York record companies and pull the same stunt, only this time let it slip that you're meeting with Johnny on April 1. This is a quick way of sowing seed in the hot soil of the A&R mind. Can't let Starmaker get a leg up! Of course I'll meet with Tandy!

Get the demo tape, first album, and press clips in the air as soon as possible. Book your flight with Mom and Dad's American Express card. In the week prior to April 1 make your final follow-up calls—"Just making sure everything is okay for the meeting, I hope you like the tape," et cetera. Be sure to extract the name of each A&R person's California counterpart (and secretary) before you get dumped off the phone. Then pull the earlier telephone routine at the Hollywood companies, making sure you mention their New York opposites by their first names as a reference, leaving a little leeway in your tone just in case they hate these people.

═══

In 1982 everyone in Georgia thought the music business was located in New York City because the B-52's struck gold there back in 1979. We always got the gray granite brush-off, but this time the reception was warmer because of our more "mature" demo tape. The New York A&R people were still noncommital, being notoriously uncertain about what might be good. They require support from other A&R people to help them confirm what's good. In the end, those who liked our demo had good things to say about it to their equally indecisive West Coast counterparts—sowing the seed, so to speak, for the next jaunt—partially justifying the next month's credit card balance. Now it was time to go West.

I floated some checks and flew to L.A. where I stayed with a friend who had just gotten a big job with a major label. I spent the next week driving around town in a rental car to the record companies and acting like I knew what I was doing. Pretending to be a manager wasn't too hard since everyone in California is pretending to be something. The feeling at the West Coast major label companies seemed much looser than in New York. Everybody was trying to come off as "just folks." Some people were enthusiastic about the demo tape ("heard some good things"), a pleasant change from the usual Manhattan chill. When I wasn't trying to impress them that I, too, was just folks and avoiding any real discussion as to the merits of my band, I was hanging around the record company with my friend.

The first thing I noticed about the record company was the large number of expensive, exotic motor vehicles on the lot. I assumed these plutomobiles belonged to the label's famous recording artists, but then I discovered they belonged to the guys who *just worked there*. There was the rumor that the monster who headed the Radio Promotion Department had been given a Rolls Royce by Kenny Rogers as a tip. The more I hung around the more I realized that record executives think *they* are the stars. The point was made for me six years later when I opened a copy of *Billboard* and caught a full-page advertisement for the movie *Field of Dreams* starring Kevin Costner. Only it wasn't an ad for *Field of Dreams*, it was a duplicate ad announcing the installation of the new president of Capitol Records, with his head in place of Costner's.

The A&R staff outside the field of hustle knew what I was doing in L.A., liked the demo tape, and never made me feel like someone toting a resumé full of lies. They stayed in touch with me after I returned home, and when we booked some gigs and got some wigs to fly in from other labels, they said that they would send someone, too.

Two labels flying in wasn't enough to constitute a "bidding war," but it did provide some incentive. The last thing you want in a bidding war—even a fake one—is for someone to put up a white flag, so I felt it was my responsibility to hint at other "interest." The hints were completely unconvincing, but that didn't stop the two A&R chiefs from flying into Raleigh, North Carolina, on January 27, 1984, to see the band perform in what formerly had been a tractor showroom and was now a nightspot called the Culture Club. Later that night one of the two A&R men said, "Let's make records." "Let's," we said.

The Means had come to The End.

Meanwhile, the American Express bill has arrived in the mail, but that's the least of your troubles. Now you're faced with decisions you've never had to make before, and they have to be made all at once. You've secured The Record Deal, but the real problems have just begun. You've become a human ping-pong ball to be batted between the record company, the attorney, the manager, the friends. Once the word gets out on the deal, people you thought were friends in the local music community stab you in the back. Hometown writers who were "behind the band" now really get behind the band—with sharpened knives. A half-drunk jackass gets in your face and says, "You need to get back to doing what you were doing before people were telling you what to do!" It's quite an adventure, all the same. You have to rely on your instincts because nothing that's happened before prepares you for this. In show biz the past is never prologue, and the future unfolds as a series of non sequiturs ad infinitum. Overnight you've gone from being a deadbeat in a rock group to being "a serious artist with a career."

Which brings me to The Attorney. It can't just be any old attorney. It has to be a Music Business Attorney (M.B.A.). In Hollywood there are many M.B.A.'s. In the hinterland, however, the attorney who can deal with the filed teeth at a record company is a rarity. When you finally find one, remember—he's working for you (and since he has an idiot for a boss, you'll probably end up working for him). Your first mistake is to act responsibly and listen to hours of legal discussions about percentage points, royalty rates, and film deals. None of this means anything unless you sell a bunch of records, and then you can holler "renegotiate!" If you don't sell a bunch of records it doesn't matter because you're going to get "dropped." Getting dropped hangs like a dagger over your head night and day. The kinds of commitments an artist really needs built into a recording contract aren't going to happen unless the artist is "established" or has a huge buzz factor. So what you should say to your new attorney is, "Listen, I don't want to hear about it. Just get as much money as you can and forge my signature." The one thing of value he tells you is, "The record company is your enemy," but you won't understand this because the record company people seem so nice and "artist-oriented" and want to spend all their spare time "developing" you.

Once you have the attorney in the bag you need to choose The Producer. There aren't many of them out there, and there's always a scheduling conflict. There's no science to this, but it helps to understand what a producer really is: he's the guy who acts as if he's "into the project," and he usually is—for about ten to twenty-five grand. There's a lot of big talk about finding someone who "can take you to the next step." Oh yeah, and he has to have a "track record," meaning some success with a prior release. With the money in your recording budget you're not going to get the heavy hitter with the multi-platinum wall and—trust me on this—you wouldn't want to be around him anyway.

Finding the right producer who can handle the budget, the recording console, and the five mental cases in the band is not easy. Eventually you have to settle on the person with whom you feel comfortable personally and artistically. We decided to make our album with the staff producer who had signed the band to the label. He brought in as coproducer an up-and-coming hotshot engineer from New York City who has since produced some very successful records. We began "pre-production" in April 1984, spending two weeks in our rehearsal space—the basement of a bar. Then in May we spent thirty days recording at a twenty-four track studio in Atlanta. Our producer kept us calm while the coproducer got down in the trenches. Making an album can sometimes be painful, but we learned valuable lessons about the way records are made. We brought the project in under budget, took the remaining money, paid off some debts (The Anti-Mogul), and bought a van.

Getting this far without a real manager was a little unusual. The day after our album was completed our producer began prodding us about it. He knew what was in store for us at the label. There's some sense to this course of action (getting a real manager) since it's impossible for a band member to take care of managerial responsibilities while touring to "support a record." Record companies don't like "dealing with the artist." The hard cases who run the label make a practice of referring to artists as though they were items for sale in a produce market. They can't make cracks about an artist's complexion or dimensions if they're "dealing with the artist." They can say anything they want to a real manager, though, in an effort to avoid cutting a check. We flew around and finally found a real manager, so the label's *accountant* could tell us through him, "I just don't hear any hits."

═══

At the beginning, when you get on the inside of a record company, the first thing you discover is that all the departments hate one another.

The second thing is that labels are in a perpetual state of renovation. The A&R man who signed you to a contract will probably be gone by the time your record is released. Here are the major departments and a brief description of their functions:

A&R DEPARTMENT	Talent Scout Hucksters
PROMOTION DEPARTMENT	Radio Airplay Hucksters
MARKETING DEPARTMENT	Get Product Into Store Hucksters
ART DEPARTMENT	Packaging Hucksters
MEDIA DEPARTMENT	"Column-Inches, Baby!" Hucksters
VIDEO DEPARTMENT	Useless-Without-One Hucksters

The Master Navigators know how to make them all work together. For the rest of us, it's like keeping fifteen pie pans spinning on cue sticks. Though the departments hate each other, a successful record can provide incentive for harmony.

Two outstanding inside lines:

(1) "It's in the pipeline, baby!" I wasn't certain what the pipeline was, but I knew it had been backing up since the 1970s. What it means is that your record has been shipped to retail outlets and radio stations. What it *really* means is that your record will probably never see the light of day. Why? Because it's in the pipeline, baby!

(2) "You need to become a priority at the label." If you have to ask what this means, you're probably not ready to become one. Asking a record company person how to become a priority often results in what Edmund Wilson called The Stalin Tic, a constant looking back over the shoulder to see if anyone is listening. Record company people are usually pretty circumspect when talking to artists about the business, and if they're not, they won't last long, or they're too powerful to care. I finally found out what becoming a priority meant, but I can't tell you because it involves a secret handshake.

People at our record company liked us at first because we made the mistake of being ourselves. Accessibility, however, is ultimately an anathema to the bogus distance of stardom. In the end, record company workers want you to be exaggerated in certain respects— that way you can dominate their unfulfilled star fantasies and they'll feel compelled to work for you even if they rightly denigrate you the second you leave their offices. So do you remain human, or do you become a beast?

THE HAMLET VARIANT. The record company, as we were constantly told, is *working for you*. I always thought that anybody working for you should be treated with at least a minor display of humanity. In show business, however, displays of humanity are a sign of weakness. Being nice is a liability, and liability not only gets you nowhere, it "hurts you." This is the high dollar quandary of potential stardom: Are you willing to sacrifice a sense of humanity for opportunity? To be or not to be nice, that is The Hamlet Variant.

After our self-titled album shot out of the pipeline, we received a good bit of critical praise in America and England (though we were predictably savaged in our hometown). Our first single elicited a "positive response from radio," and it became time to "tour in support of the record." Supporting the record means that you drive to and perform in about fifty American cities where, theoretically, the record company has a crack branch-office team making sure the album is in the stores and forcing the big radio station to play your record. Our manager was able to pull in some mysterious old favor and arrange a *support slot* on Lou Reed's first national tour in many years.

Reed is a quiet gentleman, one of the few with a large brain in the business. He treated us very well, which is more than I can say for the kingpins at our record company. Initially they had provided tour support to defer the ridiculous cost of traveling (road crew, motels, gas, etc.). With tour support you subtract the money you make each week from total operating expenses. The label picks up the difference, "recoupable," as it were, against profits from your future record sales. Halfway through the Lou Reed tour the kingpins pulled the plug on our support. I encountered The Top Pin during a three-night stand with Reed in Manhattan. Before I could say anything he quickly justified the plug pulling, saying, "I've seen the pattern many times before."

After extensive travel you begin to comprehend how big America really is in relation to your hip little scene. We came back from the Reed tour a little rubbery-legged, trying to figure out our next move. Our second single was better than our first single because record companies always choose the wrong first song to send to the radio station. Naturally it received a negative response from radio, and, with no tour possibilities imminent, our album went back into the box, one made of pine.

The dashing of our expectations made it difficult for the next few months, but by March 1985 we were back on track and flew to Hollywood to meet with Pat Benatar's husband about producing our next album. The A&R people were saying we needed to make a "competitive record." But the Hollywood trip didn't work out. Then a British producer flew in for a meeting. He was to be an unusual choice. He was best known for producing some successful "synth-pop" English bands, and we were into small electric guitar symphonies. It seemed to work, however, and we spent a total of three months making a pretty sophisticated recording. Our band was foolishly perceived by the record company to be a "garage guitar band." When the head of A&R heard what we were doing, he was flabbergasted. "What?! They're making a forty-eight track album?!" Unheard of, except for hugely successful bands. I flew to London where ours became the first record ever mastered on the world's first digital mastering console.

Once again it was to be pipeline time, and The Fog Machine was pumping full-ahead. It's The Fogger's function to divert logical inquiry and make you think that it's only some shortcoming of your own that accounts for the fact that NOTHING MAKES SENSE at the record company. Example One: In a normal business a product can't be sold to the public unless the public knows that the product exists. In the music business this goal is achieved through publicity, advertising, promotional materials (posters), videos, and radio airplay. The record company has to do these things so that John Q. Consumer knows that the product—your record—exists. When the record company doesn't do any of these things, whose responsibility is it when nobody buys the record? The artist's, of course. Why? Because NOTHING MAKES SENSE and THE ARTIST IS ALWAYS TO BLAME. Example Two: It makes sense to produce a good record for a relatively small amount of money so that the record will generate a return profit and the record company will have incentive to promote the product even more. Right? Wrong. When I suggested this to an A&R man at Capitol Records, he pitched forward into his soup. "My God," he stammered, "don't let anyone at the label hear you say that!" Why? Because you were too frugal. Unless you spend a million dollars making a record, the company won't feel compelled to promote it. Having created a masterpiece isn't enough incentive, and they won't know it's a masterpiece unless it cost a fortune. Put another way, they won't perform unless their job is threatened. The incentive is fear, and now things start to make sense.

So you have to "set up the record," and to do that your manager has to "work the label." This means he has to somehow extort commitments from the different department directors so that they'll kick in the promotion. Then at the right moment your manager has to coordinate the departments for the full-frontal assault.

A little while before our second major label release it was becoming apparent that we might not be a priority. One time we contacted the Hollywood A&R department to ask if we could send a promotional video to the company's annual convention. First, we had to convince the secretary we really were on the label. Then we were told (exasperated voice) that any promotional video would be inappropriate because "this year we're only concentrating on the big winners, the home runs."

Trouble began even before our album came out of the box. The record company's art department appropriated creative control over the packaging (the record cover). The results were preposterous, and the band was extremely agitated. Our manager pleaded with us not to "alienate the label." Meanwhile, he was too busy promoting big rock concerts and tractor-pulls to work the label on our behalf. And our big-time booking agency was doing a crack job of booking the band into clubs we'd played for years—and for about half of our usual guaranteed fee. Once we had to go on strike at show time and re-negotiate with the club owner inside of a truck while an angry mob pelted our one-man road crew with debris.

The strike was on February 21, 1986. Our new record was released two weeks later to "critical acclaim." Good press is better than bad, or none at all, but I've since discovered that terms like "Critically Acclaimed" (CA) and "Legendary" (L) often form one side of the following equation:

$$CA + L \neq \$$$

The radio airplay patterns were typically confusing. The big radio stations in Boston and Denver played the record, but The Good Guys at the big radio station in our hometown wouldn't touch it. Of course, not everything was terrible on the home front. The Atlanta chapter of a national organization presented us with the rock group category award for 1986. The awards ceremony was sponsored by a real estate firm. In our acceptance speech we expressed gratitude for the trophy but hinted that a house would have been nicer. No one was amused.

It gradually becomes clear that the full-frontal assault the manager was supposed to have coordinated has turned into Pickett's Charge. The phone calls stop being returned, even from friends like The Artist Relations Director, a nice man who's supposed to help you smooth out problems with the hierarchy. The toll-free number of the label mysteriously changes and no one seems to have the new one. Right around this time you get hit with The Star Question: Someone at the record company—usually the A&R person—asks, "Do you really *want* to be a star?" This is when you should know you're in serious trouble because somebody at the label has expressed doubts in a meeting about the band's "star quality." The irony about this is that the person in the meeting was probably talking about some other artist, but your A&R person is so paranoid he thought the guy was talking about you.

"Do you really want to be a star?" To which you respond, being naively flattered, "Yes, of course. Please push the button." Only your idea of being a star is something quite different from the record company's. Your idea is chatting on the *Dick Cavett Show* about poetry and politics. The problem with this particular star fantasy is that Dick Cavett hasn't had a show in fifteen years.

Along with The Star Question comes The Big Euphemism. The S.Q. fades away, but The Big Euphemism haunts you forever. What is The Big E.? Well, The Fog Machine is really cranking, and you can't see anything. So you start asking questions about this department's "sincerity" and that department's "commitment." They start calling you paranoid. Soon, when the dirigible bursts into flames, you'll realize that "paranoid" is The Big Euphemism for "Extremely Correct."

By the time you understand The Big Euphemism it's way too late. You'll be driving in circles around New England in July trying to find out whether or not you're playing some super-hip industry function in New York for which the record company said they'd pay, only nobody calls back to let you know one way or the other. So you head south and then you're standing in the twisted girders of a phone booth at a Howard Johnson's not far from Gettysburg and someone tells you that you're a loss to be casually cut. That's when you realize you've been re-marginalized. Certain people will soon trot out the word "bitter" and apply it to you, and you haven't even opened your mouth yet. When you do open your mouth you discover that the word "bitter" is just one more Big Euphemism for "Extremely Correct." By then you've already driven back home where they've hung a banner at the city limits that says WELCOME TO THE REAL THING, BABY! and you watch an outer-space movie and pour down twelve inches of Old Repeater that at length has no effect but you still feel better than you have in 750 days, and you go to sleep for neither the first nor the last Sunday morning as the sun comes up over America's Pop Republic.

≡≡≡≡

Time to raise the periscope, and questions and answers as well. I see a tree falling in the wilderness. No one is there to hear it. Is there a sound? Answer: Yes.

Question: If America is a level playing field, why am I always rolling downhill? Answer: Because I can't stop.

A few years ago I walked into an antique jewelry shop on the outskirts of town. The saleswoman recognized me, walked up, and said, "Thanks."

"You're certainly welcome," I said, "but I haven't bought anything yet."

She explained. Her family had owned a farm somewhere in Tennessee. Her dream had been to return after she received her college degree and establish the farm as an art therapy center for disturbed children. The previous summer, though, the mortgage on the farm had been foreclosed. Everything was to be auctioned off, including, of course, her dream. All she could do was sit on the front porch of the farmhouse every day and, while a century left her piece by piece, listen to music on her headphone set.

"Your album," said the saleswoman, "was the only hope I had, and it was the only thing that got me through."

I put my sunglasses on and bought a red ceramic bracelet from

China that had caught my eye. Then I walked outside into a storm of motes in a wide shaft of August light.

What does this mean? Everything. And everything else means nothing.

Index

Notes on Contributors

JEFF CALDER has been a singer and songwriter with the Atlanta-based rock band the Swimming Pool Q's since 1978. The Q's have recorded five albums, including the most recent "World War Two Point Five" (Capitol Records, 1989). He also performs with the group the Supreme Court. He has written for newspapers and small publications. The present piece is excerpted from his critical autobiography, "I Posed with the Gods."

ANTHONY DeCURTIS is a writer and Senior Features Editor at *Rolling Stone*, where he oversees the record review section, and the pop music critic for "Weekend All Things Considered" on National Public Radio. He coedited *The Rolling Stone Illustrated History of Rock & Roll* and *The Rolling Stone Album Guide*, both scheduled for publication in the fall of 1992. His essay accompanying the Eric Clapton retrospective, *Crossroads*, won the 1988 Grammy Award in the "Best Album Notes" category. He holds a Ph.D. in American literature and has taught at Indiana University and Emory University.

MARK DERY writes on pop culture, mass media, and the arts for the *New York Times*, *New York*, the *Philadelphia Inquirer*, and the *Chicago Tribune*. His column of cultural criticism, "Guerrilla Semiotics," appears quarterly in *Mondo 2000*. In October 1991 Miller Freeman published his nonfiction title *Cyberculture: Road Warriors, Console Cowboys, and the Silicon Underground*.

PAUL EVANS is a freelance writer working out of Atlanta. He wrote the chapter on Prince for *The Rolling Stone Illustrated History of Rock & Roll* and is also one of the four critics who compiled *The Rolling Stone Album Guide*.

GLENN GASS is a composer and Assistant Professor of Music at Indiana University, where he teaches a series of courses that he developed on the history of rock and popular music. He is the recent recipient of a grant for composition from the National Endowment for the Arts and is completing a history of rock music, which will be published in 1992.

Currently rotting in the musty catacombs of Perkins Library at Duke University where he is at least occasionally a graduate student, TRENT

HILL is or has been a hardcore musician, janitor, bankrupt, gun sales-man, and messenger boy for corporate masters at Great Satan, Inc., at different times in his life. He prefers graduate school.

MICHAEL JARRETT is Assistant Professor of English at Penn State Uni-versity, York Campus. He is currently completing *Drifting on a Read*, an investigation of jazz as a model of rhetorical invention ("euret-ics").

ALAN LIGHT is an Associate Editor at *Rolling Stone*, where he has writ-ten about virtually every major figure in the world of hip-hop. A 1988 graduate of Yale University, he majored in American Studies with a concentration in American popular music and wrote his senior thesis on the Beastie Boys.

GREIL MARCUS is the author of *Mystery Train: Images of America in Rock 'n' Roll Music* (1975), *Lipstick Traces: A Secret History of the 20th Century* (1989), and *Dead Elvis: A Chronicle of a Cultural Obsession* (1991). He lives in Berkeley, California.

ROBERT PALMER is a former chief pop music critic for the *New York Times* and a frequent contributor to *Rolling Stone* and many other publications. As a musician, he has recorded with jazz great Ornette Coleman; with Bono, Keith Richards, and Ron Wood on the anti-apartheid album *Sun City*; and with several bands, ranging from In-sect Trust in the late 1960s to the Scam and Panther Burns in the 1980s and 1990s. His documentary films include *The World According to John Coltrane*, which he wrote and co-directed, and *Deep Blues*, a tour of Mississippi juke joints for which he served as writer and music director. The latter film is based on his award-winning book *Deep Blues* (1981).

ROBERT B. RAY is Associate Professor of English and the Director of Film and Media Studies at the University of Florida. He is the author of *A Certain Tendency of the Hollywood Cinema, 1930–1980* (1985) and a member of the Vulgar Boatmen, who have released two records, *You and Your Sister* and *Please Panic*.

DAN RUBEY is Humanities Librarian and Director of the Comparative Literature Program at Lehman College, The City University of New York. He has written on medieval, Renaissance, and American literature; editing theory; and film. He reviews contemporary art and is writing books on medieval romance narratives and music video.

DAVID R. SHUMWAY is Associate Professor of Literary and Cultural Studies in the English Department of Carnegie Mellon University. He is the author of *Michel Foucault* (1989) and is currently at work on *Creating American Civilization: A Genealogy of American Literature as an Academic Field*.

MARTHA NELL SMITH, Associate Director of Graduate English at the University of Maryland, College Park, is the author of *Rowing in Eden: Rereading Dickinson* (forthcoming, 1992) and, with Suzanne Juhasz and Cristanne Miller, has coauthored *Dickinson's Comic Power: Performance and Audience* (forthcoming, 1993). She is working on a study of lesbian and gay performances in popular culture.

PAUL SMITH is Director of the Literary and Cultural Studies Program at Carnegie Mellon University. He is author of *Pound Revised* and *Discerning the Subject*, and editor with Alice Jardine of *Men in Feminism*. He has written on a variety of topics in cultural theory and is at work on a book about Clint Eastwood.

Library of Congress Cataloging-in-Publication Data

Present tense: rock & roll and culture / edited by
Anthony DeCurtis.
p.   cm.
Includes bibliographical references and index.
ISBN 0-8223-1261-1 (alk. paper): $39.95. — ISBN
0-8223-1265-4 (pbk.: alk. paper): $14.95
1. Rock music—History and criticism.   2. Music and
society.   1. DeCurtis, Anthony.
ML3534.P76   1992
781.66—dc20   92-1651